HISTORICAL DICTIONARIES OF
RELIGIONS, PHILOSOPHIES, AND MOVEMENTS

Jon Woronoff, Series Editor

23. *Islamic Fundamentalist Movements in the Arab World, Iran, and Turkey*, by Ahmad S. Moussalli, 1999
24. *Reformed Churches*, by Robert Benedetto, Darrell L. Guder, and Donald K. McKim, 1999
25. *Baptists*, by William H. Brackney, 1999. *Out of print. See no. 94.*
26. *Cooperative Movement*, by Jack Shaffer, 1999
27. *Reformation and Counter-Reformation*, by Hans J. Hillerbrand, 2000
28. *Shakers*, by Holley Gene Duffield, 2000
29. *United States Political Parties*, by Harold F. Bass Jr., 2000
30. *Heidegger's Philosophy*, by Alfred Denker, 2000
31. *Zionism*, by Rafael Medoff and Chaim I. Waxman, 2000. *Out of print. See no. 83.*
32. *Mormonism*, 2nd ed., by Davis Bitton, 2000. *Out of print. See no. 89.*
33. *Kierkegaard's Philosophy*, by Julia Watkin, 2001
34. *Hegelian Philosophy*, by John W. Burbidge, 2001. *Out of print. See no. 90.*
35. *Lutheranism*, by Günther Gassmann in cooperation with Duane H. Larson and Mark W. Oldenburg, 2001
36. *Holiness Movement*, by William Kostlevy, 2001
37. *Islam*, by Ludwig W. Adamec, 2001. *Out of print. See no. 95.*
38. *Shinto*, by Stuart D. B. Picken, 2002
39. *Olympic Movement*, 2nd ed., by Ian Buchanan and Bill Mallon, 2001. *Out of print. See no. 61.*
40. *Slavery and Abolition*, by Martin A. Klein, 2002
41. *Terrorism*, 2nd ed., by Sean Anderson and Stephen Sloan, 2002. *Out of print. See no. 96.*
42. *New Religious Movements*, by George D. Chryssides, 2001
43. *Prophets in Islam and Judaism*, by Scott B. Noegel and Brannon M. Wheeler, 2002
44. *The Friends (Quakers)*, by Margery Post Abbott, Mary Ellen Chijioke, Pink Dandelion, and John William Oliver Jr., 2003
45. *Lesbian Liberation Movement: Still the Rage*, by JoAnne Myers, 2003
46. *Descartes and Cartesian Philosophy*, by Roger Ariew, Dennis Des Chene, Douglas M. Jesseph, Tad M. Schmaltz, and Theo Verbeek, 2003

Historical Dictionary of Homosexuality

Brent L. Pickett

Historical Dictionaries of
Religions, Philosophies, and Movements, No. 96

The Scarecrow Press, Inc.
Lanham, Maryland • Toronto • Plymouth, UK
2009

SCARECROW PRESS, INC.

Published in the United States of America
by Scarecrow Press, Inc.
A wholly owned subsidiary of
The Rowman & Littlefield Publishing Group, Inc.
4501 Forbes Boulevard, Suite 200, Lanham, Maryland 20706
www.scarecrowpress.com

Estover Road
Plymouth PL6 7PY
United Kingdom

British Library Cataloguing in Publication Information Available

Library of Congress Cataloging-in-Publication Data

Pickett, Brent, 1967–
    Historical dictionary of homosexuality / Brent L. Pickett.
        p. cm. — (Historical dictionaries of religions, philosophies, and movements
; no. 96)
    Includes bibliographical references.
    ISBN 978-0-8108-5979-1 (hardback : alk. paper) — ISBN 978-0-8108-6315-6
(ebook)
    1. Homosexuality—History—Dictionaries. I. Title.
HQ75.13.P53 2009
306.76'603—dc22
                                                                        2009004763

To my three lovely girls: Jeana, Sophie, and Zoey

Contents

Editor's Foreword

Usually the term "historical dictionary" is just another way of saying encyclopedia. But in the case of homosexuality, it was necessary to produce both an encyclopedia and a dictionary, because there is still incredible confusion—and in some cases, outright controversy—about the meanings of even the most essential terms. Yet, without having some agreement on these issues, it is impossible to achieve any deeper understanding of a field that is hardly just academic, but a matter of securing a decent life, and sometimes even any life, for those concerned. This fact becomes perfectly clear when considering the history of homosexuality, a history all too often afflicted by dogma, discrimination, and even death, and where—despite considerable progress in some places in recent decades—the situation has hardly improved or may even have gotten worse. Thus, this volume has two crucial tasks: to help us understand what we are talking about with regard to homosexuality and to see what these issues and terms mean in reality.

This double task explains the contents of the dictionary section. Some of the entries explain the terminology, not just by explaining what words mean but what they have signified over the centuries for those concerned. Other entries deal with homosexuals, whether male or female, some of whom have been at the forefront of the struggle for improvement either in their writings or their lifestyles or their political efforts or all of the above. This activism has resulted in legislation and court cases, which make up a considerable share of the entries. But, for the editor at least, the most illuminating entries deal with specific countries and regions, indicating what progress has been made (or not) and showing just how spotty and tenuous this growth has been. These partial views are woven together in an excellent introduction, which should really be read before the rest, since it puts things in their proper place and makes them easier to understand. The chronology also shows that the movement has been largely in the right direction but hardly onward and upward. There are so many facets to homosexuality, and situations vary so much from one place to another, that the bibliography is a precious source of material for those who want to know more about specific aspects.

This *Historical Dictionary of Homosexuality* was written by Brent L. Pickett, who is the associate dean of the Outreach School and director of the University of Wyoming/Casper College Center and an associate professor of political science. That last function is particularly important, because much of what is covered by this book has something to do with politics. That Dr. Pickett teaches courses on comparative politics is even more important, since it is necessary to have a broad view to see what is going on in different places as well as different times, a view that is all too often lacking. Along with teaching, Dr. Pickett has written numerous articles for learned journals and submitted papers to various conferences on this topic. He has also published a very relevant book, *On the Use and Abuse of Foucault for Politics*. He has given many talks in support of gay rights, including same-sex marriage. This historical dictionary has brought together many of the strands of his activities and provides readers with an impressively strong base for further study and understanding.

Jon Woronoff
Series Editor

Preface

In order to avoid anachronism, the term "gay" is largely reserved for the post-1960s time period. While the author does not wish to take a stand, in this work, on the issue of whether there are definite categories of sexual orientation that remain largely unchanged throughout history, it is still helpful to retain historically specific language. Thus, "gay" is reserved for the time period when persons would have identified with that term, while "invert" or other terms are used for other periods. The word "homosexual," as an adjective, is used as the broadest category of persons who experience primarily same-sex attraction. From the mid-19th to the mid-20th centuries, however, "homosexual" is used as a noun. Because persons writing about their own sexuality during that era often referred to themselves as homosexuals, this writing follows their precedent.

Although it is common today in Europe and North America to include transgender issues with lesbian and gay ones, this work does not. There are several reasons for this. First, the drawing together of homosexuality and transgenderism/transsexualism is quite recent, and this work has a broader scope. Second, the conceptual framework that pushes toward bringing together these topics (and political concerns) is just one of several possible frameworks, and it is useful to keep them distinct as far as historical study. Third, and most importantly, the topic of the history of homosexuality is very large in itself. The neglect of transgender issues better allows room for the central object of study in this work, given that it is a historical dictionary of homosexuality. No denigration of transgender concerns is intended whatsoever.

Another issue within the historiography of homosexuality concerns the proper areas of emphasis. One common approach to the history of homosexuality has been to list famous homosexuals. This was especially true from the late 19th through the second third of the 20th century. Persons

xiii

like Socrates and Michelangelo were included and their achievements were then described. Authors did this to justify a denigrated sexuality, showing that in contrast to the common understanding of the day, homosexuality is not a disease; it is not debilitating, and in fact truly amazing people have been deeply attracted to persons of the same sex. Certainly another desire was to help repair an understandably impaired sense of self among homosexual readers. Some entries of this type have been included in the present volume. In part this is due to historical interest but also to give a sense of this approach. While it is less common today, it has been important in the history of homosexual historiography.

More researchers today approach same-sex historiography through time- and locale-specific studies. This volume has many country and regional entries. Individual countries that are populous or historically influential have been selected, although more emphasis is given to those in the Western tradition.

Terms in bold within an entry are cross-references. It is often the case that closely related topics are split into two or more entries. If this occurs, the reader is notified either by the use of bold in the entry itself or the *See also* reference at the end of entries.

Acknowledgments

For all of his comments and suggestions, and even more for his friendship, I want to thank Patrick Blythe. He read first, second, and third drafts; discussed larger conceptual issues with me; and encouraged me during those times when I felt like the project was not moving forward. Bill Felice also provided insightful comments upon the project at all of its stages. He pushed me to think more critically about entry selection, reviewed individual entries to ensure they were balanced, and then read over the entire manuscript. I am fortunate to have such a great pair of colleagues and friends. They improved the manuscript immeasurably. Each is also adept at combining enthusiastic support with profound criticism.

Melanie Young read much of the manuscript and offered a host of suggestions that improved it. I am grateful for her time, effort, and friendship. I also want to thank Janet DeVries and Leanne Woodfill. They lent me numerous books and magazines, offered advice on what entries I should have, and dispelled my ignorance on specific issues and contexts. They are a wonderful pair. Paul Flesher provided helpful comments on the entries pertaining to religious issues. Brian Adams-Thiess gave me insightful comments on the differences between European and U.S. gay rights movements. Jon Woronoff, my editor at Scarecrow Press, made numerous constructive suggestions without having too heavy of a hand. The Casper, Wyoming, chapter of Parents and Friends of Lesbians and Gays has been generous and welcoming; I thank all of its members.

Before I embarked upon this project, I spoke with three of the most important persons in my life about whether I could count upon their support during the writing process. Maggi Murdock, associate vice president and dean of the Outreach School at the University of Wyoming, encouraged me to continue my research even while in an administrative post. She is a great mentor, and I am fortunate to work under her leadership. Renee Woodward, Manager of University of Wyoming/Casper College (UW/CC) Center Programs, has also been very helpful during the writing process. She is a joy to work with and a marvelous colleague. Most importantly, Jeana Lam-Pickett, my wife, has been supportive even while I cluttered our house with more books and papers. I thank them all.

My colleagues and the staff at UW/CC have also been helpful during my work on this project. In particular, I would like to thank Bruce Richardson for his comments on drafts, Erin Clark for her assistance in putting together a trip for archival research, and Lana Perrotti for formatting assistance. I also want to thank Teena Gabrielson for her support and our conversations about matters political and philosophical.

Three institutions helped me access research materials. I want to thank the University of Wyoming library, especially those who work in Outreach support and Interlibrary Loans. I am also grateful to the Casper College Goodstein Library, especially Michelle DeSalvo. Finally, the ONE National Gay and Lesbian Archive in Los Angeles provided immense help during a research trip there. I would like to thank David Moore in particular.

List of Acronyms and Abbreviations

ACLU	American Civil Liberties Union
ACT UP	AIDS Coalition to Unleash Power
AIDS	Acquired Immunodeficiency Syndrome
ALI	American Law Institute
ANC	African National Congress
APA	American Psychiatric Association
ASK	Association for Social Knowledge
BSA	Boy Scouts of America
BSSP	British Society for the Study of Sex Psychology
CAMP	Campaign against Moral Persecution
CDC	Centers for Disease Control and Prevention
COC	*Cultuur-En-Ontspannings Centrum* (Culture and Recreation Center)
DOB	Daughters of Bilitis
DOMA	Defense of Marriage Act
DSM	The Diagnostic and Statistical Manual, Mental Disorders
ECHO	East Coast Homophile Organizations
ECHR	European Court of Human Rights
ENDA	Employment Non-Discrimination Act
EU	European Union
FDA	Food and Drug Administration
FOF	Focus on the Family
FRC	Family Research Council
FUORI	Unitary Front of Revolutionary Italian Homosexuals
GAA	Gay Activists Alliance
GALZ	Gays and Lesbians of Zimbabwe
GDR	German Democratic Republic
GE	*Gemeinschaft der Eigenen* (Community of the Special)

GLF	Gay Liberation Front
GLH	*Groupe de Libération Homosexuelle* (Homosexual Liberation Group)
GMHC	Gay Men's Health Crisis
HIV/AIDS	Human Immunodeficiency Virus/Acquired Immunodeficiency Syndrome
HLRS	Homosexual Law Reform Society
HRC	Human Rights Campaign
ICCPR	International Covenant on Civil and Political Rights
ILGA	International Lesbian and Gay Association
INS	Immigration and Naturalization Service
IS	*Institut für Sexualwissenschaft* (Institute for Sexual Science)
JILGA	International Lesbian and Gay Association—Japan
MCC	Metropolitan Community Church
NACHO	North American Conference of Homophile Organizations
NCGLE	National Coalition for Gay and Lesbian Equality
NGLTF	National Gay and Lesbian Task Force
OLGA	Organization for Lesbian and Gay Activists
PAC	Political Action Committee
PACS	*Pacte civil de solidarité* (civil solidarity pact)
PFLAG	Parents and Friends of Lesbians and Gays
PQ	*Politique et Quotidien* (Politics and Daily Life)
SIR	Society for Individual Rights
UCLA	University of California, Los Angeles
UN	United Nations
U.S.	United States
WHK	*Wissenschaftlich-humanitäres Komitee* (Scientific-Humanitarian Committee)
WLSR	World League for Sexual Reform

Chronology

Ca. 385 B.C.E.   Ancient Greece: Plato wrote the *Symposium*, his dialogue on eros (love/desire). Male same-sex attraction and relationships were central to the speeches in this piece and were even celebrated.

378 B.C.E.   Ancient Greece: The Theban general Gorgidas formed the Sacred Band of Thebes, a military unit several hundred strong that was composed entirely of pairs of male lovers. The unit soon became renowned for its valor in battle.

342   Rome: Co-emperors Constantius and Constans enacted a law that criminalized the passive role in male same-sex relations. There is little evidence that the law was enforced, however.

390   Rome: Emperor Theodosius proclaimed an edict that targeted male prostitutes and brothels and prescribed death by burning for those found guilty.

533   Byzantine Empire: Emperor Justinian issued a law criminalizing all same-sex acts. The law was later made part of the Code of Justinian.

Ca. 850   Europe: An anonymous author forged a series of religious documents that blamed homosexual relations for various ills. The church circulated the forgeries for centuries.

1102   Great Britain: The council of London issued a canon banning sodomy.

1233   Italy: Pope Gregory IX formally established the Papal Inquisition. Over the next several centuries, Inquisition authorities executed, tortured, exiled, sentenced to the galleys, or otherwise punished thousands of people for the crime of sodomy.

1478 Spain: The Court of the Holy Office of the Inquisition established in Spain. The two central targets of the Spanish Inquisition were Jews and homosexuals.

1532 Germany: Charles V of the Holy Roman Empire promulgated a comprehensive criminal code that mandated the death penalty for sodomy.

1533 Great Britain: Parliament passed Act of 25 Henry VIII, which criminalized anal intercourse, both homosexual and heterosexual. The act stood for centuries, with occasional alterations. It became the basis for many anti-sodomy laws across the British Empire.

1536 Portugal: The Portuguese Inquisition began.

1721 Germany: The last known execution for female sodomy in continental Europe occurred.

1730 Netherlands: A series of investigations into alleged sodomy cases quickly led to a national wave of hysteria and violence against men accused of relations with other men. Hundreds were tried and scores were put to death in just two years.

1791 France: The Constituent Assembly repealed France's anti-sodomy law. Some police harassment and surveillance continued, however.

1803 Netherlands: The last recorded execution for sodomy in continental Europe occurred.

1810 France: The Code Napoléon, a systematic codification of legal reforms since 1791, was promulgated. It maintained the decriminalization of sodomy that the Constituent Assembly had enacted almost two decades before. Given France's expansion under Napoleon, the code was deeply influential throughout Europe for decades after.

1821 Brazil: The country legalized sodomy. **Mexico:** The Inquisition ended in Mexico due to its newly achieved independence from Spain.

1836 Great Britain: The last execution for sodomy in Britain occurred.

1860 United States: Walt Whitman published the third edition of *Leaves of Grass*, which added the "Calamus" group of poems. The new section had a strong homoerotic theme and celebrated the "love of comrades" and "manly love."

1861   Great Britain: The British government dropped the death penalty for homosexual sodomy. Authorities could still impose a sentence of life in prison.

1864   Germany: Karl Heinrich Ulrichs began publishing a series of pamphlets defending same-sex love. His work strongly influenced the early homosexual rights movement.

1869   Germany: Karl Maria Kertbeny, who fought for the repeal of anti-sodomy laws, coined the term "homosexuality."

1871   Germany: Paragraph 175 of the criminal code again made criminal male-male sodomy.

1873   Japan: The government enacted a law making male homosexual sex illegal, although the penalty of 90 days in jail was considerably less than the norm in Europe.

1883   Japan: On advice from a French legal consultant, Japan repealed its anti-sodomy law.

1886   Great Britain: The Labouchère Amendment went into effect. Whereas previously only male-male anal sex was criminalized, the law made male-male oral sex punishable with two years in prison, potentially with hard labor.

1889   Great Britain: Scotland abolished the death penalty for sodomy.

1897   Germany: Magnus Hirschfeld and others founded the *Wissenschaftlich-humanitäres Komitee* (WHK, Scientific-Humanitarian Committee). Soon other chapters were established in other German cities as well as elsewhere in Europe. **Great Britain:** Havelock Ellis published the English-language edition of his *Sexual Inversion*. In it he argued that homosexuality was congenital and did not cause personal or social harm.

1914   Great Britain: Havelock Ellis and Edward Carpenter formed the British Society for the Study of Sex Psychology. The group worked to promote research and education as well as lobbied on behalf of women and homosexual rights.

1919   Germany: Magnus Hirschfeld founded the *Institut für Sexualwissenschaft* (IS, Institute for Sexual Science).

1928   Great Britain: Radclyffe Hall published her influential novel *The Well of Loneliness.* The lesbian character at the center of the novel is portrayed as an "invert" along the lines suggested by the theories of Havelock Ellis and others.

1933   Germany: Adolf Hitler came to power in Germany. Nazi storm troopers raided headquarters of the WHK and the IS. The early homosexual rights movement and the effort to reform the German antisodomy law, Paragraph 175, was quashed.

1941–1945   Germany: Between 10,000 and 15,000 homosexuals, primarily men, were deported to Nazi concentration camps, where they were identified by the wearing of pink triangles. The majority perished. **United States:** The U.S. military began screening for homosexual men and women to keep them out of the armed forces.

1946   Netherlands: The Shakespeare Club, also known as the "Amsterdam Social Club," was founded, and it in turn formed the nucleus of a larger group, the *Cultuur-En-Ontspannings Centrum* (COC, Culture and Recreation Center). It was the first European postwar homosexual rights group.

1950   United States: After a State Department official, John Peurifoy, testified to Congress about the frequency of homosexuality among those dismissed from government, the Senate launched an investigation. The subsequent report, "Employment of Homosexuals and Other Sex Perverts in Government," argued for the dismissal of all homosexual federal employees. The federal and state governments, as well as the military, increased their persecution of homosexuals.

1951   Europe: An international conference for equal sexual rights was held in Amsterdam. Held largely at the initiative of the COC, it was successful and led to the creation of the International Committee for Sexual Equality. **United States:** Henry Hay and others founded the Mattachine Society in Los Angeles. It became one of the leading homophile groups of its time.

1952 United States: The American Psychiatric Association (APA) listed homosexuality as a sociopathic personality disturbance in its first edition of *The Diagnostic and Statistical Manual, Mental Disorders (DSM-1)*.

1953 United States: A small group of persons associated with the Mattachine Society began publishing *ONE*. Unlike other homophile publications, it was relatively outspoken for its day. It aspired to expose police harassment and entrapment practices as well as defend homosexuality.

1954 United States: The Postmaster General declared *ONE* obscene and seized copies of the magazine. Its publishers filed suit. **France:** The journal *Arcadie* was launched. It quickly became an outspoken and influential pro-homosexual journal and at the forefront of the French homophile movement.

1955 United States: The Daughters of Bilitis formed in San Francisco. It was the first and foremost homophile group for lesbians.

1956 Thailand: The government repealed a five-decades-old anti-sodomy law that had never actually been used.

1957 Great Britain: The Wolfenden Report was released in the United Kingdom. It argued that consensual homosexual sex between persons 21 years of age or older should be legalized. While the report received favorable coverage in the press, the majority of the public remained opposed. **Germany:** The government of East Germany announced that it would no longer enforce its anti-sodomy law.

1958 United States: In a case arising out of the seizure of a homophile publication, the Supreme Court, in *ONE, Inc. v. Olesen*, unanimously ruled in favor of ONE, Inc., declaring that the publication could be distributed. It was the first Supreme Court case that directly addressed homosexuality.

1962 United States: In the case of *Manual v. Day*, the Supreme Court again ruled in favor of homophile publications, this time in favor of a publisher of homoerotic materials. The ruling helped bring about a more outspoken homophile press.

1964 United States: The Society for Individual Rights was founded in San Francisco. The organization marked a new, more assertive phase in the homophile movement.

1967 Great Britain: The Sexual Offenses Act decriminalized homosexual sex in England and Wales. It set the age of consent at 21, even though the age of consent for heterosexual sex was 16.

1969 Germany: The West German government decriminalized homosexual sex but set the age of consent considerably higher than for heterosexual acts. **United States:** A late June police raid on the Stonewall Inn, a Greenwich Village bar with a gay clientele, culminated in the Stonewall riots. The event helped usher in the modern gay movement. Within a few weeks, activists formed the Gay Liberation Front.

1970 Great Britain: Two activists established the Gay Liberation Front in Britain. Although short-lived, the group proved deeply influential. **Spain:** The government of General Francisco Franco enacted an anti-sodomy law, the Social Menace and Rehabilitation Act. It called for the "reeducation" of homosexuals. Under its provisions, persons were subjected to electroshock therapy and other forms of brutality.

1971 Netherlands: The government equalized the age of consent for heterosexual and homosexual sex.

1973 Netherlands: The government declared that gays and lesbians could serve in the military. **United States:** The APA removed homosexuality as a mental disorder from the *DSM*. Instead, it listed homosexuality combined with a wish to change that orientation, or otherwise being disturbed by one's same-sex attraction, as a disorder.

1975 United States: California's government repealed its felony "crimes against nature" law.

1977 United States: Anita Bryant launched a campaign to overturn a Dade County, Florida, anti-discrimination law. It was one of the first major initiatives of the religious right backlash against the emergent gay rights movement.

1979   Spain: The government repealed most of the Social Menace and Rehabilitation Act, including its anti-homosexual provisions. **United States:** Jerry Falwell founded the Moral Majority.

1980   United States: Steve Endean and others founded the Human Rights Campaign, a political action committee (PAC). Still in existence today, it is one of the largest gay PACs. Committed to funding pro-gay candidates for public office, it also lobbies on behalf of gay rights.

1981   Europe: The European Court of Human Rights, in the case of *Dudgeon v. United Kingdom*, found that Northern Ireland's anti-sodomy law violated the Convention for the Protection of Human Rights and Fundamental Freedoms. The ruling applied across all of the Council of Europe. **United States:** The Centers for Disease Control and Prevention published a report about a disease striking gay men. It was one of the first accounts of what would become the AIDS epidemic.

1982   Great Britain: Northern Ireland decriminalized sodomy. **Indonesia:** A small group of activists formed the country's first gay organization, Lambda International.

1984   Argentina: The country's leading gay rights organization, *Comunidad Homosexual Argentina*, was established. **United States:** Researchers announced that they had isolated and identified HIV, the virus that causes AIDS.

1986   South Africa: Activists formed the Organization for Lesbian and Gay Action, which in turn was accepted into the broader anti-apartheid umbrella group. **United States:** The APA removed homosexuality entirely from the *DSM*.

1987   Sweden: The country became one of the first to accord any legal status to same-sex couples. The Homosexual Cohabitants Act provided a smaller set of rights than Sweden's opposite-sex cohabitant laws.

1988   Great Britain: The government, under Prime Minister Margaret Thatcher, passed Clause 28. It forbade local governments from promoting homosexuality. **Israel:** The government repealed its anti-sodomy law.

1989   Brazil: Two states passed anti-discrimination laws covering gays and lesbians. **Denmark:** After years of lobbying efforts by the lesbian and gay community, the government passed a registered partnership law. **Israel:** The government amended its Employment Act (mandating non-discrimination) to include sexual orientation.

1992 Namibia: The government enacted an anti-discrimination law that included sexual orientation.

1993 Norway: The country established a registered partnership system for same-sex couples. **Philippines:** Activists established ProGay Philippines, a gay rights group. **United States:** Under fire from conservatives and many in the military, President Bill Clinton abandoned his campaign pledge to end the ban on gays and lesbians in the military. Members of Congress crafted a compromise, "Don't Ask, Don't Tell," that was adopted.

1994 Great Britain: The government lowered the age of consent for individuals participating in homosexual sex to 18. The corresponding age for heterosexual relations was 16. **Japan:** The Japanese chapter of the International Lesbian and Gay Association organized Japan's first gay pride march in Tokyo, in which hundreds participated. **Philippines:** ProGay Philippines organized the region's first gay pride march, which took place on the 25th anniversary of Stonewall. **United Nations:** The Human Rights Committee ruled, in the case of *Toonen v. Australia*, that Tasmania's anti-sodomy law violated the International Covenant on Civil and Political Rights.

1995 Spain: The government passed a law that forbade discrimination on the basis of sexual orientation in regard to employment, housing, or public services. **Sri Lanka:** The government added female-female relations to its anti-sodomy statute. **Sweden:** The country deepened the legal status of same-sex couples by enacting a registered partnership law.

1996 Iceland: A registered partnership law went into effect. **South Africa:** The new post-apartheid constitution went into effect. Its bill of rights specifically listed sexual orientation as a status to be protected from discrimination. It was the first constitution in the world to do so. **United States:** The U.S. government passed the Defense of Marriage

Act, which forbids the federal government from recognizing same-sex marriage in any fashion.

1997   Australia: In response to a United Nations Human Rights Committee ruling, the province of Tasmania repealed its anti-sodomy law.

1998   Costa Rica: The government enacted an anti-discrimination law protecting gays and lesbians in employment. **Ecuador:** An anti-discrimination law was added to the constitution. **South Africa:** The Constitutional Court of South Africa ruled that all anti-sodomy and unnatural acts laws were in conflict with the bill of rights' guarantee of non-discrimination on the basis of sexual orientation and thus were void. **United States:** Matthew Shepard, a University of Wyoming student, was brutally attacked outside of Laramie. He died a few days later. His slaying attracted a wave of attention about hate crimes against gays and lesbians.

1999   France: After a divisive battle between traditionalists and the ruling Socialists, the government passed a law creating the *Pacte civil de solidarité* (civil solidarity pact). It is a weak version of Nordic registered partnerships. **Mexico:** Mexico City added an anti-discrimination law covering gays and lesbians.

2000   Brazil: The social security agency issued a rule granting benefits to same-sex partners of the deceased. **Great Britain:** The Labor government equalized the age of consent for homosexual and heterosexual sex at 16. The government also allowed gays and lesbians to serve openly in the military. **United States:** Vermont enacted a civil unions law.

2001   Czech Republic: The government passed a domestic partnership law that included gays and lesbians. **Estonia:** The age of consent for heterosexual and homosexual sex was equalized. **Germany:** The government began to recognize civil unions. While initially rather narrow, the scope of this recognition has been broadened by subsequent changes. **Netherlands:** The country became the first in the world to accord full marriage rights to same-sex couples. **South Korea:** The government passed a law that forbids discrimination on the basis of sexual orientation.

2002   Argentina: The city of Buenos Aires began recognizing civil unions. **Bulgaria:** The government equalized the age of consent for heterosexual and homosexual sex. **Finland:** The government enacted a registered partnership law. **Hungary:** The age of consent was equalized for heterosexual and homosexual sex.

2003   Belgium: The government recognized same-sex marriage, although the law did prohibit adoption by such couples. **Brazil:** As a result of a court decision, the government began recognizing same-sex couples for the purposes of immigration rights. **Bulgaria:** The government passed an anti-discrimination law that included gays and lesbians. **Great Britain:** England and Wales repealed Clause 28, an anti-gay measure dating back to the Thatcher government. **Poland:** An anti-discrimination law was passed. **United States:** Connecticut passed a civil unions law.

2004   Egypt: The government launched a crackdown on men who have sex with men. Scores were jailed; others were harassed and beaten but not charged. **New Zealand:** The government passed the Civil Union Act, which confers most of the benefits of marriage to same- and opposite-sex couples. **United States:** Massachusetts began legalized same-sex marriage. In the fall elections, 11 states passed initiatives that banned recognition of same-sex marriages.

2005   Canada: The country began recognizing same-sex marriage. **Great Britain:** A weak registered partnership law went into effect, the Civil Partnerships Act. **Spain:** The Socialist government of José Zapatero passed a same-sex marriage law, including adoption rights.

2006   South Africa: In the wake of a ruling by the Constitutional Court of South Africa, the country's highest court, that mandated full recognition of same-sex relationships, the government became the first in Africa to have same-sex marriage.

2007   Nigeria: The parliament considered and then dropped a bill that would have criminalized forming or joining a gay group, going through or attending a (private) same-sex marriage ceremony, or otherwise promoting homosexuality. **Thailand:** The government banned discrimination in employment on the basis of sexual orientation. **United States:** The CDC reported that the number of HIV/AIDS diagnoses among men who have sex with men rose by 11 percent from 2001 to 2005. The prevalence among gay black men was roughly double that of gay white men. **Uruguay:** The country became the first in Latin America to recognize same-sex civil unions.

2008 **Israel:** In a controversial ruling, the country's attorney general ruled that gay couples can jointly adopt children. **Netherlands:** The country enacted a registered partnership law. **Nicaragua:** The government repealed the country's anti-sodomy law. **United States:** In New Hampshire, a civil union law went into effect. The state supreme court in California ruled that the denial of same-sex marriage was in violation of the state constitution. A ballot iniative, Proposition 8, subsequently overturned the court's decision.

Introduction

The history of sexuality is central to social history, the history of ideas, the realization or repression of human rights, and other areas of focus. This is also true about those who have had, or do have, what could be called minority sexualities. Same-sex attraction has generally been a minority sexuality; it has been the object of tremendous repression and vociferous complaint as well as praise by talented poets and philosophers. One purpose of this volume is to convey a sense of how same-sex attraction has been and continues to be deeply intertwined with the broader contours of history.

Because sexual expression is at least partially historically contingent, a difficulty faced by anyone studying sexuality in general, and homosexuality in particular, is identifying the precise scope of the subject matter. That is, the apparently simple question of what counts as homosexuality ends up being extraordinarily complex. The same is true, of course, for heterosexuality; it is not as if one form (heterosexuality) is historically invariable and thus is the proper standpoint for interrogation of an uncertain homosexuality. Context matters, especially historical context. Furthermore, the range of contexts is daunting, since many different social, religious, and legal regimes are relevant. A simplistic way of avoiding these issues would be to reduce the issue to genital contact: a person is a "homosexual" just by dint of having sex with someone of his or her own sex. There are, however, a number of problems with such an approach. Such a narrow definition misses not only cases of chaste attraction to members of one's own sex, as was idealized in medieval Spain under the Moors, but also could easily slide into ignoring the much richer emotional and cultural aspects of same-sex attraction and affection. It also lends itself to a grossly unequal treatment of homosexuality as compared to heterosexuality. For instance, Justice Antonin Scalia's dissent in *Lawrence v. Texas* discusses homosexuality purely in narrow sexual terms, just like the majority decision in *Bowers v. Hardwick*, whereas the same decisions' discussions of heterosexuality turn away from sex acts to discuss relationships, marriage, and procreation. It is simplistic and dehumanizing to ignore broader issues of relationships, families, extended circles of friends, and the cultural meanings of same-sex attraction. Surely for Justice Scalia heterosexuality means more than just genital contact with his wife; it means children, extended family, and it is an important aspect of a broader community. The same is true for homosexuality.

There is no given, a priori way of mapping sexual and emotional desire or expression. In ancient Greece, the gender of one's sex partner was less important than whether one was penetrating or penetrated. Furthermore, the nobility of character and physical beauty of one's partner were also seen as of great significance. For citizens, being the one penetrated was unseemly, but the superior position was relatively unproblematic, yet for one to take the passive or penetrated role as a young man or older boy was acceptable. Furthermore, there was arguably not an understanding of one having a "sexual orientation," unless the concept is broadened to include men who consistently and willingly took the passive role—something deeply troubling to status-conscious ancient Greeks.[1] An analogous type of understanding is common in the Arabic world today, although it is fair to say that sexuality in general is much more stigmatized among today's Arabs than among ancient Greeks. The question for both is, or was, much more one of acts than of identity, and also whether one is the active partner or the passive one. Likewise, some understandings focus on gender roles rather than sexual object choice. That is, one is seen as "normal" if one's behavior accords with traditional interpretations of gender role regardless of the sex of one's partners. Thus, a man who is masculine is, in this interpretation, not marginalized even though he consistently chooses men for sex partners, as long as he takes the "manly" role in the act.

TYPOLOGIES OF HOMOSEXUALITY

It is possible to construct a typology of homosexual relationships. Two of the most common have already been mentioned. Like the ancient Greeks, many societies have structured same-sex erotic relationships as occurring between a man in a conventional gender role and one who is in a lesser position, often due to young age or perhaps social status. Medieval Japan is another example of this. Another recurring type pairs individuals where one adheres to conventional gender roles and the other person does not. Examples would include butch/femme relationships, the American Indian berdache, and many pre-colonial African tribes. Finally, there is the type that is the norm in contemporary developed countries, which involves persons of roughly the same age and status forming relationships. None of these, in turn, connect neatly to the issues of social role and identity. In ancient Greece, men who ardently pursued youths were usually married and had children. Adolescent boys in pre-colonial Africa who had older man–youth relationships almost always later married and had children in adulthood. In Asia today, millions of persons have same-sex erotic relationships or encounters yet also have fulfilled their social duty of opposite-sex marriage and procreation. It is only at some times, and in some places, that erotic attractions and acts become a defining aspect of identity and perhaps a distinct social role. The contemporary West is one of those times and places; societies with the role of gender nonconformist in homosexual relations have frequently been another. For other societies, same-sex behavior is confined to a portion of one's life, but many persons in the culture experience it. The idea that persons have a lifelong orientation toward members of only one sex, and that this orientation is partially definitive of the self and identity, is culturally specific to the contemporary West and is an idea that would strike many around the world as odd.

The typology of age/status, gender role, and egalitarian forms of homosexuality can be further divided, such as by how formalized the relations and norms are. In some societies, the most common type of same-sex relationship is highly structured and institutionalized. For instance, age-structured forms of homosexuality have been viewed by some tribes as a form of care for boys coming of age. Inseminating them with semen (or smearing their bodies with ejaculate, etc.) is how they become masculine. In others, such as early modern Italy, age-structured homosexuality was largely furtive and not institutionalized within mainstream society. In other societies, religious ceremonies and roles have been the basis for institutionalization. For instance, some societies have assigned berdache important religious or medicinal roles. Hence there have also been formalized, gender-based examples of homosexuality, such as with female-dressing shamans, and non-formalized yet still gender-based homosexuality.

An additional complicating aspect comes from differences between the sexes. Many, such as the poet and essayist Adrienne Rich, argue that lesbianism is not just a mirror image of male homosexuality. Rich contends that lesbians are doubly oppressed due to their sexuality and their gender. For her, women whose actions embody resistance to a system of compulsory heterosexuality are in a broad sense "lesbian," even if they do not engage in female-female sexual acts. Thus, 19th-century women who passed as men, or those who refused marriage and instead had intense friendships with other women, fall into a broad "lesbian continuum." Many also object to the term "lesbian" being used in cross-cultural contexts, arguing that it is a historically contingent and culturally specific understanding. Although the specifics of her argument are controversial, Rich, the historian Lillian Faderman, and others have put forward understandings of lesbianism that downplay its sexual aspects.[2]

SEXUALITY: SOCIALLY CONSTRUCTED OR SET BY NATURE?

Some look at the broad variation in understandings of sexuality, including same-sex attraction, and are struck by what they see as profound discontinuity. Michel Foucault is one of the foremost examples of this. For him, sexuality is socially constructed, primarily by the power regime that runs in such a tight capillary manner through the social body but also by how resistance fights and eludes that regime. There is no cross-cultural sexuality that is simply given, whether by genes or other aspects of nature. Instead, cultural understandings, and even subjective interpretations of bodily drives and urges, are historically specific and often strikingly dissimilar from one historical era or culture to the next. In contrast, others contend that there is still continuity, and today's gays and lesbians can rightly derive satisfaction and pride from the forebears. Examples of this view include some noteworthy students of history such as John Boswell and Louis Crompton.

One response to these theoretical issues is to speak of "homosexualities," rather than just homosexuality. This terminological shift is an effective way of gesturing at the discontinuity and variations involved while still preserving some common element. While this historical dictionary of homosexuality does not take a stand on the continuity versus discontinuity issue, there is a crucial terminological problem that cannot be dodged. Were ancient Greek men "gay," or does that impute to them an identity that is limited to the modern world, primarily to the contemporary West? It seems that to use the terms "gay" and "lesbian" regardless of time and place does at least prejudge the issue. Thus this work does not use, for example, the term "gay" across all societies and historical eras. At times this does make the language more cumbersome, but it also makes it more historically and conceptually accurate. Thus, when talking about post-Stonewall movements in the United States, it certainly makes sense to speak of gays and lesbians. In other historical contexts, it makes more sense to write of same-sex attraction or love and use other types of locutions that avoid terms specific to a different time and locale.

Any work in the history of sexuality, including the present volume, will at least implicitly take a stand to the question of what counts as sexuality and, in this case, homosexuality. A good approach is inclusive. Genital contact is not decisive, although it is significant. Same-sex relationships which are intimate and passionate, and perhaps even the dominant aspect of a person's life, move persons along the continuum toward homosexuality, even when they are not overtly sexual. Many writers use the term "homosocial" to get at these sorts of relationships. This neologism usefully captures the idea, given that the issue is that those relationships do not have an overt or consummated sexual dimension but do have a pronounced same-sex aspect. Furthermore, the history of homosexuality certainly should include those cultural expressions of same-sex sexuality where the participants do not see it as "homosexual" in the modern, Western sense. Otherwise, such a study falls even more deeply into cultural blindness, taking the specifics of one's own milieu and imputing it to others.

PRIMITIVE AND ANCIENT SOCIETIES

Evidence about the earliest forms of same-sex eroticism primarily comes from 20th-century anthropological studies of tribal societies.

For example, analyses of such societies in New Guinea have found that 10–20 percent of them have initiation rites for younger males that involve being penetrated by older men. Since societies were structured primarily along tribal or clan lines for most of human history, the study of the organization of sexual behavior among such peoples has historical and anthropological relevance.

Yet the profession of anthropology itself has been plagued by many of the issues of bias already discussed. One way in which anthropology's shortcomings have been manifested is in the relative dearth of cross-cultural studies of female same-sex sexuality. This is despite the fact that two of the foremost 20th-century anthropologists, Margaret Mead and Ruth Benedict, were lovers. Feminist scholars in the 1970s, and later lesbian scholars, subjected the field to insightful criticism about its male and Western-oriented viewpoint. Still, the research into female-female sexuality is inadequate and well behind male-male research.

As noted above, many non-state societies have, or had, male same-sex ritual practices. Anthropologists have observed only a few female same-sex rituals. Aboriginal Australians would initiate girls at menarche. This involved dancing and public ceremonies with overt homoerotic conduct. This tradition largely died out in the second half of the 20th century. Other early 20th-century field reports recorded female-female homoerotic rituals on some islands in Melanesia. Anthropologists have more frequently observed same-sex erotic play among adolescents, both male-male and female-female. Some cultures have seen this as a rather safe way to learn about sexuality, since such play cannot produce children. Others, such as the !Kung San in the Kalahari Desert, generally disapprove, yet do not make any serious efforts to stop it.

Some tribal societies with strongly defined, dichotomous gender systems had formalized transgender roles. For instance, persons with female bodies could adopt male roles as far as behavior and the division of labor and could marry women. Given strong definitions of gender and their importance for kinship lines and other crucial social norms, persons had to fit either gender role, but not necessarily one that accorded with their biological sex. Since the pursuit and marriage of women was understood as part of the male role, women who engaged in this were generally recognized by others, and saw themselves, as male. The same set of background conditions created the possibility of the adoption of the female role by biological men. Several cultures accorded great respect for transgender persons, seeing them as especially powerful shamans or mystics. For instance, at least two tribes in 19th-century Siberia recognized women in male roles and recognized their marriages to women. Similar practices were reported in some North America tribes. Anthropologists have also recorded transgender roles in Asia, such as in Thailand and Indonesia, although those societies often accorded persons in such roles less social acceptance.

Some primitive societies have, or had, well-established intimate relationships between women. Often they were between a somewhat older woman and a younger one, one or both of whom were in opposite-sex marriages. In cultures such as the Azande in central Africa and the Nama further south, these relationships were publicly recognized and sealed by rituals. Southern African tribes practiced "mummy-baby" friendships, formed between two young women. The older was the "mummy," and she was expected to be more generous in her gift giving. These relationships often had a sexual component (though recognizing that the participants themselves often defined "sex" as only something that a women and man could do, since they saw it as requiring a penis and vagina). The women in mummy-baby relationships usually married but often maintained the close friendship. Some celebrated their relationship by inviting persons to a feast.

Extensive records about same-sex relations in ancient societies only extend to ancient Greece, China, and Rome. Furthermore, the records are incomplete and primarily only address male same-sex relations, in part because literacy was often limited to men. Ancient Greek attitudes toward same-sex sexuality varied significantly by locale, but the type of idealized relationship recorded, even celebrated, between men and older youths in some city-states has proven to be a leitmotif in Western culture. For centuries, attractive young men were sometimes called Ganymedes, in reference to the myth of the comely young Trojan that Zeus abducted to be his cupbearer and lover. Michelangelo made a black chalk drawing entitled *The Rape of Ganymede*. Another Italian Renaissance artist, Benvenuto Cellini, crafted a beautiful sculpture of Ganymede in the early 16th century. Ancient Greek and Roman mythology portrayed several gods as pursuing relations with both sexes. In addition to Zeus, the Greek tradition had Apollo, Hercules, Orpheus, Dionysus, and others engaging in same-sex relations. Tradition also told of the Amazons, who were women who rejected the company of men, except for once a year in order to reproduce. These tales, however, generally involve the conquest of the Amazons and the reassertion of what the Greeks saw as the natural order of male primacy.

Not every ancient society accepted or tolerated same-sex relations. There is some evidence of social views opposed to same-sex sexuality in ancient Egypt. Since records are scant and the society in question existed for such a long time and surely shifted in its social norms, it has been difficult for scholars to reconstruct attitudes toward sexuality with precision. Clearly for at least some time, ancient Egyptians over-laid gender roles on sex, so that men who penetrated other men were manly and virile since they took the "male" role. Men who allowed themselves to be penetrated, or who were forced to do so, were made into women, which was a mark against them in a patriarchal society. Early ancient Hebrews forcibly suppressed cult prostitution, much of which was same-sex, but that perhaps was driven by a nationalistic ardor to drive out foreign sects, rather than opposition to homosexuality. Clearly, however, in the fourth and third centuries B.C.E., Hebrews were sharply critical of male-male relations, as recorded in the book of Leviticus and elsewhere.

THE MIDDLE AGES

The fall of Rome and the dissolution of its empire in the fifth century ushered in an era of tribalism and warfare. Although records from this era are fragmentary, there is some evidence that Germanic tribes encouraged close relations between men and older youths and may have had formalized pederastic relations like in ancient Greece. In the early Middle Ages, there is little evidence of intolerance toward homosexuality outside of Visigothic Spain, where Christian influence was strong. The diffusion of Christianity across Europe did not immediately provoke sentiment against same-sex sexuality. It did, however, slowly and only partially alter the background mental framework. Around 850, an anonymous author produced a number of forgeries that blamed homosexuality for various troubles and invoked the story of Sodom as a warning about the consequences of God's wrath. One of the documents called for death by burning for those caught in what the author saw as unnatural acts. The Church circulated the forgeries for decades. A few penitentials, which guided priests in assigning penance for confessions, laid out some of their strongest penalties for same-sex relations. Yet secular authorities did not respond quickly, nor does it appear that popular attitudes changed significantly until the 12th and 13th centuries. Only in the later part of this time frame did secular authorities begin enacting laws criminalizing same-sex acts. At the same time, the Church established the Inquisition, which targeted "sodomites" along with heretics, especially in Spain and Portugal.

There are few records or texts that pertain to female-female relations during the Middle Ages, and most of those appear in the latter part of the era. A 12th-century French treatise, written by a man named Fougères, described "unnatural" relations between women. He called for death for those caught in such activities. The German theologian Albertus Magnus and his student, Thomas Aquinas, argued that same-sex relations are inherently immoral and included female-female relations in that description. A few medieval romances describe women passing as men who fall in love with other women. The revelation of the cross-dressing, however, always draws the relationships to an end.

The slow turn in Europe from apparent disregard of same-sex relations to overt hostility stands in contrast to feudal Japan. There, relations between warriors and older boys were idealized and institutionalized. Likewise, in Imperial China, same-sex relations, often between men and older boys, were enshrined in literature. Poetry and stories related tales of youths and men who were disinterested in women and deeply devoted to their beloveds. Also, in contrast to most ancient literature, receptive males were sometimes depicted as deriving pleasure from being penetrated. In Fujian province, there were male-male marriages. In Beijing, male actors sometimes served as prostitutes.

THE MODERN ERA

The medieval era in Europe had a broadly Christian theological interpretive schema for sexuality in general, and thus a harsher view toward same-sex love than was common in China or Japan. In contrast, the modern era in Europe (roughly from the 17th century on) has seen the partial replacement of that perspective with a naturalistic, secular framework. This change certainly has not necessarily meant acceptance for homosexuals, but it has profoundly changed the ways in which persons have tried to interpret same-sex love. Furthermore, some of the modern world's central characteristics—such as labor mobility, the rise of cities, the decline of the importance of rural regions and extended families, as well as a new emphasis on companionate love arising out of free, personal choice—have all had profound implications for the availability and experience of same-sex relationships. The individual, increasingly liberated from an all-encompassing social architecture that had determined where one would live, how one would worship, and who one would be able to marry, was able to enter into relationships and contracts (whether of an economic or marital sort) more freely. Sexuality, by becoming less directly attached to theology and procreation, has become an area of life marked by increasing degrees of freedom over time. All of these profound changes in society, initially focused within Western Europe, have dispersed widely over time.

There have been corresponding developments in law. The social contract theories of the 17th century both reflected the profound changes under way in Great Britain and the Dutch Republic as well as sowed the seeds for further changes. The idea that all persons are born with inalienable rights and that political societies are founded to protect those rights has been, quite literally, a revolutionary doctrine. Of course, the legal and social changes that are the hallmark of the modern West have been wildly uneven in their effects upon those attracted to their own sex. In fact, more effective states and bureaucracies often worked to the detriment of homosexuals, regardless of the ideological framework underpinning them. Apart from the Inquisition, only modern states have systematically hunted down and persecuted those attracted to members of their own sex. The fact that such persons, due to the changes that partially define modernity, often had no extended family or religious community to fall back upon only made the assaults more brutal and their effects more tragic. Yet the slowly broadening scope of application of equal rights—to male racial minorities, then women, then religious minorities—had by the latter part of the 20th century led to strong pressures for the inclusion of gays and lesbians into the realm of equal citizenship.

The changes brought forth by the increasing role of science in society help to illustrate this. While the medieval world in Christendom primarily had recourse to the story of Lot while condemning "sodomites," the centrality of this type of language was displaced during the Enlightenment. French thinkers, such as Voltaire, substituted terms drawn from law to refer to homosexuals. Others soon followed suit, such as Cesare Beccaria in Italy. Yet the impulse to scientifically explain and categorize human actions soon took center stage in the effort to name and describe same-sex attraction. In the 19th century, investigators of sexuality put forward a variety of terms in their attempts to denote human sexual variety. Persons attracted to their own sex were called, among other things, inverts, uranians, or homosexuals. The attempt to describe homosexuals scientifically led to efforts that seem humorous today. A Dr. Meagher, writing in 1929, stated that "active male homosexuals" enjoy "pleasant artistic things." He continued, "They are poor whistlers. Their favorite color is green."[3] Some, however, reached more sinister conclusions. Dr. La Forest Potter, in a book that had six printings, argued that while some homosexuals could be "cured," others needed "permanent restraint." And he added, "Some we would probably kill."[4] While this pseudo-scientific thinking clearly was reflected in the Nazi killing of homosexuals, it is important to note that it was influential outside of Germany as well.

THE DEVELOPMENT OF THE GAY RIGHTS MOVEMENT

The first modern homosexual rights movement emerged in the late 19th and early 20th centuries in Europe. Its intellectual center was in Germany, but Great Britain played an important role as well. The movement failed to achieve any real success in altering social attitudes or public policy, and ultimately the dislocations of the Great Depression and World War II caused it to fall apart. Yet the movement served as an important precursor and produced ideas and publications on which later generations drew.

Within a decade after the end of World War II, a number of disparate homosexual organizations formed in various Western countries. Some, such as *Arcadie* in France, were basically social groups, while others had a more political bent. This new generation of homosexual rights groups is usually called the homophile movement. What the early homosexual rights and homophile movements show is that there are a number of preconditions for the emergence of such groups, as well as for their success.[5] The patterns revealed there have continued into the current, post-Stonewall era and may be replicated when, or if, the gay rights movement moves forward in Africa and the Middle East.

In the formation of a gay rights movement, there initially needs to be a background set of ideas and the social space that allows those attracted to members of their own sex to form an identity as a distinct group. In the late 19th century, the role of medical and scientific discussions was prominent, but so too were literary works such as Walt Whitman's *Leaves of Grass*. Memoirs, journals, and other records recount persons not having any name or fixed idea about their sexuality until someone asked them if they were a homosexual or an invert. After having the idea explained to them, they would say, "Yes, that is what I am." Furthermore, the rise of cities and especially the transient nature of ports such as New York, London, and San Francisco, created specific locales that became cruising areas for men. People established gay bars and dance halls. In this social context, repression fostered a political attitude for homosexuals. Severe repression, however, prevented the emergence of any type of movement.

Also, national gay and lesbian movements have a long history of learning from one another. The early homosexual rights movement formed groups such as the Scientific-Humanitarian League, which had chapters across several countries, and the World League for Sexual Reform, which had an international membership. This pattern continued during the homophile movement era and increased after the Stonewall riots in 1969. Today, the existence of groups such as the International Lesbian and Gay Association (ILGA) work on behalf of gay rights in the developing world. While these groups are sometimes accused of having a "neo-colonial" attitude toward developing countries, it is likely that they will help foster the background conditions conducive to the creation of a local movement.

There are also broad similarities as far as the causes for which lesbian and gay rights groups work. They try to carve out private spaces in which it is safe to meet others attracted to their own sex, whether for social or sexual purposes, and create networks of social support. Given the frequency of social and legal repression—the need to hide one's attractions from family, friends, and members of one's places of employment and worship—it is unsurprising that gays and lesbians have often bonded and formed groups with the implicit or even explicit aim of fostering a strong, undamaged sense of self. In addition, these groups have fought to exchange ideas and freely engage in discussions in various public forums. These efforts for freedom of association and the press are crucial to the long-term viability of the movement and its prospects for further successes. Thus, homophile groups have worked against police harassment and entrapment, the practice of chain confessions, and raids on gay bars. They have fought, and sometimes won, legal battles to protect gay publications. As these battles are won, the fight usually shifts to public space, such as the right to hold gay pride parades and other events. Gay rights groups also fight against public discrimination. Initially, this usually takes the form of working against the practice of firing those who are outed as gay or lesbian, or evicting them from apartments. Again, success changes the nature of the fight, so that today in most Western countries the battle has turned to the issue of passing laws outlawing discrimination against gays and lesbians, in effect giving sexual orientation the same protected status as race, ethnicity, gender, and so forth, and the same legal recognition of same-sex relationships.

A critical stage for gay rights movements has historically come with the repeal of anti-sodomy laws. Such laws have proven poisonous for organizing and for the cause of gay rights in general. While such laws remain on the books, all organizing, whether political or just for coffee klatches, can be taken as attempts to promote illegal activity. These laws lead to police harassment and intimidation, since prosecutions of consensual sex are difficult to obtain without resorting to such tactics. Anti-sodomy laws promote discrimination in employment and housing, since such discrimination is targeting "mere criminals." They often dissuade middle- and upper-class persons from joining groups and movements, due to the fear of arrest and the resulting loss of employment and status, thereby robbing organizations of financial resources and greater mainstream legitimacy. They justify keeping out of the country persons who admit to homosexual relations, since they are by definition criminals. They underpin refusing naturalization to those who similarly confess, in addition to justifying agents of the state even asking questions about the most intimate of actions. Finally, anti-sodomy laws keep the issue of same-sex relationship recognition off the agenda since the physical expression of those relationships is a crime.

The contemporary (post-1969) gay and lesbian rights movement must be counted as one of the most successful movements of the past half century in the developed world. That movement, despite its significant internal divisions, has played a key role in moving most Western countries from a norm of criminalization of homosexual acts, police harassment, and open discrimination—often codified in law or regulatory practice—to one where homosexual relations are not only legal, but also where discrimination is often illegal. Some sort of legal recognition of same-sex relationships is also increasingly common, although it is usually less than that available to opposite-sex couples. Despite the success, gays and lesbians in the West are not consistently treated as full and equal members of society. Discrimination persists, although it is now typically covert. Relationships most frequently have less status, both legally and socially, and in some areas are scorned or even provoke hostility. Revealing one's sexuality is still a fraught process. Hate crimes against gays and lesbians are still frighteningly common. The higher rates of suicide among gay teenagers are testimony to this lack of full acceptance.

CULTURAL FRAMEWORKS AND THE STATUS OF HOMOSEXUALITY IN NON-WESTERN REGIONS

The West's movement on gay rights stands in stark contrast to the general trend in the Arab world over the past century and a half. In many locales, the 19th-century approach to same-sex relations was fairly relaxed. The cultural norm saw courtship between men or between a man and an older boy as quite normal. Yet consummation was more problematic, likely due to the influence of Muslim scriptural edicts against such carnality. Even then, some cities (such as Tangiers) developed a reputation for extensive same-sex sexuality. While this situation continued in the first couple of decades in the 20th century, the trend toward religious conservatism and even fundamentalism in the latter half of the century sharply curtailed same-sex sexuality. Thus, while the West was taking its first tentative moves toward openness to same-sex relations, the Arab world was moving away from it.

Most places in the developed world have a distinction between gender, understood as one's social role as according to either female or male norms (or mixing those in a manner that is androgynous), and sexuality, where one is attracted to members of the same sex, opposite sex, or both. For instance, in the United States it makes sense to describe someone as manly (gender) and gay (sexuality). Yet in some regions, such as in Latin America, what is often taken in the developed world as an unproblematic distinction between sexuality and gender is, in contrast, mixed together. Gender roles shape the interpretation of sexuality. Thus a man who is an *activo*, by virtue of playing the penetrative role in sex acts, is manly. Men who are penetrated are effeminate, and in a patriarchal society they are therefore discredited. While the gay rights movement is certainly alive in Latin America, it is weaker than in Europe or the Anglophone world. The conceptual schema here, of *activo* versus *pasivo* (or *ativo* and *passivo* in Portuguese), is likely at least part of the reason, since it inclines *activos* to not identify with and perhaps even denigrate *pasivos*, even when the active partner largely or solely prefers men. The gender overlay itself, however, is complicated by several factors. For instance, same-sex sexual relations are less problematic for younger men but become more so as one rises in age or social status. Another issue is the multitude of perspectives within Latin American society itself, across countries, between urban and rural areas, and so forth.

Similarly, in much of modern Asia, the identities of those engaged in same-sex relations have often differed in important ways from those common to the West. One of the most pointed examples of this is the *hijras* of Bangladesh, northern India, and Pakistan, the large majority of which were born as men. *Hijras* are devotees of the mother goddess Bahuchara Mata and many undergo castration to embody their devotion to the goddess. They have a ritualistic function, blessing newborns and performing at weddings. Yet many also engage in prostitution, and in some *hijra* communities that is the primary source of income. Another example of the combination of ritualistic functions with gender transformation comes from northern Siberia, where the Chukchi tribe has had shamans who, while born male, were made into an ambiguous gender. Some shamans went on to take a husband. Indonesian society has traditionally had men who adopted a feminine gender role and had sex with men. In China, persons attracted to the same sex typically get married, reflecting the importance of family and the obligation to marry and reproduce in traditional Confucian culture. Globalization, however, is changing the nature of sexual identities in Asia, especially among those who engage in same-sex relations. Women and men in places such as Indonesia, China, and India are being exposed to and in many cases adopting self-understandings of homosexuality that are frequent in the West and transmitted by media and travelers.

From this thumbnail sketch certain inferences can be drawn. As mentioned above, the development of the idea of a "sexual orientation," in the sense that the modern West has, ultimately proved critical for the development of the modern homosexual rights movement. In contrast, different understandings have been prevalent in much of Africa, Asia, and the Middle East, though this does not imply one is correct or superior to the other. There are meaningful intra-regional differences as well, which connects to another important change. Increasingly it makes sense to speak of the globalization of the gay rights movement. Since Western media, economies, and higher educational institutions have been dominant in the recent past, Western ideas of sexuality and the corresponding set of appropriate rights have been exported to new areas. Thus Lebanon, which is rather open to Western companies and media and sends many of its citizens abroad, has a nascent gay rights movement. In contrast, Egypt is more closed and does not have such a movement. Similarly, persons from China, Singapore, Indonesia, and elsewhere in Asia who have gone to the West to pursue higher education have sometimes brought back with them Western ideas of sexual orientation and the need to organize around that identity.[6] While the first modern homosexual rights movement quickly achieved internationalization, it was not truly global since it was confined to one region of the world. In contrast to that early 20th-century movement, the past two decades have witnessed the creation of a truly worldwide effort linking national and international groups and campaigns.

Another important factor is a society's attitude toward minorities. As noted above, persons with same-sex attraction and Jews have historically been subjected to persecution by the same regimes, whether clerical- or state-based. The reverse also has generally proven to be true: societies that are tolerant of minorities generally treat persons attracted to the same sex well, too. More precisely, when societies go through periods of tolerance, it typically includes those with minority sexualities. Homosexuals have historically been among the first to be persecuted by regimes or movements bent upon thoroughgoing social control, usually aimed at imposing a homogeneous culture. For instance, when it came to power, the Chinese Communist Party declared homosexuality a bourgeois, decadent practice and harshly repressed it. Homophobia is analogous to racism. There are often hysterical qualities to both, with strange attributes imputed to those one hates. Gays are accused of being obsessed with dirty sex; anti-gay, right-wing websites in the United States today refer to "studies" about how gay men ingest large quantities of fecal matter in their sex lives. There are obsessive qualities, such as anti-gay fanatics picketing the funerals of gay men and women. Furthermore, for centuries the propensity to engage in same-sex relations has often been described as literally foreign. Europeans attributed homosexuality to other countries or to an Italian city. This continues today. The president of Iran claimed that his country has no homosexuals, and other Middle Eastern leaders have said that homosexuality in their countries is solely caused by foreign, Western influence.

As noted above, the diffusion of largely Western media is causing change in social norms and identities elsewhere, especially in Asian urban areas. This in turn is likely to affect the gay and lesbian rights movement. In 2008, 86 United Nations member countries had laws that criminalized same-sex relations.[7] African and Middle Eastern countries constitute a majority of those. Seven countries have the death penalty. The more closed nature of many of those societies, combined with religious fundamentalism, makes it unlikely that the widespread nature of these laws will change soon. In the West, pro-gay changes in law and social norms are often contested as well, especially in the United States. While the vastly increased acceptance of gays and lesbians in Western Europe seems more secure, some worry about immigrants, often from the Middle East or northern Africa, ultimately changing those societies, too. Yet the influence is likely to run both ways. Many Lebanese have spent time in Europe, and Lebanon is the only Muslim-majority Middle Eastern country to have a meaningful gay rights movement. Looking to the future, the only certainty is that the identities and social and legal status of those who pursue and engage in same-sex affections and relations will continue to be intertwined with the broader contours of historical change.

NOTES

1. David Halperin argues that the ancient Greeks did not have a concept of "sexual orientation," even with this broadened definition. The ancient Greeks did not have any concept similar to the particular constellation of items that we capture with the term. See his "Sex before Sexuality: Pederasty, Politics, and Power in Classical Athens," in *Hidden from History: Reclaiming the Gay and Lesbian Past*, ed. Martin Duberman, Martha Vicinus, and George Chauncey Jr., 37–53 (New York: Meridian, 1990).

2. See Adrienne Rich, "Compulsory Heterosexuality and Lesbian Existence," in *The Lesbian and Gay Studies Reader*, ed. Henry Abelove, Michèle Aina Barale, and David M. Halperin, 227–255 (New York: Routledge, 1993).

3. Quoted in Byrne R. S. Fone, *Homophobia: A History* (New York: Henry Holt, 2000), 383.

4. Fone, *Homophobia*, 387.

5. This section draws upon the work of Barry Adam, Jan Duyvendak, and André Krouwel, eds., *The Global Emergence of Gay and Lesbian Politics: National Imprints of a Worldwide Movement* (Philadelphia: Temple University Press, 1999).

6. See Erick Laurent, "Sexuality and Human Rights: An Asian Perspective," in *Sexuality and Human Rights: A Global Overview*, ed. Helmut Graupner and Phillip Tahmindjis (New York: Haworth Press, 2005).

7. Daniel Ottosson, "State-Sponsored Homophobia: A World Survey of Laws Prohibiting Same-Sex Activity between Consenting Adults" (an ILGA Report, May 2008).

The Dictionary

– A –

ACT OF 25 HENRY VIII (1533). In 1533, the English Parliament passed a law that made "buggery" a crime punishable by hanging. It applied to heterosexual and male homosexual anal intercourse. The probable impetus for the statute was Henry VIII's fight with the Catholic Church and his desire to limit the scope of ecclesiastical courts within England. He also used the law to buttress charges against monasteries in order to seize their wealth, even though there were very few actual prosecutions under the law during his reign. Henry's Catholic daughter, Queen Mary, subsequently repealed the law as part of the repeal of most of the legislation passed by the Protestant Parliament. In 1564, however, Queen Elizabeth reinstated the act.

The act stood for centuries. In 1861, the government reduced the punishment from death by hanging to life imprisonment. In 1967, the **Sexual Offenses Act** repealed the law. While the law was rarely the basis for charges under Henry VIII or Queen Elizabeth, in the 18th and 19th centuries dozens of men were hanged and hundreds were imprisoned. Given the deep influence of English Common Law throughout the British Empire, the act was also the basis for anti-sodomy laws across the English-speaking world, as well as in Nigeria, Kenya, **India**, Malaysia, and elsewhere. *See also* AFRICA; ANTI-SODOMY LAWS; ASIA; AUSTRALIA; CANADA; GREAT BRITAIN; LABOUCHÈRE AMENDMENT; LATIN AMERICA; UNITED STATES.

ADOPTION. In **ancient Rome**, one way that men could establish a formal same-sex union was through adoption of one another as

1

brothers. In fact, the phrase "adopt a brother" was slang, during the Roman Empire, for establishing a homosexual relationship. Such adoptions had legal consequences, such as the granting of inheritance rights and citizenship. While some were not sexual or intimate emotional friendships, many were.

While adoption in ancient Roman law created a relationship of greater legal equality than heterosexual marriage, adoption in the contemporary West typically does not, in part because it is rarely the adoption of another adult. A few theorists, such as **Michel Foucault**, have argued for formal, legal recognition of same-sex relationships through adoption. More commonly, advocates for gay and lesbian rights defend **same-sex marriage** laws that include a right to adopt children. A few countries have adopted such laws, primarily in **Europe**.

Even in the absence of formal same-sex marriage, **registered partnership**—or **civil union** laws that provide a degree of legal protection for families formed by same-sex couples—and the increased prevalence and acceptance of same-sex relationships in much of the developed world have made adoption much more common over the past several decades. The **religious right** has campaigned against such adoptions; **Anita Bryant**'s Save Our Children campaign was behind Florida's enactment, in 1977, of a law forbidding adoption by gays and lesbians. Mississippi and Utah ban adoptions by gay couples but not by gay and lesbian individuals; Arkansas voters passed a similar law in 2008. A substantial proportion of married same-sex couples have children, whether from previous relationships, adoption, or other means. *See also* ASSIMILATION; FRANCE; SPAIN.

AFRICA. The history of same-sex sexuality in sub-Saharan Africa prior to the influx of Western missionaries and then colonialism is obscure. Anthropological evidence, the records of early missionaries, and other sources allow for some inferences, but the conclusions are often tentative. There also clearly was a lot of regional variation across tribes. General patterns stand out, however. Before Westerners came to Africa, many tribes strictly separated the sexes for most activities. Men and older boys would spend weeks and, if they were a largely hunting or militaristic tribe, even months together without the presence of women. As a result, same-sex sexual contact seems to have been common and was often seen as acceptable, with some considering it an appropriate precursor to heterosexual relations. There are reports of numerous same-sex relations among such tribes as the Nuba, Tutsi, and Hutu. Another factor contributing to same-sex relations was a scarcity of prospective wives for younger men, given the frequency of polygamy. Yet there was a strict social imperative to marry and procreate since many African communities measured wealth by the number of persons connected to a household, rather than by possessions. Thus, exclusive homosexuality was not a viable option for most.

There was some room for exceptions to the general prohibition on exclusive homosexuality. Most tribes envisioned the community as extending to ancestral spirits. Odd behavior therefore could be explained as possession by such a spirit. A possessed woman could thereby dress as a man and marry a woman; the same held for men. The Konso had four words for such women-spirit-possessed men. In some tribes, men possessed by female spirits served as medicine men and thus had high status. Also, some tribes accorded a magical or spiritual aspect to same-sex relations. The exchange of semen, such as through anal sex, could be a sacred ritual or a sharing of medicine.

Colonialism disrupted and often ended the military practices and polygamy that had promoted homosexual behavior. Yet the introduction of Western capitalism, in conjunction with ruthless colonial masters, forced many men to relocate to industrial and mining centers, thereby creating new opportunities for situational homosexuality. One important example of this was the practice of "**mine marriage**," which was common in many southern African mines in the first half (or longer) of the 20th century.

Given how traditional African society has been generally inhospitable ground for homosexuality, at least as an identity that in turn can be accepted and given space, the first homosexual rights groups formed among white South Africans. The movement there emerged in the late 1960s, reflecting the sharp trend toward the internationalization of the gay rights movement, at least among those tied into global media and economic currents. Another precipitating factor was a proposed law that would have broadened the country's antisodomy laws to include private, consensual sex. Yet the movement largely dissolved once the government gave up on the centerpiece of the proposed law, even though it did manage to raise the **age of consent** for male-male sex to 19. A deeper sense of gay community developed in the 1970s, although it was sharply divided in the ways that South African society was along lines of race, ethnicity, and class. In black society, the community was largely made up of members of the middle class. Many groups formed in the 1980s in a wave of organizing that proved historically important, although some did not last for long. Lesbians in Love and Compromising Situations was primarily white, and its founders had been inspired by the formation of the Gay and Lesbian Association on a university campus. In 1986, a group of activists formed the Organization for Lesbian and Gay Activists (OLGA), which then allied itself with the cause of black liberation and the end of apartheid rule. The African National Congress (ANC) umbrella group accepted OLGA into its ranks, which helped to sow the seeds for the ANC's later support of gay rights. The Gay and Lesbian Association of the Witwatersrand also was active in the anti-apartheid movement and was interracial in its membership.

In 1994, leaders of more than two dozen gay and lesbian groups agreed to form the National Coalition for Gay and Lesbian Equality (NCGLE). This umbrella group worked to ensure that South Africa's post-apartheid constitution included sexual orientation as a protected status in its bill of rights, along with such things as race and ethnicity. NCGLE was successful and the final constitution, in 1996, included sexual orientation. The next year, NCGLE took the lead in a court case to have all of South Africa's anti-sodomy, unnatural acts, and other anti-gay laws struck down as unconstitutional. In 1998, the Constitutional Court of South Africa agreed that the laws contradicted the constitution and hence were void. The next year, the court mandated that same-sex relationships be recognized in **immigration and naturalization law**. The court went further in 2005, mandating that the country enact a **same-sex marriage** law. The government did so the next year. Despite the legal equality for gays and lesbians in South Africa, which ranks among the best in the world, the day-to-day situation is much more tenuous. Many segments of society still view homosexuality as "un-African." As a consequence, ostracism by families, the threat of violence in some neighborhoods, and other forms of discrimination are still common.

In contrast to the (sometimes grudging) acceptance of gay rights by the South African anti-apartheid movement, and then by the ANC-led government, elsewhere in southern and central Africa the gay rights movement has only begun to form or has not emerged at all. In 1989, Gays and Lesbians of Zimbabwe (GALZ) formed as a social group and support network. Robert Mugabe's government banned GALZ from participating in the 1995 Zimbabwe International Book Fair. Mugabe himself delivered a stridently anti-homosexual speech at the opening of the book fair. Yet the publicity ultimately increased GALZ's membership and international backing. It was able to participate in the 1996 fair. In the 1990s and the first decade of the 21st century, a number of other groups have emerged and are trying to assemble a regional movement. For example, LAMBDA (of Mozambique) and the Coalition of African Lesbians held a joint leadership institute in early 2008. More typical is Tanzania, where a weak set of informal groups exists underground out of fear of violence and police repression.

Many countries maintain sharply punitive anti-sodomy laws. In Uganda, sodomy is punishable by life in prison. The government has subjected leaders of the central gay rights group, Sexual Minorities Uganda, to **police harassment** and intimidation. Similar accounts can be found from other countries. In Botswana, male-male relations are punishable by up to 7 years in prison; in Tanzania, up to 14. In Nigeria, Islamic anti-vice squads target persons thought to be homosexual or who do not conform to gender roles. In some of the country's provinces, persons are tried under traditional Islamic family law, sharia. In 2007, the government considered but did not pass an anti-gay bill. Sodomy is already punishable by death in the country; the proposed law threatened up to five years in prison for those who form or attend gay organizations, go through or attend a same-sex marriage ceremony, or do anything to publicize, even indirectly, same-sex love.

Many African political leaders denounce homosexuality as a threat to cultural traditionalism. Likewise, religious leaders have been outspoken in their opposition to same-sex relations. Conservative, evangelical Christianity has flourished in the southern half of Africa. Muslim leaders have also been hostile. While awareness of homosexuality has clearly increased in sub-Saharan Africa over the past quarter of a century, it has often not led to acceptance or even tolerance. Violence and the threat of violence against persons thought to engage in homosexual relations are common. Men have raped lesbians to "punish" them for their sexuality. Family members have taken others to traditional healers for cure. Treatment might consist of burning, or cuts, with herbs then rubbed into the wounds, or other invasive actions. International gay and lesbian groups have worked aggressively to protect those who engage in same-sex relations, although often without success. *See also* CHRISTIANITY; MIDDLE EAST; MILITARY SERVICE; *NATIONAL COALITION FOR GAY AND LESBIAN EQUALITY V. MINISTER OF JUSTICE*; SOTADIC ZONE.

AGE OF CONSENT LAWS. Many countries that do not have **anti-sodomy laws** had, or still have, unequal ages of consent for heterosexual versus homosexual relations. For example, **France**, during World War II, raised the age of consent for same-sex relations to five years higher than opposite-sex acts. Some countries enacted unequal age of consent laws upon repealing anti-sodomy laws. **Great Britain** did so in 1967, West **Germany** in 1969. Gay and lesbian rights groups, among others, have argued for decades that such unequal laws are a form of discrimination. These laws stigmatize same-sex relations, implying that the consequences of same-sex acts are more serious and take a greater degree of maturity. Since they threaten to penalize adolescents for **coming out**, theses laws thereby worsen an already difficult time for young persons.

Most countries in the developed world have now equalized their age of consent laws. France did so in 1982, Germany in 1994. Great Britain only did so in 2000. In the many countries in **Africa**, the **Middle East**, and elsewhere that criminalize same-sex relations, the issue of equality in ages of consent is moot. In **Asia**, Indonesia has unequal ages of consent. Hong Kong has a higher age of consent for male-male relations but not for lesbian ones. *See also* HOMOPHILE MOVEMENT; SEXUAL OFFENSES ACT.

AIDS. *See* HUMAN IMMUNODEFICIENCY VIRUS/ACQUIRED IMMUNODEFICIENCY SYNDROME.

AIDS COALITION TO UNLEASH POWER (ACT UP). Founded in 1987, in New York City, the AIDS Coalition to Unleash Power profoundly influenced the gay rights movement in the **United States.** Even though strictly speaking ACT UP is a **human immunodeficiency virus/acquired immunodeficiency syndrome** advocacy group, its militancy, theatricality and media savvy, and use of civil disobedience tactics quickly set a new tone for the entire gay rights movement. It also spurred changes in the Food and Drug Administration's (FDA) drug approval process for those medicines shown to be safe, yet with unproven effectiveness.

The account of ACT UP's founding is now one of the key stories of the post-**Stonewall** era. In early 1987, **Larry Kramer**, a playwright and gay activist, spoke at the Lesbian and Gay Community Center in New York City. He forcefully addressed the crowd of several hundred about the AIDS crisis, denounced the FDA, and contrasted the political influence of mainstream groups with the relative impotence of the gay movement. Within days, activists had formed ACT UP as an AIDS patients' advocacy group, rather than as a gay rights group. Its members decided to focus upon pressuring the FDA to release all experimental anti-AIDS drugs. ACT UP quickly put together a protest on Wall Street, criticizing both the FDA and Ronald Reagan's administration. Activists founded chapters in other large American cities, such as Los Angeles. Soon after, activists in other countries founded chapters, including in **Great Britain** and **France.**

ACT UP brought a new level of media sophistication to gay rights and AIDS awareness groups. Influenced by persons such as the former gossip columnist Michelangelo Signorile, as well as Village Voice writer Michael Musto, ACT UP organized demonstrations that had national import, yet also fed small-town reporters local angles in order to maximize coverage. It developed an eye-catching pink triangle on black background logo that read, "SILENCE = DEATH." Much of its vibrancy came from the diversity of its membership, many of whom were HIV-positive young men in their 20s, as well as older radicals who had participated in the New Left, along with lesbians long experienced in the feminist movement and anti-apartheid campaigners. Over time, however, ACT UP suffered from internal divisions over whether it was too radical or not radical enough. Some gay rights activists and persons sympathetic to ACT UP have criticized some of its actions as counterproductive. For instance, members of ACT UP publicly denounced Catholic leaders including Cardinal Joseph Ratzinger, later named Pope Benedict XVI, disrupted celebrations of mass, and stomped on communion wafers.

ACT UP is still active, although its membership and its militancy have declined. For its 20th anniversary in 2007, ACT UP held a demonstration on Wall Street that demanded universal health care. The change in focus is part of an overall strategy to increase membership. *See also* CHRISTIANITY; OUTING; QUEER NATION.

AMENDMENT 2. In 1992, Colorado voters passed a ballot initiative that struck down local **anti-discrimination laws**. The Supreme Court subsequently struck down this constitutional amendment, known as Amendment 2, in the case of *Romer v. Evans* (1996). In 2008, the majority of voters in Florida approved a ballot proposal to ban same-sex marriage in their state. It also was called Amendment 2. *See also* NAVRATILOVA, MARTINA.

AMERICAN PSYCHIATRIC ASSOCIATION (APA). In 1952, the American Psychiatric Association published the first edition of its comprehensive listing and description of mental illnesses and pathologies, *The Diagnostic and Statistical Manual, Mental Disorders (DSM-I)*. It listed homosexuality under sociopathic personality disturbances. This description reflected the dominant approach to homosexuality within psychoanalysis at the time, which contended that homosexuality was caused by overbearing mothers, or perhaps seductive ones, or detached fathers, or some other sort of severely dysfunctional parental role models. In 1956, however, a California psychologist, **Evelyn Hooker**, published an influential paper, which argued that homosexuality was neither a cause nor a manifestation of pathology. Her work prompted other researchers to analyze the topic. The second edition of the *DSM*, published in 1968, changed the listing of homosexuality to the category of non-psychotic mental disorders, along with several types of sexual behavior, such as masochism.

In 1973, the board of trustees of the APA revisited the issue and this time voted to strike the listing of homosexuality as a mental disorder. At the same time, it created a new category for those who felt ashamed by or wanted to change their sexual orientation. A group of anti-gay psychiatrists fought the de-listing and managed to get a referendum of the APA's membership. Nevertheless, in 1974 a large majority of the respondents in the referendum voted to uphold the board's decision striking homosexuality as a disorder. The *DSM-III R*, published in 1986, removed all references to homosexuality. *See also* ETIOLOGY; KAMENY, FRANK; MEDICAL MODEL OF HOMOSEXUALITY; REPARATIVE THERAPY.

ANCIENT CHINA. Reliable evidence concerning homosexuality in ancient **China** goes back to the Eastern Zhou dynasty (722–221 B.C.E.), and then only for a small political and social elite. Over the next several centuries, however, a wealth of records accumulated. In part, this is due to cultural norms allowing frank discussion of sexuality, including in literature and art. These records reveal a long tradition of openness to homosexuality, though as is the case with other ancient societies, the historical accounts almost exclusively concern male-male love, omitting lesbianism.

As early as the sixth century B.C.E., there are records of rulers engaged in love affairs with other men. Several stories from this era became standard references to male homosexuality. One is the tale of Duke Ling, who loved Mizi Xia. When Mizi gave him a half-eaten peach, the duke exclaimed about his lover's thoughtfulness and devotion. Another tale concerns a king whose lover, Long Yang, cried bitterly one day when the two were fishing. When asked why he was upset, Long said that just like catching a larger fish makes one want to throw back an earlier, smaller fish, so too finding a greater beauty would make the king want to throw back Long. The most famous anecdote comes from the later part of the Han dynasty (206 B.C.E.–9 C.E.). Emperor Ai's lover, a man named Dong Xian, had fallen asleep on the emperor's robe. Rather than wake him, the emperor cut off his sleeve and then appeared in public in his altered robe. For centuries, there are references to shared peaches, the passion of Long Yang, and cut sleeves, often as stand-ins for homosexuality in general. The Emperor Ai was also noted for his exclusive preference for men. This stands in sharp contrast to an age where the norm was for an emperor to have a large number of wives and concubines, in addition to male lovers. As in **ancient Greece**, many assumed that beauty in either sex could elicit an erotic response, and thus Ai was significant for falling outside this norm of bisexuality.

The tradition of emperors and local rulers having male lovers continued for centuries and in a public enough fashion that they were noted even by official court historians. The Han dynasty's first 10 emperors all had male lovers. Some were influential at court; many were rewarded with land or wealth. Political intrigue often swirled around these favorites. For example, the Emperor Ai tried to make Dong, of the cut sleeve, his successor. Since this was a non-traditional succession, it lacked legitimacy and Dong was forced to kill himself.

The three great religions that deeply influenced ancient China—Taoism, Buddhism, and Confucianism—did not overtly condemn homosexuality. Confucianism puts great emphasis on family and thus promotes heterosexual marriage. It also values social order and hierarchy, and the norms and correct public demeanor to uphold those. Even with these aspects, however, there is no denunciation of homosexuality, as long as persons operate within those constraints. The lack of a religious tradition opposed to homosexuality contributed to the openness and prevalence of homosexual sex and relationships.

It is after the Han dynasty that historical evidence becomes available for the broader Chinese culture. In the third century, a pair of writers, the poets Xi Kang and Ruan Ji, had an enduring relationship. Xi was one of the most influential intellectual figures of his century. Contemporaneously, there are accounts of male prostitution as common, with wealthy male patrons having their favorites. The prevalence of male prostitution during the Song dynasty (960–1280) led the regime to try to suppress it. As in ancient Greece, the sexual passivity of a male in a sex act was seen as troubling. The Song passed a law requiring lashes and a large fine for convicted male prostitutes. The law was rarely enforced. Nevertheless, the law reflected a growing conservatism in Chinese society, largely driven by neo-Confucianism. *See also* JAPAN; LITERATURE, HOMO-SEXUAL MALE.

ANCIENT GREECE. The ancient Greeks wrote openly about sexual matters, as well as provided frank depictions of sexuality in their artwork. Consequently, there is a wealth of material to draw on in discussions of ancient Greek sexuality, although almost all of it was written or made by men. The following brief discussion describes the general outlines of ancient Greek understandings of sexuality, but it is worth noting that there were substantial regional variations. For example, in parts of Ionia there were strictures against same-sex eros, while the people of Elis and Boiotia approved of and even celebrated it.

Aside from the works of **Sappho**, there are only a few scattered references to female-female sexuality. Several vases and plates depict female-female intimacy. These works sometimes include courtship rituals common to male-male relations, such as the touching of a chin. One depicts the sacrificing of a hare to Dionysus, suggesting that religious rites might sometimes have been the occasion for female-female intimacy. The visual images show women of roughly the same age, yet Plutarch and other writers sometimes referred to pederastic female-female relations. In the Hellenistic era, Nossis wrote poetry that implies lesbian eroticism. While either she did not write more explicit poems or they were lost in antiquity, she wrote about the beauty of women, declared herself a follower of Sappho, and generally ignored men in her works.

The ancient Greeks did not have terms or concepts that correspond to the contemporary dichotomy of heterosexual/homosexual. Probably the most frequent assumption that the ancient Greeks had concerning what people today would call sexual orientation was that persons, or at least men, could respond erotically to beauty in either sex. Diogenes Laertius, for example, wrote of Alcibiades, the Athenian general and politician of the fifth century B.C.E., "in his adolescence he drew away the husbands from their wives, and as a young man the wives from their husbands" (quoted in Greenberg 1988, 144). Some persons were noted for their exclusive interest in persons of one gender. For example, Alexander the Great and the founder of Stoicism, Zeno of Citium, were known for their exclusive interest in boys and other men. Such persons, however, were generally portrayed as the exception. Furthermore, attraction to one gender was seen as a matter of taste or preference, rather than as a moral question. A character in Plutarch's *Erotikos* argues that "the noble lover of beauty engages in love wherever he sees excellence and splendid natural endowment without regard for any difference in physiological detail" (Greenberg 1988, 146).

Even though the gender that one was erotically attracted to in any specific instance, or as part of a pattern, was not important, other issues were salient. One concern was whether a person exercised moderation in his sexual practices. Social status was also important. Since only free men had full status, they were allowed sex with those of lesser status, such as women and male slaves. Sex between free men, however, was potentially troublesome. The central distinction in ancient Greek sexual relations was between taking an active or insertive role, versus a passive or penetrated one. The passive role was acceptable only for social inferiors, such as women, slaves, or male youths who were not yet citizens. Hence, the cultural ideal of a same-sex relationship was between an older man, probably in his 20s or 30s, known as the *erastes*, and a boy whose beard had not yet begun to grow, the *eromenos* or *paidika*. In this relationship there was a courtship ritual, involving gifts such as a rooster, and other norms. The *erastes* had to show that he had nobler interests in the boy, rather than a purely sexual concern. The boy was not to submit too easily, and if pursued by more than one man, was to show discretion and pick the nobler one. There is also evidence that partners often avoided penetration by having the *erastes* face his beloved and place his penis between the thighs of the *eromenos*, which is known as intercrural sex. The relationship was to be temporary and should end when the boy reached adulthood. To continue in a submissive role even while one should be an equal citizen was considered troubling, although there were certainly many adult male same-sex relationships that were noted and not strongly stigmatized. There were also male youth-youth relations, as made clear in vase paintings and in the writings of persons such as Pindar. While the passive role was seen as problematic, to be attracted to men was often taken as a sign of masculinity. Greek gods, such as Zeus, had stories of same-sex exploits attributed to them, as did other key figures in Greek myth and literature, such as Achilles, **Ganymede**, and Hercules. **Plato**, in the *Symposium*, has a character argue for the creation of an army composed of same-sex lovers. Such an army did in fact exist, as the **Sacred Band of Thebes**. *See also* ANCIENT CHINA; ANCIENT ROME; ARISTOTLE; CARPENTER, EDWARD; ELLIS, HAVE-

LOCK; ESSENTIALISM; EUROPE; FOUCAULT, MICHEL; JA-
PAN; LITERATURE, HOMOSEXUAL MALE; LITERATURE,
LESBIAN; MIDDLE EAST; MILITARY SERVICE; NATURAL
LAW; PEDERASTY; SAME-SEX MARRIAGE; SOCIAL CON-
STRUCTIONISM; SOTADIC ZONE; SYMONDS, JOHN ADD-
INGTON.

ANCIENT ROME. Although deeply influenced by **ancient Greece**,
ancient Roman society did not have an idealized view of same-sex
relations, unlike in many Greek city-states. Romans tolerated male
same-sex relations, but generally stigmatized the passive (penetrated)
partner. The attitude toward female-female relations was more consistently negative. There also was considerable variation over time in
social norms about same-sex eroticism.

The ancient Etruscans founded a civilization based in what is now
Tuscany, **Italy**, but which for a time extended considerably further
north and south. Little of Etruscan culture is still extant except
for some of their artistic works, many of which depict homoerotic
themes or same-sex sexual acts. They were eventually defeated by
their longtime rivals, the Romans.

During the time of the early Republic, Roman culture was rather
prudish in its mores. In contrast to the Greeks, they did not celebrate
male nudity and the patriarchal nature of society constrained female
sexuality. Yet male same-sex relations seemed to be common, at
least according to a Greek historian who traveled to Rome, since
he observed that most young men had male lovers. During the late
Republic, some of the leading literary figures wrote about same-sex
love. There was also a frequent assumption that men could respond
erotically to beauty in either sex. Catullus, for instance, wrote poems
about same-sex and opposite-sex love. Again, however, concerns
about status and role are central. Penetrating another person, male or
female, was permissible for a freeborn male since ancient Romans
took this as connoting power and possession, and hence an appropriate status. Those penetrated, however, were typically women or
slaves. Catallus' writings reflect this, as he combined expressions of
deep affection and longing for beautiful boys alongside demeaning
language for his enemies, calling them *cinaedus* (faggot) and threatening to rape them. Politicians frequently alleged that their enemies

had engaged in same-sex liaisons, including as the passive partner, yet such taunts did little harm.

Rome's newfound wealth during the time of the Republic had made possible the rise of a cultured class marked by leisure and conspicuous consumption. This new elite was also more accepting of same-sex love. All of this created cultural conflict, however, with some worrying that a cultured elite, unfamiliar with traditional virtues and crafts, and with more permissive sexual mores, would contribute to societal decline. Cicero, a leading political and legal figure during the waning days of the Republic, argued against same-sex love. His work marked an advance for **natural law** theory. Decades later, Musonius Rufus echoed Cicero, arguing that same-sex relations are contrary to nature. There was no resolution to this conflict during the early empire, although it seems clear that most still at least tolerated same-sex relations that conformed to what were seen as appropriate role and status concerns. Plutarch's *Erotikos*, composed early in the second century, reflects this broader social conflict, with one protagonist defending the superiority of men loving youths while another denounces such affections. The Emperor Trajan, who ruled from 98 to 117 C.E., had a well-known pederastic relationship. He was then succeeded by Hadrian, who had a passionate same-sex affair that ended tragically. Hadrian erected statues in memorial to his lover who had drowned in the Nile. Contemporaries and historians have rated both emperors highly.

The first overt discussions of female same-sex relations from ancient Rome come from the early empire and were written by men. The tone is consistently hostile. Poets like Martial depicted lesbians as masculine persons who violate acceptable social roles. They take the active role during sex, often with the use of devices. One author from the later empire even used the general abhorrence of lesbianism as an argument against tolerating male-male love, since, he contended, to accept one means accepting both.

Over time more persons converted to **Christianity**, which helped to change attitudes about sexuality. Early church writers, such as Clement of Alexandria and Tertullian, were hostile to any non-procreative sex, as well as to procreative sex in marriage that was conducted with lust. Thus, to their minds, by definition same-sex acts were immoral. In the fourth century, Emperor Constantine changed Rome's official policy toward Christianity to one of tolerance. While serving as co-emperors, his sons decreed a law that criminalized the passive role in male same-sex acts, although it does not appear to have been frequently enforced. Enacted in 342, the law was later incorporated into the Theodosian Code in 438. An edict in 390 also strongly condemned the passive male in same-sex relations and targeted male prostitutes. The prescribed penalty was death by burning. Yet in the same year, a Roman general who took action against a charioteer in Thessalonica for having relations with a male slave was murdered as a result of his throwing the man into jail. Some of the general's officers were killed as well. In revenge, Theodosius launched a massacre against the people of the town in northern Greece. Thousands were killed. *See also* ADOPTION; ANTI-SODOMY LAWS; AUGUSTINE; ETIOLOGY; EUROPE; FOUCAULT, MICHEL; FRANCE; LITERATURE, HOMOSEXUAL MALE; LITERATURE, LESBIAN; MIDDLE EAST; SAME-SEX MARRIAGE; SPAIN; TRIBADE.

ANTI-DISCRIMINATION LAWS. A long-standing goal of gay rights groups in **Europe** and the **United States**, and increasingly around the world, has been enacting protections against discrimination on the basis of sexual orientation. Legal protections are generally sought in regard to employment (by both public and private employers), housing, and public accommodations, such as with hotels and bars. More recently, persons with **human immunodeficiency virus/ acquired immunodeficiency syndrome** have also sought protection from discrimination. Sexual orientation anti-discrimination laws have been enacted in large parts of Europe, but only in some states and municipalities in the United States. An anti-discrimination legal regime is often called equal protection status in the United States, after the language of the 14th Amendment and subsequent civil rights law. While such status could have been conferred via judicial interpretation of the Constitution and lower law, state and municipal legal enactment has so far been more frequent and effective.

While members of the **homophile movement** sometimes expressed a desire for anti-discrimination laws, it took the radicalism and confidence of the post-**Stonewall** era to push this onto the political agenda. The first significant gains were in the 1970s. In the United States, several cities passed sexual orientation anti-discrimination laws, including the District of Columbia, Iowa City, and Los Angeles. Yet it was in Europe in the 1970s and the next two decades that even more significant laws were passed. Several countries passed anti-discrimination laws, such as **France**, Denmark, Norway, Ireland, and the Netherlands. The European Union has passed a resolution calling upon all member states to pass such laws.

In the United States, the movement to pass anti-discrimination laws moved slowly in the 1980s. There were some successes, such as in Lawrence, Kansas, as well as Chicago and a statewide law for Wisconsin. The 1990s, however, was a time of significant action. Connecticut, Vermont, Minnesota, and New Hampshire all passed laws banning discrimination on the basis of sexual orientation in private employment, public accommodation, and other areas. A large number of cities also passed such laws. The momentum has continued, albeit more slowly, in the first decade of the 21st century. *See also* AFRICA; ASIA; AUSTRALIA; *BOY SCOUTS OF AMERICA V. DALE*; BRYANT, ANITA; CANADA; CHINA; CLOSET, THE; EMPLOYMENT NON-DISCRIMINATION ACT (ENDA); FALWELL, JERRY, SR.; FAMILY RESEARCH COUNCIL; FOCUS ON THE FAMILY; GAY ACTIVISTS ALLIANCE; GERMANY; HUMAN RIGHTS CAMPAIGN; ITALY; JUDAISM; MILK, HARVEY; NATIONAL GAY AND LESBIAN TASK FORCE; NATURAL LAW; NAVRATILOVA, MARTINA; PARENTS AND FRIENDS OF LESBIANS AND GAYS; RELIGIOUS RIGHT; *ROMER V. EVANS*; RUSSIA.

ANTI-SODOMY LAWS. The term "sodomy" historically has not had a precise meaning. Relatedly, anti-sodomy laws have varied considerably in their application and interpretation. Some of the narrowest have applied only to male-male anal sex that included emission of semen, perhaps only for the male taking the passive role; others have criminalized any form of non-procreative sex, including heterosexual relations. Anti-sodomy laws have often been used to political ends, with the state charging opposition figures with unlawful intercourse rather than political crimes. Romania's Communist government frequently relied upon this tactic. Such laws have also served to justify entrapment and other forms of **police harassment**. Since consensual sodomy is difficult to prove, agents of the state have resorted to posing as homosexuals, spying, or obtaining coerced confessions in order to gain convictions. Other laws help buttress anti-homosexual legal regimes. Lewd and lascivious behavior, disorderly conduct, and related laws often garner as many if not more convictions against targeted populations.

Historically, anti-sodomy laws in **Europe** date back to **ancient Rome**. The **Code of Justinian**, enacted in 533, broadened the scope of the previous laws and laid out a penalty of death. The most influential anti-sodomy law was **Act of 25 Henry VIII**. The English Parliament passed the law in 1533. The law was narrow in focus, criminalizing only male-male anal sex, but the punishment it laid out was death by hanging. The law applied in British colonies such as **Australia** and was typically adopted by countries even after independence from the Crown. The government of **Great Britain** repealed the law in 1967 with the **Sexual Offenses Act**.

In the **United States**, the formative influence during the colonial era was British law. As a consequence, most colonies only criminalized male-male anal sex. The same was true for the United States' first century. Yet the increasing prominence of medical discourse and classification led to a focus upon gender roles. One consequence of this change in perspective was a new emphasis on the control of oral sex between men as part of an overall concern about the violation of gender roles. In 1879, Pennsylvania amended its anti-sodomy law to include male-male oral sex. Over the next three decades, about a dozen states followed suit, or created new statutes that criminalized oral sex. In other states, supreme courts reinterpreted existing anti-sodomy statutes to cover male-male oral sex. Most remaining states followed in subsequent years, until the legal norm around the nation was the criminalization of all forms of male homosexual sex. Therefore, the number of sodomy arrests and convictions increased steadily after 1880. Likewise, Britain enacted the **Labouchère Amendment** in 1885; it too criminalized male homosexual oral sex.

In 1955, the American Law Institute (ALI) released an influential draft version of its model penal code, which omitted any anti-sodomy statute. In 1961, the state of Illinois repealed its anti-sodomy law. The next year the ALI released its final version, which retained its support for the decriminalization of sodomy. Connecticut repealed its anti-sodomy law in 1969. In the 1970s, most states either repealed their anti-sodomy statutes or reduced them to misdemeanor offenses. The Supreme Court, in the 1986 decision of *Bowers v. Hardwick*, ruled that same-sex sodomy laws were constitutional. By that point, only a handful of states, primarily in the South, still had such laws on the books. In 2003, the Court reversed itself. In *Lawrence v. Texas*, it held that the right to privacy extended to same-sex sexuality and therefore struck down all anti-sodomy laws.

Some countries are notable for their lack of regulation of sodomy. **Japan** for centuries had a tradition that celebrated at least some forms of same-sex love. In 1873, however, the government did pass an anti-sodomy law with a penalty of 90 days in jail upon conviction. It repealed the law a decade later.

Today, anti-sodomy laws are common in the **Middle East** and, to a lesser extent, in **Africa**. Uganda and Tanzania stand out for the harshness of their penalties. The rise of **Islam** and the resulting push to implement sharia, or Islamic family law, has also led to the adoption of anti-sodomy laws, often on an informal, local basis. Several countries in **Asia** also have such laws, including Bangladesh and Sri Lanka. As has often been the case historically, vaguely worded laws are also used to prosecute those who have same-sex sexual relations. For instance, Mongolia's law criminalizes the "immoral gratification of sexual desires," which some authorities equate to engaging in same-sex relations (Laurent 2005, 178). *See also* AGE OF CONSENT LAWS; BENTHAM, JEREMY; BRITISH SOCIETY FOR THE STUDY OF SEX PSYCHOLOGY; CANADA; CHINA; CHRISTIANITY; CLOSET, THE; CODE OF JUSTINIAN; CODE NAPOLÉON; ELLIS, HAVELOCK; ENLIGHTENMENT, THE; EUROPEAN COURT OF HUMAN RIGHTS; FAMILY RESEARCH COUNCIL; FREUD, SIGMUND; GERMANY; HIRSCHFELD, MAGNUS; INDIA; ITALY; JUDAISM; KAMENY, FRANK; KINSEY, ALFRED; LATIN AMERICA; MATTACHINE SOCIETY; MEDICAL MODEL OF HOMOSEXUALITY; MILITARY SERVICE; *NATIONAL COALITION FOR GAY AND LESBIAN EQUALITY V. MINISTER OF JUSTICE*; NATIONAL SOCIALISM; NATURAL LAW; RELIGIOUS RIGHT; RUSSIA; SOCIETY FOR INDIVIDUAL RIGHTS; SOTADIC ZONE; SPAIN; ULRICHS, KARL HEINRICH; UNITED NATIONS; *WISSENSCHAFTLICH-*

HUMANITÄRES KOMITEE/SCIENTIFIC-HUMANITARIAN COMMITTEE; WOLFENDEN REPORT.

AQUINAS, THOMAS (1225–1274). Thomas Aquinas set out the most influential statement of **natural law** theory, which today stands as the most common defense for the unequal legal (and social) treatment of gays and lesbians. Integrating **Aristotle**'s philosophy with the theology of **Christianity**, Aquinas emphasized the centrality of certain human goods, including marriage, procreation, and the raising of children. While Aquinas did not write much about same-sex sexual relations, he did write at length about various sex acts as sins. For Aquinas, sexuality was only permissible and good if it was within the bonds of marriage and helped to further what he saw as the distinctive goods of marriage, mainly love, companionship, and legitimate offspring. Aquinas did not argue that procreation was a necessary part of moral sex; married couples could enjoy sex without the motive of having children. Sex in marriages where one partner is or both partners are sterile is also potentially just, given a motive of expression and cultivation of love. It is worth noting that Aquinas' view at this point need not rule out homosexual sex. For example, a Thomist could embrace same-sex marriage, and then apply the same reasoning, simply seeing the couple as a reproductively sterile, yet still fully loving and companionate union. Andrew Sullivan sympathetically explores a natural law position from this type of perspective.

Aquinas, however, added the requirement that for any given sex act to be moral it must be of a "generative" kind. Since only the emission of semen in a vagina is potentially reproductive, only sex acts of that kind are generative, even if a given sex act does not lead to procreation. The consequence of this addition, of course, is to rule out the possibility that homosexual sex could ever be moral, even if done within a loving marriage. Aquinas did not spell out a justification for this generative requirement, and many contemporary natural law theorists continue to struggle with this area of Thomist thought. *See also* EUROPE; RELIGIOUS RIGHT.

ARISTOTLE (384–322 B.C.E.). One of **Plato**'s students, Aristotle played a crucial role in shaping **natural law** theory. **Thomas Aquinas**

drew upon Aristotle for his account of practical reason, human goods, and the role of virtue in the best life. While natural law theory is central to contemporary intellectual denunciations of gays and lesbians and the defense of anti-gay laws and social norms, there is no good evidence that Aristotle shared this hostility to same-sex sexuality. Aristotle seldom discussed sexuality. When he did, the general picture is along the lines typical of **ancient Greece**. Sexuality is simply one appetite among several. One should not be greedy or gluttonous; likewise, one should manage one's sexual appetites.

Several contemporary neo-Aristotelian philosophers defend equal rights for gays and lesbians. Their arguments focus on the importance of love and companionship in life and on how gay and lesbian relationships are equivalent to heterosexual ones in realizing those goods. Two noteworthy examples are Martha Nussbaum and Michael Sandel. *See also* EUROPE.

ASIA. There is an extensive history of same-sex sexuality in Asia, even leaving aside **China**, **India**, and **Japan**. Early Western explorers and later anthropologists have recorded a variety of institutionalized or ritualized forms of same-sex sexuality among tribal peoples in places such as New Guinea and Melanesia. This has often taken the form of age-structured relations, involving an adolescent or older boy who is taken in by a specified older male (frequently a non-blood relative) upon leaving his childhood home. As such, this form of relation involves initiation to manhood or other rite-of-passage aspects. The older partner takes the penetrative role, although whether that is to be orally or anally varies by tribe. The practice is interpreted as the transmission of the vital and masculine life force to maturing boys. Among some, such as the Etoro and the Marind-Anim, the relationship is to last for years. As a full adult male, the man is to in turn take the other role. In such tribes, much of a man's sexual life will be same-sex focused at least during a specific period of his life, although this rarely precludes marriage and procreation.

Modernization and the disruption it brings to traditional forms of life have caused the dissolution of some tribes and many tribal practices. An example of this is the role of the *manang bali* among some tribes in Borneo and Malaya. Similar to the **berdache**, they would adopt feminine dress, have relations with men, and often worked as shamans. Common in the late 19th century, the role had virtually disappeared by the latter half of the 20th.

Outside of tribal areas, many Asian societies tolerated same-sex conduct and transgender roles. The indigenous religious traditions do not have clear, sharp denunciations of same-sex relations, unlike in the West. In many places, the 19th- and early 20th-century norm allowed for same-sex relations, as long as they did not become too public. What Westerners would call bisexuality was frequent; men saw themselves as engaging in "play" with one another, but "sex" with women. Western influence in Asia brought with it a sharper distinction between same-sex- and opposite-sex-oriented sexuality and stronger condemnation of the former. Some **anti-sodomy laws** in the region, such as Sri Lanka's, were originally imposed under colonial rule.

The experience of same-sex attraction and eroticism today varies dramatically across the region, as would be expected with such a large and diverse area. As a gross generalization, however, in much of Asia there is an expectation that persons will marry and have children. There is often a religious context for this imperative, such as with Confucianism. The effects of these informal norms are more pervasive in rural settings, where sexuality is easily policed by neighbors and extended family. Crowded cities often do not afford privacy, but they do grant anonymity. Since identity is often deeply intertwined with social status and role rather than sexuality, marriage and parenthood need not rule out same-sex relations. Often there is a norm that as long as a person keeps his or her same-sex erotic life hidden and still fulfills his or her roles, it is not an issue.

In Indonesia, the **butch/femme** dichotomy is prevalent among middle- and working-class lesbians. Some butches even pass as men. Lesbian circles there tend to be divided by ethnicity and class, while that is less true among men. The penetration of global media and the sharp rise in international travel to and from the country has led to widespread exposure to Western ideas of sexual orientation. Notions of "gay" and "lesbian" in the Western sense are increasingly common. Traditional versions of nonconformist sexuality continue, however. Although lesbianism is rather invisible in mainstream Indonesian society, **transgenderism** and same-sex sexuality among men is not. *Waria*, or gender-nonconforming men (the term is a portmanteau word from woman, *wanita*, and man, *pria*), are common in urban areas, especially among the poor.

In 1982, three gay men formed the first Indonesian gay organization, Lambda Indonesia. A few years later, activists formed *Kelompok Kerja Lesbian dan Gay Nusantara* (Lesbian and Gay Archipelago Working Group). Both have functioned largely as social and support groups, with the latter also working as a larger, umbrella organization. The social and support group focus is a result of the lack of overt state repression. Since the first legal code was drawn up during the period when most of Indonesia was a French colony, the **Code Napoléon**, which did not criminalize sodomy, was the basis for law. Most gays and lesbians fear the effects of informal social controls, such as family ostracism, rather than the police. The first lesbian organization formed in 1992 during a wave of increased publications and organizing. Indonesia now has one of the largest and oldest gay movements in Asia, complete with national conferences and gay pride parades. Jakarta and Bali have vibrant gay subcultures and nightlife. Still, the prevalence of Islam, the state's constant references to Indonesia as "one big family" (designed to counter separatist impulses across a vast and varied archipelago), and norms of marriage and reproduction combine to make gay and lesbian life frequently invisible and socially difficult.

Taiwan, like many other Asian countries, shares a deep cultural expectation of marriage and reproduction, which arises from a strict version of neo-Confucianism. This in turn has contributed to the historical invisibility of same-sex love there, since persons face strong pressures to marry even if they are attracted to members of their own sex. The Nationalist regime, founded in 1949, did not lay down any anti-sodomy laws, but the government closely policed sexuality, including cruising areas and bars. The relative obscurity of homosexuality continued mostly unbroken until the 1980s. The end of authoritarian rule, general societal liberalization, and the rise of the **human immunodeficiency virus/acquired immunodeficiency syndrome** epidemic all combined to bring same-sex sexuality out of the margins. The *Tongzhi* (Comradeship) gay movement that emerged gained influence quickly. In the 1990s, activists founded the first Chinese-language lesbian group in Asia, the number of gay and lesbian bars increased, a gay publishing house was founded, and a Chinese-language gay magazine began. Even though the *Tongzhi* movement struggles with the still-widespread disapproval of homosexuality in Taiwanese society, as embodied by gay pride marchers in Taipei wearing masks to hide their identity, it has lobbied aggressively for policy changes. The government banned discrimination on the basis of sexual orientation in education in 2003. It expanded the ban to the workplace in 2007. While President Chen Shui-bian's government proposed a **same-sex marriage** law in 2003, it stalled due to widespread opposition.

Mainstream culture in Thailand shares the general expectation of heterosexual marriage; it has also historically been tolerant of other sexual and social roles. Thai culture traditionally has had a conceptual schema that put together **transvestism**, transgenderism, and same-sex sexuality. With greater exposure to Westerners, however, some men began to self-identify as gay in the 1960s. In turn, that altered the traditional categorizations of sexuality in broader Thai culture. Most Thais, especially outside the heavily Muslim south, are from a Buddhist background that privileges heterosexuality but does not condemn same-sex relations. Alternative sexualities (including gender roles) are less regulated in rural areas than is commonly the case in Asia. Still, mainstream culture and media often denigrate homosexuality as shameful and inappropriate.

An early 20th-century king, influenced by Westerners, criminalized homosexual relations, including between women. The law was never actually used. The government repealed it in the 1950s. A gay subculture grew in the wake of persons self-identifying as gay, especially in the 1990s. Today Thailand has one of the most vibrant gay subcultures in Asia, centered primarily in Bangkok. There is a strong commercial element, with gay bars and prostitutes, yet there is not a correspondingly robust network of community, political, or lobbying groups. As a consequence, there has been little effort to pass **anti-discrimination laws** or recognize same-sex relationships. In 2005, the government changed policy to open **military service** to gays and lesbians.

Most other Asian countries today have gay and lesbian groups. Increasingly today there is international cooperation and information sharing between them, with international congresses and other venues for information exchange. Activists formed Progay Philippines in 1993. The group organized Asia's first gay pride march, which was held in June 1994 on the 25th anniversary of **Stonewall**. Other countries also now have gay pride marches. The scale of the movement does not come close to what is found in most Western nations, however. In many countries the groups are weak, and there are few gay publications outside of Thailand. There is also a debate throughout the region about whether the movement should follow a Western gay rights model.

Several countries have **anti-sodomy** laws. Malaysia and Pakistan, both strongly influenced by Islam, have harsh penalties. Convictions can bring up to 20 years in jail in the former; persons have been publicly lashed in the latter. Bangladesh's law calls for up to 10 years in jail. Sri Lanka added female-female relations to its anti-sodomy law in 1995. Prosecutions under the law are very infrequent, however, and the statute has mainly served as a basis for **police harassment**. Cambodia, the Philippines, South Korea, and Vietnam do not have anti-sodomy laws. In 2001, the South Korean government passed a new human rights law that forbids discrimination based on sexual orientation. *See also* AGE OF CONSENT LAWS; AUSTRALIA; IMMIGRATION AND NATURALIZATION LAW; KORAN.

ASSIMILATION. The social ostracism, marginal legal status, workplace and housing discrimination, and outright fear of physical assault that most gays and lesbians faced throughout societies in the West, particularly in the **United States**, helped to forge a distinctive gay cultural identity, often focused in specific geographical locales and neighborhoods. The lessening of **homophobia** has led to worries in the gay community about the loss of this identity and the threat of mass assimilation into mainstream culture, although some celebrate the prospect of the mainstreaming of gay life.

Gay authors on the political right, such as Andrew Sullivan and Bruce Bawer, have argued for years that key political and social institutions, such as the military and marriage, should be open to gays and lesbians. Since they are not arguing for the change of those institutions, just the broadening of who can access them, their positions are in many ways conservative. Having gay and lesbian couples who are monogamous and responsible living side by side with straight, married couples in suburban tracts is helpful to the cause of gay liberation, according to this line of thinking. Some gay radicals fiercely resist this, contending that the distinctive aspects of gay culture (and what features get highlighted as the definitive ones vary) are valuable precisely because they defy a mainstream culture that is objectionable and deserving of resistance.

The geographical aspect of the assimilation issue concerns the waning of gay enclaves in major metropolitan areas. At least from the 1950s through the 1980s, many men and women who lived in places with a lot of homophobia, especially those from rural areas, would move to cities such as San Francisco and Los Angeles. Gay neighborhoods, or "gayborhoods," resulted, such as the Castro district in San Francisco or West Hollywood. Yet the waning of the social forces that helped to create them threatens to change the character of these neighborhoods. In addition, the sharp reduction in the availability of low-cost housing in places such as the Castro has led to the eviction of **human immunodeficiency virus/acquired immunodeficiency syndrome** patients, struggling gay artists, and others with a marginal economic existence. In the first decade of the 21st century, even as the rest of the United States has become slightly more urban, the evidence is that same-sex couples have become more suburban in their residential patterns. *See also* FRANCE; GREAT BRITAIN; SAME-SEX MARRIAGE.

ASYLUM. Many countries, especially in the developed world, regularly accord refugee status to those who are fleeing political, racial, or religious persecution in their home country, as laid out in the 1951 Geneva Convention on Refugees. Activists and groups such as the **International Lesbian and Gay Association** (ILGA) have lobbied for the expansion of the grounds of refugee status to include persecution based on sexual orientation. While international law has not been amended in this fashion, some countries have granted asylum. In 1990, **Germany** granted refugee status to an Iranian lesbian who faced the death penalty if she returned to her country. In 1994, a formal tribunal in **Great Britain** laid out that persons subjected to persecution on the basis of sexual orientation may qualify. Other countries that have similarly accorded asylum include **Austria**, **Canada**, and the **United States**. *See also* IMMIGRATION AND NATURALIZATION LAW.

AUGUSTINE (354–430). Born in North Africa on the outskirts of the Roman Empire, Augustine eventually became one of the most important theologians in **Christianity**. While his mother was a devout Christian, Augustine was a pagan in his youth, devoted to Manicheanism, which was then an important dualistic faith. In his autobiography, *The Confessions*, Augustine wrote about a male friend he had in his youth. The friend died and Augustine suffered profound grief. Many have interpreted the relationship as homosexual, due to the manner in which he wrote about the friendship and his mourning. Certainly Augustine had extensive sexual experiences, with his wife and mistress, and wrote frankly about his struggle with lust.

Against the early Patristic writers, Augustine argued that lifelong celibacy was unnecessary. Instead, sexual expression governed by reason is moral while that dictated by the appetites is not. Augustine's account emphasized procreation as the natural outcome of the proper use of genitalia, and other uses as unnatural. From this, he argued that marital heterosexual sex out of a desire to have children is acceptable, as long as it is done without lust. This theological view placed an emphasis on the gender of one's partner, in contrast to previous understandings in **ancient Rome**, and ruled out the possibility of moral same-sex sexuality. Augustine was also one of the first to argue that the story of Lot, from the Old Testament, was a denunciation of homosexuality. *See also* SODOMITE.

AUSTRALIA. White settlement of Australia began in the 1780s. For the first several decades, there was a large imbalance between the number of men and women, with the former greatly outnumbering the latter. Since there was also a frequent segregation by sex, there were numerous reports of homosexuality and some prosecutions under the **anti-sodomy laws** common to the British Empire. In 1843, the lieutenant governor of what is now Tasmania reported how the women in a female-only factory have their "lovers, to [whom] they are attached with quite as much ardour as they would be to the opposite sex" (Dynes, Johansson, Percy 1990, 94). Something similar could be said about many of the male penal colonies and barracks. Britain continued to transfer criminals to Australia into the 1840s. In some of the prison barracks, boys went by female names. Some inmates reported that those who did not share in the general norm of homosexuality were abused and even beaten. Inmates informally recognized **same-sex marriages** in some of the camps.

As a British colony, the **Act of 25**, passed by Henry the VIII, as well as the **Labouchère Amendment**, were law. Consequently, the most common source of records about homosexuality comes from the police and the courts. For instance, in the 19th century there were prosecutions of several women who were passing as men, even to the point of being married to women. In the 20th century, consensual homosexual sex acts were more often prosecuted under lesser charges, such as lewd or offensive conduct. In the 1950s and 1960s, entrapment and **police harassment** were common. Australia did not have a **homophile movement** to help expose these police practices or to campaign for the repeal of anti-sodomy laws. In 1970, the Campaign against Moral Persecution (CAMP) was formed, "camp" then being common Australian slang for "homosexual." It was the first prominent gay rights group in the country and it emphasized the need for gays and lesbians to come out of the closet.

After a prominent murder case involving gay bashing, the state of South Australia in 1972 partially decriminalized homosexual sodomy. Other states followed suit and, slowly, over the next quarter of a century all of Australia legalized gay sex. In 1977, New South Wales passed an **anti-discrimination law**. Some other states have followed, but the strength and scope of the laws vary significantly. There is no federal anti-discrimination law. In 1991, Australia recognized same-sex relationships for the purposes of **immigration and naturalization**. The next year it allowed open gays and lesbians to serve in the military. In 2004, the conservative government of John Howard amended federal family law to specify that marriage is between a man and a woman, and also inserted language to prevent government recognition of same-sex marriages. In contrast, most state governments do recognize same-sex relationships. *See also* ASIA; UNITED NATIONS.

– B –

BENTHAM, JEREMY (1748–1832). The founder of utilitarianism, Jeremy Bentham worked throughout his life for legal reform. As befitted someone with his philosophical outlook, Bentham argued that laws should be evaluated by whether they contribute to happiness or alleviate pain. Beginning in his 20s and continuing throughout his life, Bentham wrote extensively about same-sex love and **anti-sodomy laws**. He argued that same-sex relations gave pleasure to those involved and for reform in social attitudes about homosexuality, since in the absence of superstition and bigotry, such relations would not cause pain to others. Unlike all of his British contemporaries, Bentham sought to understand this antipathy to homosexuality, instead of seeing same-sex attraction as needing explanation. In his late 60s and early 70s, Bentham returned to the issue and wrote a lengthy treatise on homosexuality, especially in regard to Christianity and the Bible. This work, *Not Paul but Jesus*, praised male same-sex love. Complaining about the baleful effects of the terminology of the day, Bentham sought to develop a neutral set of words and phrases about homosexuality.

Bentham realized, however, that his arguments were wildly at odds with public opinion in Britain. He noted how the mere act of defending the abolition of anti-sodomy laws would subject him to accusations of homosexuality. The animus that homosexuality provoked in the Britain of his day was irrational and violent, he argued. "On this subject a man may indulge his spleen without control. Cruelty and intolerance, the most odious and most mischievous passions in human nature, screen themselves behind a mask of virtue" (quoted in Crompton 1978, 385). Due to these risks, and out of a sense of hopelessness of changing opinion and law, Bentham chose to not publish his writings on homosexuality. It was not until 1931 that any of his voluminous work on the subject appeared.

BERDACHE. Many North American Indian tribes had established roles for persons who were born male yet whose social role as adults either mixed male and female elements or was primarily female. The broad umbrella term for such persons has generally been "berdache," which comes from a Persian word (*bardaj*) that was then adopted in Spanish and French. Since the word carried negative connotations in all of these languages, and because the French *bardache* and Spanish *bardaja* refer to a man who takes the passive role in homosexual sex, rather than referring to a social role outside of a strict male/female dichotomy, many have begun referring to such persons as "two-spirits." Some also just refer to them by the tribe-specific term, such as *winkte* among the Sioux and *nadle* among the Navajo. While such persons did not always have same-sex relations, many did, although apparently berdache-berdache relations were unheard of. Many tribes recognized marriages between a man and a berdache. The men who married berdaches were not seen as different from other men and did not have any term to refer to them, illustrating how the conceptual schema involved focused more on gender and social role, rather than what the contemporary West would call sexual orientation.

Among the over 100 American Indian tribes that had the berdache role, many accorded these individuals great respect or saw special powers inherent in them. The Cheyenne saw two-spirits as having special powers to cure and thus included them in war parties. The Navajo had them prepare special sacred meals; the Sioux had them confer sacred names on children. Some tribes, such as the Cheyenne, had them act as matchmakers.

Roles akin to the berdache have been common among indigenous peoples in other parts of the world, including Siberia, Southeast **Asia**, and Polynesia. In North America, European colonization largely destroyed the tradition. Missionaries denounced the practice, and **United States** agents and schools for American Indians tried to stop it as well. Some authorities used violence or the threat of it to force berdaches to adopt a traditional masculine role. By the early 20th century, the tradition was largely dead. Over the past couple of decades, some American Indian gay groups have worked to re-establish two-spirit people as an indigenous tradition.

BIBLE. By 400 C.E., Christians had chosen the group of writings that constitute the New Testament and deemed them divinely inspired and canonical. A series of religious meetings united those writings to the Hebrew Bible (including the **Torah**) and other Jewish holy books. Many passages in the Old Testament show a clear appreciation of male beauty or otherwise imply same-sex desire. Saul and David are praised for their beauty. The First Book of Samuel describes David in a relationship with Jonathan, complete with expressions of undying devotion. Upon Jonathan's death, David composed a dirge that he commanded be read throughout Israel. In it, David describes his love for Jonathan as surpassing the love of women (2 Samuel 1:17–26).

The New Testament contains several passages that may refer to male homosexuality, although the evidence is mixed. Most of the relevant passages come from the Pauline Epistles. Paul's letter to the Romans (1:26–32) has the only clear, unambiguous reference. The passage begins by condemning women who exchange natural relations for unnatural ones, and then continues on to a pronounced denunciation of male-male relations. It concludes with a call for death for those guilty of such relations, echoing the language from the Old Testament book of Leviticus. Traditionally many have taken the reference to women who exchange unnatural for natural relations as a reference to lesbianism. If correct, it is the only such reference in the New Testament. Yet the language is vague, only condemning the turning away from "natural use." The discussion of male relations is more pointed and clearly refers to same-sex relations. The close juxtaposition of the two is one reason for taking the vague description of women as a reference to female-female relations.

The New Testament does not depict Jesus of Nazareth as ever addressing same-sex relations. Even though **Christianity** is ostensibly founded upon his teachings, there is no good evidence that Jesus shared Paul's hostility to same-sex love. Jesus does refer on several occasions to Sodom, but he implies that the city's sin was its lack of hospitality. Such a view was in line with the dominant understanding within **Judaism** at the time. *See also* JAMES VI AND I; SODOMITE; UNITED STATES.

BILLING CASE. In 1918, Noel Pemberton Billing, an independent member of Parliament in **Great Britain**, alleged that the German secret service had a book containing the names of 47,000 homosexual English citizens. He first made the charge in the pages of his right-wing magazine, which was well-known for its anti-Semitism, and then on the floor of the House of Commons. An unsigned piece in the magazine subsequently alleged that an actress and dancer, Maud Allen, was one of the 47,000. She was about to appear in a play written by **Oscar Wilde**. Allen sued, charging libel. The trial provoked a great deal of media attention. Billing was acquitted and many saw him as a patriot. The case both reflected and contributed to the cultural divisions in British society at the time. On the one hand were those who saw themselves as patriotic citizens, who worried about how homosexuality, treason, and degeneracy might be linked. On the other were those who believed, like Wilde, that homosexuality was no evil and that art should not be yoked to the cause of advancing traditional values. The perceived link between homosexuality and treason was to remain an undercurrent in British political culture for much of the 20th century.

BOSTON MARRIAGE. Originally used in the late 19th-century **United States**, the term "Boston marriage" referred to women who were together in long-term relationships, often establishing common residences. The rise of these relationships reflected increased economic and social independence for middle- and upper-class women, especially in New England. Henry James wrote a novel, *The Bostonians*, about such a relationship. His sister, Alice, was in a Boston marriage. Even though it is unclear whether many of these marriages had an overt sexual aspect, undoubtedly the women in them had much of their intellectual and emotional lives vested in their partners. *See also* LESBIAN CONTINUUM.

***BOUTILIER V. IMMIGRATION AND NATURALIZATION SERVICE* (1967).** Born and raised in **Canada**, Clive Michael Boutilier moved to the **United States** as a young man. In 1963, he applied for citizenship at the age of 30, but admitted to the Immigration and Naturalization Service (INS) that he had a prior arrest, but no conviction, for sodomy. Upon further questioning, Boutilier related that he had had several same-sex sexual encounters per year for over a decade. The INS then moved to deport him, but Boutilier filed an appeal. The case, *Boutilier v. INS*, ultimately went before the Supreme Court. The majority decision upheld the INS' deportation order. Justice Tom Clark's majority opinion argued that the INS was correct in interpreting "psychopathic personality," the term from Congress' 1952 **immigration and naturalization law**, as barring foreign homosexuals from residence or naturalization. Thus, the mere admission of past homosexual relations constituted grounds for deportation.

***BOWERS V. HARDWICK* (1986).** In 1982, a Georgia police officer entered the residence of Michael Hardwick in order to serve a warrant. There he found Hardwick engaged in oral sex with another man. The patrolmen arrested both men, and they were charged under Georgia's **anti-sodomy law**. The law criminalized heterosexual and homosexual oral and anal sex, which the American Civil Liberties Union (ACLU) attorneys working on behalf of Hardwick tried to use to their advantage. Yet a lower court dismissed a heterosexual couple added to the suit as lacking standing. Furthermore, when the case reached the **United States** Supreme Court, Justice Byron White's majority opinion argued that the only constitutional issue before the court was permissibility of state regulation of homosexual sodomy. While the majority and concurring decisions' treatment of heterosexuality referred to relationships, marriage, and children, their discussions of homosexuality were reductive and focused exclusively on sex acts.

The majority voted to uphold Georgia's anti-sodomy law, at least in regard to its criminalization of homosexual sodomy. Many today regard the decision as a blemish upon the Court's recent jurisprudence. The Court overturned *Bowers v. Hardwick* with its *Lawrence v. Texas* (2003) decision. *See also ROMER V. EVANS.*

***BOY SCOUTS OF AMERICA V. DALE* (2000).** James Dale joined the Cub Scouts at the age of eight and later became a member of the Boy Scouts of America (BSA). He later rose to the level of Eagle Scout. After graduating from high school, he applied to become an adult member of the BSA, which the group granted. While attending Rutgers, Dale became an outspoken member of a gay group. As a consequence, the BSA revoked his membership. He filed suit for reinstatement, under New Jersey's public accommodations law that prohibited discrimination on the basis of sexual orientation. The U.S. Supreme Court ultimately ruled in favor of the BSA in a 5–4 decision.

While there was some dispute in the case about how clear the BSA had been in its anti-gay policy, the central constitutional issue concerned whether the application of New Jersey's public accommodation law violated the BSA's First Amendment right to freedom of association. The majority decision, written by Chief Justice William Rehnquist, held that it did. The BSA had a right to express its values by excluding persons from its associations. Such exclusions, at least in this case, did not amount to an invidious discrimination, as presumably would have been the case if the basis were race or ethnicity. Justice John Paul Stevens' dissent, in contrast, argued that the inclusion of Dale and persons like him would not constitute a substantial burden upon the BSA, nor did it find the BSA anti-gay policy central to the values it tries to uphold and promote.

Dale was motivated in part to take a public role opposing anti-gay discrimination out of a concern for the difficulties faced by gay and lesbian adolescents. While the majority decision notes this in passing, it does not go into the implications of such discrimination, such as violent assaults and higher suicide rates for gay teens. The ruling marked the first time the Supreme Court ruled against a state's **antidiscrimination law** in favor of a group's desire to exclude.

BRIGGS INITIATIVE. In 1978, a conservative California state senator successfully led an effort to put an initiative on the statewide ballot that would have banned gays and lesbians, or anyone who supported gay rights, from teaching in public schools in the state. Proposition 6 was generally known as the Briggs Initiative after the senator, John Briggs, who backed it. Although polls showed initial strong support, gay groups, teachers' unions, civil libertarians, and others created a strong coalition against the initiative. Even some conservatives, such as Ronald Reagan, came out against it, in part because it placed heterosexual teachers' jobs at risk simply on the basis of political beliefs. The measure ultimately failed by a significant margin in that fall's election.

The Briggs Initiative took place at a time of growing conservative backlash against the fledging gay rights movement. The year before, **Anita Bryant** had led a successful effort to repeal a gay rights law in Dade County, Florida. Also in 1978, other anti-gay initiatives and referenda succeeded in cities such as Eugene, St. Paul, and Wichita. Briggs' failure helped galvanize the gay rights movement on a national level. *See also* ANTI-DISCRIMINATION LAWS; MILK, HARVEY; RELIGIOUS RIGHT.

BRITISH SOCIETY FOR THE STUDY OF SEX PSYCHOLOGY (BSSP). Begun in 1914, the BSSP was probably inspired by a speech given in London by **Magnus Hirschfeld**. **Havelock Ellis** and **Edward Carpenter** were present and knew about the Berlin-based homosexual rights organization that Hirschfeld had helped form, the *Wissenschaftlich-humanitäres Komitee* (Scientific-Humanitarian Committee). Carpenter served as the first president of the BSSP. The group later changed its name to the British Sexological Society.

The BSSP set itself a broad mandate of promoting research and educational activities, including the issuing of pamphlets and lobbying as well as hosting frequent public talks. In addition to homosexual rights, it fought for the rights of women and general sexual freedom, seeing all of these issues as connected. The group worked on behalf of women's suffrage, the repeal of **Great Britain**'s **anti-sodomy law**, and access to birth control. Among the many pamphlets it published were essays by Havelock Ellis and the influential British feminist Stella Browne. Browne's work was notable in that, unlike most British feminists of the time, she offered a qualified defense of lesbianism. Many leading British progressives joined the group, including George Bernard Shaw, Bertrand Russell, and the novelists E. M. Forster and **Radclyffe Hall**. Its influence, however, was limited. Like other groups in the early homosexual rights movement, the rise of Fascism and the dislocations of World War II led to the group's demise. *See also* EUROPE.

BRYANT, ANITA (1940–). A beauty queen, singer, and spokesperson for Florida orange juice, Anita Bryant took a central role in the 1970s backlash against the gay rights movement. She helped lead a group, Save Our Children, which was behind an effort to repeal a Dade County **anti-discrimination law**. By a lopsided initiative vote, the citizens of the county, which includes Miami, overturned the law. The success of their effort further encouraged social conservatives and those on the **religious right**. It also galvanized gays and lesbians across the country to launch a boycott of Florida orange juice. The Florida citrus industry lobby soon dropped their contract with Bryant.

In 1980, Bryant announced that she had changed her views and now had a more tolerant stance. She also expressed regret for some of her anti-gay remarks. Her central legacy, however, is that the Save Our Children campaign showed that anti-homosexual politics could be popular and a means of encouraging social conservatives to turn out in elections. *See also* ADOPTION; BRIGGS INITIATIVE; FALWELL, JERRY, SR.

BURTON, SIR RICHARD. *See* SOTADIC ZONE.

BUTCH/FEMME. Butch and femme are stylized forms of self-presentation and relationship roles found among some lesbians. The origins of butch/femme (or sometimes "fem") are unclear, but solid documentation is found at least as far back as 1930s America. Each role has its own code of dress, style of walk, and range of gestures. What was a very clear dichotomy in the mid-20th century, however, has changed over time and "butch" and "femme" today are often used in a more colloquial, informal sense simply to refer to lesbians who could be considered either mannish or very feminine.

The roles of butch/femme were most fully elaborated in working-class lesbian bars in the 1940s through the 1960s. Butches often had short haircuts, sometimes slicked back. They wore men's clothes, with black butches preferring an upper-class look complete with three-piece suits and formal collars. Femmes wore the traditional female dress of the times. Butch/butch and femme/femme relationships were considered unacceptable. Women who did not fit into the stereotypes were called "kiki," which was considered a put-down and often made those women feel as if they did not fit in. In the oral and written accounts from the time, those who self-identified with butch or femme describe the roles as being much more than a replication of traditional heterosexual male/female roles. Instead, they describe a world in which love, erotic attachment, and a sense of being at ease with one's self were all within reach. Those who found it difficult to self-identify with either role paint a different picture, where the oppression characteristic of the traditional gender division was replicated in the lesbian subculture.

In the 1970s, lesbian feminists argued that butch/femme roles replicated patriarchy and thus should be avoided. Since most lesbian feminists of the time were white and middle class, the class and racial lines in perceptions of butch/femme were only sharpened. Black and Latino neighborhoods and bars, as well as white, working-class ones, maintained the roles more frequently. *See also* ASIA; STEIN, GERTRUDE; TRANSVESTISM.

– C –

CANADA. As a colony of **Great Britain**, Canada and its early settlers were subjected to **Act of 25 Henry VIII**, which laid out penalties for those convicted of homosexual sodomy. While there are a few reported convictions from the 17th century, the penalties fell short of death. Settlers in the western part of the country were accorded greater latitude. For instance, there are recorded examples of some women regularly dressed as men, although whether this involved any corresponding sexual aspect is unknown. The social reform movement that arose in North America in the late 19th century, however, reduced this freedom in the name of social "purity." In 1892, Canada amended its **anti-sodomy laws** to cover all male same-gender sex acts. The law included flogging as a possible penalty, in addition to jail.

World War II threw together thousands of men and women into sex-segregated environments in the military and factories, respectively. Especially for those from rural environments, the war provided a level of sexual freedom that was previously unimaginable. After the war, gay enclaves arose in some of the bigger cities, such as Toronto and Montreal. In the 1950s, however, the paranoia and persecution characteristic of **McCarthyism** in the **United States** also swept through Canada. **Police harassment** and entrapment were also common. Anti-sodomy statutes were amended to include lesbian sex acts. In 1964, a Canadian **homophile** organization was formed—the Association for Social Knowledge (ASK). Like other groups in the **homophile movement**, ASK avoided confrontation and reached out to experts in the medical and psychological fields in the hope that they would be effective advocates for legal and social reform. ASK opened North America's first gay and lesbian community center in Vancouver, British Columbia. It also published a newsletter and maintained informal ties with some chapters of the **Mattachine Society**, the **Daughters of Bilitis**, and other U.S. homophile organizations. The same year that ASK was formed in Vancouver, two magazines began in Toronto. *Gay* was the first periodical to use that term in its title. The magazine *Two* drew its title from the Los Angeles–based *ONE*.

British legal changes had long been influential in Canada, and thus the debate brought about by the **Wolfenden Report**, and the subsequent decriminalization of sodomy in England and Wales in 1967, helped spur legal reform in Canada. Another factor was the arrest and incarceration of Everett Klippert. Under Canadian law at the time, a person who had engaged in homosexual sex and was deemed likely to do so again was to be incarcerated indefinitely as a "dangerous sexual offender." The Canadian Supreme Court upheld the authorities' jailing of Klippert. It quickly became a cause célèbre and helped turn public opinion against anti-sodomy laws. Prime Minister Pierre Trudeau came out in support of legal reform, and in 1969 Parliament passed a comprehensive revision of the criminal code. Homosexual sodomy was decriminalized, although the age of consent was set higher than for heterosexual sex. Two years later Klippert was released.

In 1977, the province of Quebec passed an **anti-discrimination law** that included sexual orientation. The next year the federal government passed a new immigration law that removed gays and lesbians from its list of classes of inadequate persons. Some forms of harassment remained, however. The Pink Triangle Press, which put out a gay publication, *The Body Politic*, was charged in 1978 with obscenity. The series of trials and lawsuits that followed contributed to its closing in 1986. In 1981, police raided several bathhouses in Toronto. They arrested 300. The next night, 3,000 marched in protest in what soon was called "Canada's **Stonewall**."

The Canadian Charter of Rights and Freedoms was added to the Canadian constitution in 1982. It was designed to protect citizens in their basic rights and freedoms. While the section prohibiting discrimination in employment and housing does not include sexual orientation, a series of subsequent court decisions, including by the Canadian Supreme Court, in effect added that protection. In 1996, the government added sexual orientation to its Human Rights Act. By that point the government had also lifted its ban on gays and lesbians in the military. In the mid-1990s, Ontario changed its policy to allow gay and lesbian couples to adopt children together, and most provinces have since followed. In 1999, the Canadian Supreme Court ruled that gay and lesbian couples should have the same rights as heterosexual common-law couples. The federal government amended many federal laws in accordance with the decision. In 2003, Ontario and British Columbia began recognizing **same-sex marriages**. A federal law recognizing same-sex marriages passed in 2005. *See also* ASYLUM; LITERATURE, LESBIAN; MILITARY SERVICE.

CARPENTER, EDWARD (1844–1929). A consistent advocate of path-breaking ideas in his time, such as feminism, vegetarianism, and homosexual rights, Edward Carpenter was deeply influenced by **Walt Whitman**'s *Leaves of Grass*. He encountered the book while in his 20s and was deeply moved by its praise of the "love of comrades." In combination with a trip to Italy that awakened him to the beauty of the male nude, Carpenter abandoned his plans of a religious vocation.

A prolific author, Carpenter published books that were widely read and translated. These included *Love's Coming of Age* and *Intermediate Sex*, both published in the first decade of the 20th century. Carpenter argued that the widely held view that sexuality should be closely connected to procreation resulted in the oppression of women and homosexuals. He was an early and forceful proponent of linking the feminist and homosexual rights movements. Along with **Havelock Ellis**, he helped to found the **British Society for the Study of Sex Psychology** and served as its first president.

Carpenter also had a broad network of prominent friends and acquaintances. He corresponded with Whitman and eventually traveled to America and met him. E. M. Forster took a trip to Carpenter's home in **Great Britain**, which became a matter of pilgrimage for many advocates of progressive causes and which Carpenter shared with his male partner. The trip and his hosts inspired Forster to write his novel *Maurice*. Carpenter was also friends with **John Addington Symonds**. For both Carpenter and Symonds, the example of same-sex love in **ancient Greece** provided evidence that the wide acceptance of homosexuality and bisexuality is compatible with the highest levels of civilization and cultural achievement.

CHINA. Given the strong Confucian tradition that developed in **ancient China**, for centuries it was common that those who pursued same-sex relationships were also married, in order to uphold their familial obligations. During the Ming dynasty (1368–1644), emperors continued the tradition, dating back over a millennium, of rulers having overt same-sex relationships and lovers while also having wives and concubines. An editor (or editors) compiled what is likely the first-ever comprehensive anthology of historical records, stories, and anecdotes about same-sex male love. It is entitled *Duan xiu pian*, or *Records of the Cut Sleeve*, a reference to perhaps the most famous story of homosexual love from ancient China. The first reliable accounts of lesbianism also date from the Ming dynasty. Sex manuals detailed lesbian sex acts, albeit only as a way for a man with many concubines to enliven his erotic life. There were also pornographic drawings depicting women together. The author Li Yu, born during the waning years of the Ming dynasty, wrote a play sympathetic to lesbianism, *Pitying the Perfumed Companion*. In at least one province, Guangdong, a form of female **same-sex marriage** was established. In the female-only Golden Orchid Associations, women could propose to one another and, if accepted, go through a formal ceremony. The marriage was then recognized by members of the association, even to the point of having association members assault those who were seen as betraying a spouse.

During the same period of the Ming dynasty, a form of male same-sex marriage came into being in southern China. An older man would form a relationship with a younger man. They would live together, in the older man's house, and be known as the "adoptive older brother" and the "adopted younger brother." Extended family often recognized the relationship, which sometimes endured for decades. Again, however, Confucian duties still won out and the marriage would sometimes be dissolved due to obligations of heterosexual marriage or procreation. Upon the dissolution, the older adoptive brother was to pay the full price to find a good bride for his younger adoptive brother.

Western explorers traveled throughout China late in the Ming dynasty. Though many of their reports are positive, some were shocked at how public same-sex relations were. A Jesuit complained about how such relationships were conducted everywhere and without shame. In 1644, the Qing (or Manchu) dynasty came to power. Religious and political leaders launched a socially repressive agenda, including the passage of an **anti-sodomy law**. Compared to European laws of the same era, however, its punishments were mild. The dynasty later moderated its stance and there are even reliable accounts of later Qing emperors having male lovers. Male prostitution was common, especially in larger cities. Relationships were often formed between masters and servants, and between scholar-officials and actors. *Tan* actors, many of whom were patronized and courted by government officials, often portrayed female theatrical roles. Chen Sen captured this world in a well-regarded novel, not yet available in translation, *Pinhua baojian* (*Precious Mirror for Gazing at Flowers*).

For well over a millennium, Chinese culture exhibited a truly striking degree of acceptance of homosexuality. Love between men, in particular, was widely acknowledged and discussed, often in terms of something neither laudable or evil in itself, but rather as a setting in which persons can reveal themselves as noble or ignoble. After such a long history, mildly disrupted by the early Qing, Chinese culture abruptly changed direction under the Communists, although the translation of works by Western anti-homosexual sexologists in the early 20th century had already begun to change attitudes. After its rise to power in 1949, the Chinese Communist Party worked aggressively to punish and suppress homosexuality. During the Cultural Revolution in particular, homosexuals were sent to labor camps for "reeducation" or simply executed. One of the great ironies of Chinese history is that the culture with the longest recorded history of tolerance of homosexuality and bisexuality came to denounce same-sex love as a Western invention and foreign contagion within China.

More recently, Chinese authorities have reduced their attacks on homosexuality. Sodomy was decriminalized in 1997. In 2001, Chinese medical authorities removed homosexuality from their official listing of mental disorders. Gay websites have proliferated, as have gay bars, saunas, and tea houses. These venues, however, are occasionally subjected to **police harassment**. State-run media vary from indifferent to sometimes hostile in their treatment of gay and lesbian issues. As is often the case around the world, gays and lesbians have a more difficult situation in rural areas. In Hong Kong, there are active gay rights groups that were able to get the age of consent for homosexual sex lowered to that for heterosexual sex. While a few persons have lobbied for **anti-discrimination laws** and same-sex marriage, the prospect for either is dim in the near future. *See also* ASIA; LITERATURE, HOMOSEXUAL MALE; LITERATURE, LESBIAN; MILITARY SERVICE.

CHRISTIANITY. Several of the most important early Christian theologians, collectively known as the Patristic writers, harshly denounced same-sex relations and looked upon any type of sex as immoral. Their role in shaping early Christian doctrine, including attitudes toward sexuality, helps explain **ancient Rome**'s increased hostility to same-sex relations after Christianity became the Roman Empire's dominant religion subsequent to the rule of Emperor Constantine. The early church also held that several writings from before the birth of Jesus of Nazareth were divinely inspired and thus incorporated those writings into the Christian **Bible** as the Old Testament. This included the **Torah**. Yet early Christian writers argued that Sodom's sin was homosexual lust, in contrast to the common Jewish understanding that emphasized the sins of pride or inhospitality. **Augustine** and his contemporary John Chrysostom were early proponents of that Christian reinterpretation. Chrysostom was especially influential in the Eastern Orthodox branches of the faith. His works and sermons are notable in part for being an early example of the melding of anti-Semitism with a loathing of same-sex love. He spoke extensively about the book of Romans and argued for interpreting the vague language about women turning away from "natural use" as a denunciation of lesbianism. He defended death by stoning for the sin of sodomy.

Christianity's rise in influence, combined with its strong opposition to same-sex eroticism, resulted in a series of **anti-sodomy laws**. These began in ancient Rome, in the fourth century, and continued with the **Code of Justinian** in the Byzantine Empire, in the sixth. Direct Christian persecution of same-sex relations reached a peak during the **Inquisition**, even though the clerical authorities frequently turned their cases over to secular courts for prosecution. The Inquisition continued through most of the 18th century and was only formally abolished in the first decades of the 19th.

There is a broad variety of views today within Christianity on the morality of same-sex relations. The rise of the gay movement in recent decades has compelled Catholics and Protestants to clarify and in some cases alter their official doctrines.

The Eastern Orthodox Church, which is influential in countries such as **Russia** and Romania, where there is much less of a movement or open subculture, is openly hostile to homosexuality. While the Catholic tradition has shared that hostility, there has been some shift in official doctrine. In the 1970s, the Catholic hierarchy started addressing the issue of homosexuality more overtly. In 1986, Cardinal Joseph Ratzinger published "The Pastoral Care of Homosexual Persons." Ratzinger, who later became Pope Benedict, argued that for many, homosexuality is an innate condition and therefore, since it is not chosen, it is not a sin. Homosexual sex, however, is sinful and can never be moral, even in the context of loving relationships. Prior to this point official Catholic doctrine had never allowed that some persons could be homosexual by nature, though the substantive result of the doctrine is the same. There is a gay and lesbian Catholic group, Dignity, which fights to change the hierarchy's official doctrine. Started in 1969, Dignity also serves as a support group and has chapters across the **United States**.

Protestant sects have tremendous diversity in their views on the morality of homosexuality. Fundamentalist and evangelical groups, such as the Baptists, see homosexuality as evil and as the result of hedonism or some other grave personal failing. These groups therefore argue that homosexuality is a threat to morality, the family, and community. Yet since homosexuality does not exist by nature, it can be cured and Baptists and similar groups help finance the **reparative therapy** movement. Other denominations, ranging from Episcopalians to the **Metropolitan Community Church**, see homosexual relations as on par to heterosexual ones. Neither form is inherently moral, but loving, companionate, long-term unions are at their best realizations of the highest aspects of humanity. The Anglican Church is deeply divided over homosexuality and issues such as the ordination of gay ministers.

In general, those countries that have high churchgoing rates are more hostile to homosexuality than those with low rates. This is true across all three main branches of Christianity (Catholic, Eastern Orthodox, and Protestant). Evangelical Protestant versions of Christianity have spread widely in **Africa** over the past few decades, which will likely affect attitudes toward same-sex relationships in sub-Saharan regions for decades to come. *See also* AQUINAS, THOMAS; EUROPE; FALWELL, JERRY, SR.; FAMILY RESEARCH COUNCIL; FOCUS ON THE FAMILY; JUDAISM; LITERATURE, HOMOSEXUAL MALE; RELIGIOUS RIGHT.

CIVIL UNIONS. In the **United States** and **Europe**, the divisive fight over **same-sex marriage** has led to the construction of forms of legal recognition of same-sex relationships, such as civil unions, that confer most of the benefits and responsibilities of marriage without the use of the term. Civil unions in the United States have only been implemented at the state level. The various rights and privileges accorded by the federal government therefore do not apply, such as Social Security benefits, favorable tax treatment, and **immigration and naturalization** rights. Furthermore, since most states do not recognize same-sex unions at all, couples remain legal strangers in the majority of the country.

Vermont was the first state to enact a civil union law for same-sex couples, doing so in 2000. The law was prompted by the Vermont Supreme Court's decision in *Baker v. State* (1999) in which the majority ruled that the denial of legal recognition of same-sex relationships was in contradiction to the Vermont constitution. In 2005, Connecticut's representative branches enacted a civil union law that was notable in part because it was not in response to a judicial decision, although a subsequent court decision mandated the legal recognition of same-sex marriages. New Jersey and New Hampshire also have civil unions and more states are likely to pass similar laws in the future. Just as with same-sex marriage, the implications of these unions for other states will be the subject of significant litigation. *See also* ADOPTION; DOMESTIC PARTNERSHIP; ITALY; LATIN AMERICA; REGISTERED PARTNERSHIP.

CLAUSE 28. In the early 1980s, several local governments in **Great Britain** began to recognize homosexual groups and financially supported their efforts, for example, through financing the creation of gay and lesbian community centers. The most prominent example of this was in London, under the leadership of Ken Livingstone. In response, the government led by Prime Minister Margaret Thatcher introduced a provision to the Local Government Act—known as Clause 28—which forbade local councils from promoting homosexuality. It also contained language preventing local councils from recognizing same-sex relationships, since they are "pretended family relationships" (quoted in N. Miller 2006, 473). The draft legislation prompted great controversy. In part, this was due to the legislation's ambiguous language, which left both sides free to speculate about its consequences.

The proposal outraged gay and lesbian communities. In response, many prominent Britons, especially in the arts community, came out of the closet. What had previously been a fractured movement was given a newfound unity by its opposition to the legislation. The law passed in 1988. Its consequences proved slight. Teachers had been concerned that they would be censored; the leaders of gay and lesbian community centers were convinced they would lose a major source of funding, but neither occurred. There were some instances of self-censorship, but funding was reinterpreted as "welfare spending" and other loopholes were found.

Even though the Conservative Party most likely launched the Clause 28 fight in order to weaken local government and whip social conservatives into a political fever, the real long-term consequence was for gay communities in Britain. The battle proved to be a watershed. Aside from high-profile gays and lesbians who came out, it also re-energized gay political movements. Gay men and lesbians once again found common cause. The fight also linked together gays and lesbians with other groups, such as teachers and supporters of local government.

CLOSET, THE. The central contemporary metaphor for when one hides one's minority sexual status, the closet is constructed through social and legal restrictions of sexuality alongside efforts to resist those. On the one hand, the closet can be contrasted with simply being "out" about one's sexuality. That is, **coming out** or being out involves disclosing or making no effort to hide one's attractions, status, or relationships. On the other hand, the closet is also different than trying to repress or change one's sexuality. The closet is an awareness of one's minority sexuality while trying to hide it from at least some, such as family or work colleagues, but likely not from everyone. As a consequence, there are also varying levels of being closeted. A person might be out to friends and co-workers, but not to family members, or only out to a select circle of friends.

Keeping secret one's attraction to members of the same sex has been common in societies that punish same-sex eroticism. Yet the modern combination of seeing a person's "sexual orientation" as a centerpiece of personal identity and a state that is more effective and intrusive made the closet more constant or enveloping. In the early 19th century, a person attracted to his or her own sex likely needed to hide some behavior. In North America and **Europe**, however, during and especially after the latter part of that century, the closet for many was more akin to a constant effort at hiding much of oneself. The growth of homosexual subcultures in the late 19th and early 20th centuries in urban areas, however, made possible a "double life," in the language of the time. More often men, but sometimes also women, would be out among a narrow circle of friends, at gay bars, or in certain cruising areas. The rest of a person's life was closeted or, in the parlance in the **United States** from the 1930s and 1940s, required "wearing the mask."

After **Stonewall**, many activists in North America and Europe strongly encouraged gays and lesbians to come out of the closet. The arguments in support of this are that the closet is often psychologically debilitating and prevents gays and lesbians from achieving a positive sense of self. The closet is also politically crippling, since it prevents gays and lesbians from showing their true numbers and lobbying as effectively as they otherwise could. Finally, heterosexuals most often have their **homophobia** challenged by friends and family members who come out to them, and thus the closet preserves anti-gay attitudes.

The abolition of **anti-sodomy laws** in most of the developed world, often combined with the enactment of **anti-discrimination laws** and some form of recognition of same-sex relationships, has made coming out of the closet less treacherous. The weakening of social and legal punishments in the 1970s was central to the new-found prominence of gay enclaves in that decade, a change that was built on the erosion of the closet. The closet has weakened further in subsequent decades, even in more conservative rural areas. In contrast, most countries in the **Middle East** today still have severe punishments for sodomy, in addition to strong social pressures to marry. Such a regime of compulsory public heterosexuality makes it so that many gays and lesbians in the region feel that the closet is their only option.

From an analytical perspective, the closet functions in a paradoxical manner. As William Eskridge has pointed out, for persons attracted to their own sex, the closet is simultaneously protective and threatening. It protects against punishment by the authorities or dismissal from a job, yet threatens one's sense of self and the integrity of core personal relationships. For heterosexuals, the gay closet is protective and threatening, too. It is protective in that it allows straight society to not be confronted by unsettling gender roles and sexualities, and threatening in that many see it as a secretive refuge for criminal behavior and dangerous nonconformity. Hence 1950s America lurched between a panic about homosexuality and its alleged links to Communism, and a determination to not face homosexuality, the work of **Alfred Kinsey** notwithstanding. Also, many contemporary arguments against same-sex marriage, for example, claim that public acceptance of gay relationships is socially harmful. In this aspect, they express a desire for the closet as protective of straights. *See also* "DON'T ASK, DON'T TELL"; GAY LIBERATION FRONT; OUTING; QUEER NATION.

CODE OF JUSTINIAN. In 527 C.E., Justinian rose to power as the emperor of the Byzantine Empire. He was deeply committed to **Christianity** and the study of its theology. Soon after coming to power, he ordered the closing of the Academy in Athens, a school founded by **Plato** almost 900 years earlier.

In 533, Justinian decreed that same-sex acts were punishable by death. He subsequently issued two additional decrees on the topic, both of which invoked the need to avoid God's wrath and the destruction of cities as reasons to extirpate same-sex love. The language of both laws was broad and theological in its self-justification, but the first one implied that male same-sex love was the central concern. The second one did not mention gender. Justinian's edicts criminalized all same-sex relations, rather than just the passive role as had previously been the case under the Roman Empire. The central legacy of his regime was the compilation and formalization of the law, known as the Code of Justinian. The code included the prohibition against same-sex acts upon penalty of death. Justinian's code stood as the basic law of the empire for hundreds of years. Later, medieval rulers looked to the code as a means of resurrecting Roman law.

Justinian's **anti-sodomy laws** were used against citizens of the empire during his reign. There is some evidence that the regime used them as a tool to punish leaders of an opposing political faction or those who had offended the leadership. There is also evidence that the laws, which established inquisitors to root out those who engaged in same-sex relations, allowed those figures to extort money and otherwise engage in tactics similar to **police harassment**. *See also* ANCIENT ROME; ITALY.

CODE NAPOLÉON (1810). In 1791, the Constituent Assembly in **France** abolished all penalties for sodomy as part of an overall reform in criminal law. In 1804, Napoleon Bonaparte, the newly made emperor of France, named Jean-Jacques Cambacérès as his archchancellor. Cambacérès, who was homosexual, oversaw the drafting of the Code Napoléon, which was the formalization of the various legal changes enacted since the beginning of the French Revolution. The code retained the assembly's criminal statute reforms, including its abolition of penalties for same-sex relations. It became law in 1810.

The **Enlightenment** provided the decisive impetus for the Constituent Assembly and hence the code's liberalization of criminal and sexual laws. Napoleon gave this codification of law prestige by putting his name on it. As Napoleon's armies moved across **Europe** in the early 19th century, the practical impact of the code also spread. Various German states abolished their **anti-sodomy laws** due to the Code Napoléon. In 1810, France annexed the Netherlands and hence the code became law there. It was also deeply influential in Italian legal reform, as well as other European Catholic states, leading them to repeal their anti-sodomy laws. *See also* ASIA; GERMANY; LATIN AMERICA; LITERATURE, HOMOSEXUAL MALE; SOTADIC ZONE; ULRICHS, KARL HEINRICH.

COMING OUT. Gay subcultures in the **United States** have used the term "coming out" for close to a century, although the term has undergone significant changes in meaning over time. In the 1930s, "coming out" meant entering the gay subculture. Just like a young socialite might enter society at a debutante ball, so too a homosexual might enter the world of gay bars and homosexual circles. During World War II and immediately after, the term was often used as slang to refer to a person's first same-sex sexual encounter. By the mid-1960s, most gays and lesbians used the term to refer to a person's revealing his or her same-sex attraction to others.

Just as there are degrees of being in the **closet**, so too are there levels of coming out. A person may come out only to gay friends and acquaintances, in which case coming out is akin to the 1930s meaning. Today, however, the term is generally used to refer to the process of disclosing, or no longer hiding, one's same-sex attraction, whether to family, friends, or co-workers. That is, the contemporary understanding of coming out is more demanding since it is no longer just disclosing one's sexual identity to members of a subculture.

Many gay liberationists have argued for coming out as an act of personal liberation and political action. They contend that ordinary gays and lesbians coming out by the millions is the only way to end the closet. Often seen as radical in the 1970s, this view is more mainstream today. *See also* AGE OF CONSENT LAWS; HOMOPHOBIA; LITERATURE, HOMOSEXUAL MALE; OUTING.

CONVERSION THERAPY. *See* REPARATIVE THERAPY.

– D –

DAUGHTERS OF BILITIS (DOB). In 1955 a group of eight women, led by Del Martin and Phyllis Lyon, formed the Daughters of Bilitis in San Francisco. Over time, it proved to be the most important **homophile** group for women. The group's name came from a book of poems, *Songs of Bilitis*, some of which referred to love between women. The DOB was influenced by the **Mattachine Society** to be a political group rather than just a social club. In 1956, the DOB began publishing a journal, *Ladder*, even though the group's membership was still very small. The group slowly expanded and there were chapters in New York, Los Angeles, and Chicago by 1960. The DOB also began holding biennial conventions that year.

The group never achieved a significant size, with chapters numbering a few dozen members at best. While its emphasis on reaching out to experts, promoting understanding, and abstaining from confrontation fit with the early **homophile movement**, as the 1960s wore on it increasingly seemed like an anachronism. Some members tried to push the DOB toward social activism, but with few exceptions it refused to adopt the more confrontational stance that some Mattachine Society chapters were taking. In the late 1960s, it was also torn by dissension over whether it should ally itself with the feminist movement. Largely because of these internal conflicts, the DOB dissolved in the early 1970s. *See also* CANADA; KAMENY, FRANK; SOCIETY FOR INDIVIDUAL RIGHTS; UNITED STATES.

DEFENSE OF MARRIAGE ACT (DOMA). In 1996, a Hawaii state court decided in the case of *Baehr v. Lewin* that denial of **same-sex marriage** was unconstitutional sex discrimination under the state's constitution. It looked as if a state would recognize same-sex marriage. As a result, the **United States** Congress passed the Defense of Marriage Act, which President Bill Clinton then signed. The law states that the federal government will not interpret federal statutes as applying to same-sex marriages or otherwise recognize same-sex couples. Thus it mandates that same-sex spouses will not be eligible for Social Security benefits or enjoy other rights (or liabilities) of marriage under any federal program or agency. It also gives states a similar discretion to not recognize same-sex marriages performed in other states.

Hawaii's case was preempted by the legislature placing a referendum banning same-sex marriage before the state's voters. It passed. Massachusetts, however, started recognizing same-sex marriages in 2004 and Connecticut in 2008. This, in turn, raises federalism issues touching upon DOMA, especially in its provision for the lack of interstate recognition of same-sex marriage. The law, therefore, is likely to be the subject of future litigation. *See also* PARENTS AND FRIENDS OF LESBIANS AND GAYS.

DOMESTIC PARTNERSHIP. One form of recognition of same-sex relationships (and sometimes of opposite-sex as well), domestic partnerships are part of an expanding range of state and private options for conferring legal benefits short of marriage. Domestic partnerships lack the clarity or scope of **same-sex marriage** or the **registered partnerships** common to northern **Europe**. In contrast to those, domestic partnerships vary dramatically in the range of legal rights and benefits they accord; often they are rather minimal. Some private firms provide for domestic partnerships. Employees and their partners can register and thus the partner can receive health insurance coverage and a few other allowances such as pension rights or spousal discounts. Other domestic partnership arrangements are through local or state governments and cover a much larger range of rights. There have also been cases when an initial domestic partnership law according few rights has been subsequently broadened to the point that it becomes close to the registered partnership or **civil union** model. In the **United States**, California has had a domestic partnership law that explicitly likens partners to spouses, including in terms of legal rights and responsibilities. In 2008, the California State Supreme Court ruled that the law was insufficient and held that same-sex marriage was mandatory under the state constitution, although Proposition 8 subsequently overturned the court's ruling and ended same-sex marriage in the state. *See also* FOCUS ON THE FAMILY.

"DON'T ASK, DON'T TELL." In 1993, President Bill Clinton tried to lift the ban on gays and lesbians serving in the **United States** military. Many conservatives as well as some senior uniformed personnel strongly criticized the president's proposal, arguing that it would threaten unit cohesion. Clinton struck a compromise, known as "Don't Ask, Don't Tell." It prevents the military from asking about the sexual orientation of those who join, yet it also prevents gays and lesbians from being open about their sexuality. Certainly from the perspective of those who want gays and lesbians to be able to serve openly, the "Don't Ask, Don't Tell" policy has been a failure. Not only does the policy overtly keep gays and lesbians in **the closet**, the rate at which the military discharged gays and lesbians increased in the late 1990s. The number of those discharged for homosexuality declined during President George W. Bush's presidency, especially since the invasion and occupation of Iraq. Discharges under "Don't Ask, Don't Tell" have fallen by more than half, likely due to personnel shortages in the military. Still, from 1993 to 2007, the U.S. military used the policy to discharge 12,000 service members. The armed forces disproportionately apply the policy to women. Although women constitute only 15 percent of U.S. Army and Navy personnel, in 2007 they made up almost half of the 627 persons discharged.

Roughly contemporaneous with President Clinton's attempt to lift the ban in the United States, several other Western nations changed policy to allow gays and lesbians the opportunity for **military service**, including Israel and many European countries. The evidence from those countries is that the unit cohesion is unaffected. There is evidence that the senior U.S. military leadership is moving toward support for lifting the ban, although the political support for such a move is more uncertain.

– E –

EDWARD II (1284–1327). Edward I, the king of England, introduced his son, the prince of Wales and future Edward II, to Piers Gaveston. At the time, the prince was in his early teens and Gaveston was only a year older; the two became lovers for the rest of their lives. Years later, Edward I exiled Gaveston in order to end the relationship and improve his son's behavior, a move with some historical irony since the king had originally introduced the two in order to improve the prince's character. A few months later, however, the king died and Edward II quickly welcomed Gaveston back from exile. As king, Edward lavished favors and titles upon his lover, which offended the English nobility due to Gaveston's low birth. Several influential barons were able to force the king to exile Gaveston on two subsequent occasions. In 1312, upon his return from his third exile, Gaveston was captured and executed by his enemies.

Edward II's reign was tumultuous and unsuccessful. After Gaveston's death, he selected a father and son, the Despensers, as advisors, but they proved deeply unpopular. Many suspected Edward of romantic involvement with the son. Edward's estranged wife and her lover led an army against the king. Edward was deposed and captured. According to the most famous account of his execution, Edward was killed by having a red-hot plumber's iron inserted into his rectum. According to the contemporary official who recorded this event, Edward's killers used this method in order to avoid visible wounds. His execution, and the manner of it, long stood as warning to other monarchs and their favorites. Edward II's life and reign were the subject of a play by Christopher Marlowe. *See also* LITERA-TURE, HOMOSEXUAL MALE.

ELLIS, HAVELOCK (1859–1939). A political progressive and liberal social reformer in **Great Britain**, Havelock Ellis wrote extensively about sexuality. In 1892, **John Addington Symonds** approached Ellis about the possibility of their collaborating on a work in the emerging field of sexology. Symonds passed away the next year, but an essay he had prepared on sexuality in **ancient Greece** was included in the first version of Ellis' book, *Sexual Inversion*. British publication was initially suppressed, in the wake of the **Oscar Wilde** trial.

Like **Karl Heinrich Ulrichs** and **Karl Maria Kertbeny**, Ellis argued that the basic contours of sexual attraction were congenital and that same-sex love did not cause harm to individuals or society. Yet while Ulrichs held that those attracted to their own sex have the personality traits of the opposite sex, in effect that homosexual men are psychologically female and vice versa, Ellis put forward case studies that showed that male "inverts" are the same as heterosexuals. Ellis did, however, portray lesbians as typically masculine, athletic, and ill-suited to domestic tasks.

Ellis argued for the repeal of **anti-sodomy laws**. He worked with **Edward Carpenter** to found the **British Society for the Study of Sex Psychology**. He also collaborated with persons in the early homosexual rights movement in **Germany** to found the World League for Sexual Reform, which worked on behalf of women's rights, the right to legal contraception and abortion, and the abolition of anti-sodomy laws. *See also* HALL, RADCLYFFE; HIRSCHFELD, MAGNUS; MEDICAL MODEL OF HOMOSEXUALITY.

EMPLOYMENT NON-DISCRIMINATION ACT (ENDA). A longtime bill before the **United States** Congress, the Employment Non-Discrimination Act would protect gays and lesbians from discrimination in employment. Support for ENDA has increased over time in Congress, but it has yet to pass. Even though ENDA would apply to corporations, they have generally been silent about or even supportive of the measure. Instead, social conservatives and the **religious right** have led the opposition to it. Opponents typically make three types of arguments against ENDA, or local or state equivalents. First, they argue that sexual orientation is a behavior, while other **anti-discrimination laws** protect status, such as gender. ENDA supporters, however, point out that religious status, which is protected, is a mixture of belief and behavior analogous to sexual orientation. Second, opponents argue that sexual orientation protections would create "special rights" that would undermine traditional civil rights protections. ENDA supporters, however, argue that anti-discrimination protections do not work in a zero-sum fashion. Broader protections actually shore up support for civil rights laws in general, since it makes more persons identify with them. Finally, ENDA critics argue that it will cause a wave of frivolous lawsuits. There is no evidence of that having occurred in states and municipalities that have enacted such laws, however.

One divisive issue is whether gender identity should also have protected status. Gender identity protection has less political support and thus some see it as impeding the passage of ENDA. In 2007, ENDA co-sponsor Representative Barney Frank, a longtime supporter of gay rights, introduced two versions of the legislation, one for sexual orientation and the other for gender identity. Many gay rights groups were critical, while some praised the political pragmatism of his move.

ENLIGHTENMENT, THE. It is difficult to assign precise dates to a large intellectual movement such as the Enlightenment. Roughly, however, it extended from about the Glorious Revolution in England, in 1688, to the French Revolution, in 1789. It was strongest in western and northern **Europe**, England, Scotland, and, later, in **Italy** and the American colonies. The legacy of the Enlightenment has been a matter of fierce debate since at least the French Revolution. That is still the case today, as well as the closely related debate over how to best characterize the Enlightenment. Still, a few central features stand out. Enlightenment thinkers emphasized individual freedom, including freedom from arbitrary power and religious authorities. They also embraced secularism, and many professed a belief in natural rights.

A number of Enlightenment thinkers overtly addressed the issue of homosexuality, including legal punishment for its sexual expression. Montesquieu, in his influential *The Spirit of Laws*, noted that **anti-sodomy laws** are prone to abuse by despots, in that accusations of sodomy have been an effective way for rulers to persecute their opponents. Furthermore, he lumped sodomy in with sorcery and heresy as the few crimes still subject to punishment by fire. Montesquieu's tone in the passage is sharply negative; while still expressing disdain at sodomy, he strongly implies that these laws should either be abolished or have much weaker penalties. He suggests that a better approach would be to have educational institutions as the main venues for the discouraging of homosexuality. Voltaire, a friend of **Frederick II**, publicly expressed repugnance at homosexuality, yet argued that same-sex sexuality should not be a matter of law.

Cesare Beccaria, an Italian author, wrote a very influential analysis of criminal law, *Dei delitti e delle pene* (*Of Crimes and Punishments*). Published in 1761, it implied that the use of torture in sodomy cases, which was still widespread, often compelled the innocent to admit to a crime he or she had not committed. More broadly, Beccaria's work helped spark a widespread movement of criminal law reform. For him, punishments should not be a matter of vengeance but rather a means of deterrence; what counts as a crime should involve real harm to society, rather than imaginary harm or offense; punishments should be proportional to the crime. Beccaria's work helped to end torture as a means of inquisitorial investigation, and prompted many, such as Thomas Jefferson, to oppose the death penalty.

While most Enlightenment thinkers either ignored same-sex love or expressed a traditional repugnance about it, their arguments clearly pushed in the direction of reduced penalties. They did not invoke the story of Sodom and Gomorrah, nor did they support ecclesiastical authorities shaping the law. At the beginning of the Enlightenment, many countries had laws that called for the death penalty for sodomy and used torture to extract confessions. By 1800, many had abolished those laws, with the significant exception of **Great Britain**, and the use of torture had become rare. While those attracted to their own sex were still subjected to **police harassment**, imprisonment, and social ostracism, the Enlightenment did provide a significant improvement in at least the legal situation. It also changed the basic mode of thinking about sexuality. A secular framework displaced the traditional theological one. The term "**sodomite**" was on its way to becoming outmoded. Naturalistic analyses of sexuality, as reflected by such Enlightenment philosophes as Diderot, rose in influence. *See also* CODE NAPOLÉON; ETIOLOGY; FRANCE; MEDICAL MODEL OF HOMOSEXUALITY.

ESSENTIALISM. Among those who conduct research into the history of sexuality, especially in academic circles, there are disagreements over methodology. These historiographical debates have gone through several iterations. Some of the earliest modern researchers into sexuality put forward lists of famous historical figures attracted to persons of the same sex. This implied, in effect, a common historical entity underlying sexual attraction or orientation, including same-sex attraction, whether one called it "inversion" or "homosexuality." This approach, or perhaps more accurately a closely related family of positions, is commonly called essentialism. John Boswell later gave it a new level of theoretical and historical sophistication, although his position in the debate shifted to the point of virtual agnosticism. In contrast, in the 1970s a number of researchers, often influenced by Mary McIntosh or **Michel Foucault**, argued that class relations, the human sciences, and other historically constructed forces create sexual categories and the personal identities associated with them. This approach is commonly called **social constructionism**, although leading advocates more recently have preferred "historicism." Since the 1970s, essentialists and social constructionists have had a heated debate, although few scholars embrace the term "essentialist" as a self-description. The contours of the debate have changed significantly over time, yet several of the key contentions have not changed.

Essentialists claim that categories of sexual attraction are observed rather than invented. For example, while **ancient Greece** did not have terms that correspond to the heterosexual/homosexual division, persons did note men who were exclusively attracted to only one sex. Thus the lack of terms for a distinction does not equal an inability to make the distinction, and hence the social constructionist emphasis on the particularity of modern terminology does not actually prove their point, according to essentialists. Furthermore, essentialists not only grant that there can be better or worse taxonomies of sexual attraction, they also contend that only their position has the theoretical resources to sort out which ones are better and why. Since their key contention is that there is a reality that the categorizations are trying to get at, they have a foundation from which they can criticize inadequate taxonomies.

Essentialists also criticize the social constructionist approach, arguing that the end result of the historicist approach will be to undermine the very idea of a "gay history." Instead, the field of investigation becomes other social forces and how they "produce" a distinct organization of sexual perceptions and relations. According to essentialists, the social constructionist approach needs to be avoided in order to maintain the project of gay history, and minority histories in general, as a force for political liberation. Some persons in various gay rights movements have articulated essentialist views. For example, lesbian feminists, especially in the 1970s, often defended essentialist accounts of identity and sexuality. Lesbian separatists in particular argued that women's natures were superior, but the only way to realize that essence was through withdrawal from all men, gay or straight, in a deeply patriarchal world. *See also* SODOMITE.

ETIOLOGY. People have speculated about the cause or causes of same-sex attraction and eroticism for millennia. While opposite-sex relations can produce children and thus appear less in need of explanation, same-sex relations seem more obscure in origin. Arguments about the cause or causes of homosexuality frequently have been intertwined with defenses or denunciations of same-sex relations. In the modern era, speculations about the origins of homosexuality, often with at least a scientific veneer, have been closely connected with the **medical model of homosexuality**. In recent decades, however, research into the etiology of homosexuality has more frequently been disconnected from the goal of portraying homosexuality as a sickness.

Authors in **ancient Rome** offered accounts ranging from astrological to inheritance to mental illness. In medieval **Italy**, authors again connected same-sex attraction to astrology, contending that birth during specific astrological conjunctions was the likely cause. In the late 13th century, William of Saliceto attributed female-female attraction to a disease that causes fleshy growths on the body. He recommended clitoridectomy as a cure.

Influenced by the **Enlightenment**, the modern era has searched for naturalistic explanations for same-sex attraction. In the 18th century, a few authors contended that masturbation caused a number of illnesses and mental pathologies, including an "unnatural" desire for same-sex relations. Writers of the 19th century, especially in the latter half, focused on congenital factors. **Karl Heinrich Ulrichs** argued that development in utero was decisive, which in turn supported his view that homosexuality is natural and should not be criminalized or sanctioned.

In the early 20th century, **Magnus Hirschfeld** hypothesized that hormone levels may affect sexual orientation. Yet early sexologists, such as Hirschfeld, arguably did not affect general public opinion as much as broader streams of thought, such as social Darwinism and its degeneracy explanations for crime, mental illness, and homosexuality. Darwinism ultimately culminated in support for forced sterilization or execution for those afflicted, lest they contaminate the overall population.

Psychological accounts also were influential throughout the 20th century. **Sigmund Freud** developed a rich account of personal development, which implied that persons are by nature bisexual but that the natural completion of the process is heterosexuality. To this thinking, homosexuality is a psychological abnormality caused by an interrupted psychosexual development, but not an illness. Many of Freud's followers, however, argued that homosexuality is a form of illness in need of treatment.

Biological explanations again rose in prominence in the latter half of the 20th century. In the 1960s, the endocrine system again became the focus. Combining Ulrich's and Hirschfeld's approaches, researchers argued that in utero hormonal levels strongly influenced adult sexual expression, an account that is still explored in recent articles in the scientific press. Genetic factors have also garnered attention in the past couple of decades. Studies have found that homosexuality is much more likely to be shared between identical twins than siblings. Scientists have proposed a specific area in a chromosome and its influence upon brain development as the mechanism. While the popular press latched upon the idea of a "gay gene," the evidence for such has so far been very thin. Other studies have contended that there are subtle but real differences in the brains of straight and gay persons, but this too has been the subject of much dispute. Future research is likely to explore further the complicated interactions between genes; early hormonal exposure, including in utero; and early familial and cultural experiences. *See also* AMERICAN PSYCHIATRIC ASSOCIATION; TRIBADE.

EUROPE. The evidence about ancient European cultures' attitudes about homosexuality is thin, with the exception of **ancient Greece** and **ancient Rome**. In the first millennium B.C.E., the Celts occupied areas, at their peak, from central and southern Europe to what is today **France** and **Great Britain**. The ancient Greeks had contact with the Celts; **Aristotle** discusses the Celts and their homosexuality positively in the *Politics*. Other ancient Greek writers noted the Celtic propensity for male same-sex relations, even to the point of stating that while Celtic women are beautiful, Celtic men still prefer other men. As the Roman Empire expanded, the Celts lost their independence and influence. The Etruscans in northern **Italy**, from the ninth century to the second century B.C.E., had a strong homosexual component to their art. Not only did they draw and sculpt numerous male nudes but also frank depictions of male homosexual sex acts.

With the decline of the Roman Empire and its replacement by various barbarian kingdoms, a general tolerance of homosexual acts prevailed, with the exception of Visigothic **Spain**. Europe had few secular laws against homosexuality. Although the Christian hierarchy denounced non-procreative sexuality, including same-sex acts, a genre of homophilic literature, especially among the clergy, developed in the 11th and 12th centuries. The latter part of the 12th through the 14th centuries, however, saw a sharp rise in intolerance toward homosexual sex and relationships, alongside persecution of Jews, Muslims, believers in nonconforming versions of **Christianity**, and others. While the causes of this shift are somewhat unclear, it is likely that increased class conflict alongside the Gregorian reform movement in the Catholic Church were two important factors. The church itself started to appeal to a conception of "nature" as the standard of morality, and drew it in such a way so as to forbid homosexual sex, as well as extramarital sex, non-procreative sex within marriage, and often masturbation. This appeal to **natural law** became very influential in the Western tradition, especially as formulated by **Aquinas**.

For the next several centuries, some areas of Europe had strict laws and frequent punishments, while others had laws but no punishments or even no laws against homosexual sex. While Spain suffered through the **Inquisition**, Denmark did not even have an **anti-sodomy law** until 1683 and no prosecutions for decades after that. Starting in the mid-16th century, the city-state of Geneva prosecuted and killed persons accused of same-sex relations, including lesbianism, with a vigor that rivaled or surpassed the Spanish Inquisition. The degree to which same-sex attraction, relationships, and sex were accepted often varied by class, with the middle class taking the narrowest view, while the aristocracy and nobility often accepted public expressions of alternative sexualities. At times, even with the risk of severe punishment, same-sex-oriented subcultures would flourish in cities, sometimes only to be suppressed by the authorities. There were also differences by gender. Male homosexuality was usually subjected to greater prosecution. Even though lesbians were sometimes put to death, or whipped and otherwise punished, the scale of surveillance and prosecutions and the degree of penalties imposed were generally less. For example, the Netherlands had a sudden outburst of anti-homosexual hysteria in 1730. The authorities prosecuted hundreds; scores were executed by strangling, drowning, or hanging. Torture was used to gain confessions, and boys as young as 14 were put to death. Dutch cities had smaller-scale episodes over the rest of the century. In 1803, the authorities put to death yet another person for same-sex relations, but that might have been the last execution for sodomy in Europe. Yet over the seven decades of intermittent hysteria and repression within the Dutch republic, not a single lesbian was put to death.

In the late 18th century and throughout the 19th, there was a significant reduction in legal penalties for sodomy, in part due to the influence of the **Enlightenment**. The **Code Napoléon** decriminalized sodomy, and with Napoleon's conquests the code spread. Furthermore, in many European countries where homosexual sex remained a crime, the general movement at this time away from the death penalty meant that sodomy was usually removed from the list of capital offenses. In many places, however, the reduction in the severity of penalties often meant that the number of convictions rose, as judges and juries increasingly felt comfortable with the less draconian punishments. During the same period, the overtly theological framework for perceiving sexuality was superseded by secular arguments and interpretations. Probably the most important secular domain for the discussions of homosexuality was in medicine, including psychology. Instead of confessing one's sexuality to a priest in a confessional, or as part of an inquisition, sexuality seen as deviant became a medical or psychiatric issue. Judges called doctors into court to examine sex crime defendants.

At the same time, the dramatic increase in school attendance rates, and the average length of time spent in school, reduced transgenerational contact and hence the frequency of trans-generational sex. In contrast to much of European history, same-sex relations between persons of roughly the same age became the norm. Furthermore, as capitalism promoted labor mobility, and ever-growing cities helped ensure anonymity, self-identified communities of homosexuals became increasingly common in urban centers.

Modern Europe's turn to naturalistic explanations, and the concomitant rise in the influence of medicine, helped spur the exploration of biological and psychological explanations of homosexuality in the mid to late 19th century. Several early figures were overtly sympathetic to same-sex attraction, such as **Karl Heinrich Ulrichs**. By the early 20th century, however, analyses that posited homosexuality as a form of sickness or pathology were dominant. Richard von Krafft-Ebing played a key role in this transformation. A German psychiatrist who wrote the influential treatise *Psychopathia Sexualis*, Krafft-Ebing described homosexuality as a perversion and a symptom of degeneracy. Yet as he altered his work for later editions, he moderated his stance on homosexuality. He also supported the effort to repeal **Germany**'s Paragraph 175, which made illegal male-male sexual relations. Other early sexologists were much more scathing (and less clinical) than Krafft-Ebing, blaming homosexuality for all sorts of social ills and even military defeats. **Sigmund Freud**'s work, and the corresponding rise of psychoanalytic theory in the early 20th century, deeply influenced the debate over the etiology of homosexuality.

Magnus Hirschfeld was influenced by Ulrichs' writings and he helped to start the early homosexual rights movement, which began in Germany but had an international impact. In 1897, Hirschfeld and others formed the ***Wissenschaftlich-humanitäres Komitee*** (Scientific-Humanitarian Committee), which was the first homosexual rights group. It fought for the repeal of anti-sodomy laws and for educational efforts to overcome fear and ignorance about homosexuality. It also supported women's rights. Over the next two decades, chapters formed in a number of German cities and in other countries, and the group inspired the formation of like-minded organizations, such as the **British Society for the Study of Sex Psychology**. While the early homosexual rights movement failed in its stated goals of repealing anti-sodomy laws in Western Europe, it did mark the first time individuals banded together and outspokenly worked on behalf of the legal, social, and political interests of homosexual men and women. The rise of Fascism, however, and World War II caused the demise of the homosexual rights movement.

Throughout Europe, the late 1940s and the 1950s were a time of relative public silence about homosexuality, combined with continued repression. In Eastern Europe, various Communist governments jailed and harassed homosexuals as part of a general disregard for personal liberties. The Soviet Union and its official anti-homosexuality stance were influential in setting the tone for other states, such as Poland and Czechoslovakia. While homosexuals were more able to associate freely in Western Europe, in most countries they still faced a sociolegal landscape with anti-sodomy laws and where others knowing one's same-sex attraction would endanger career and status. In the Netherlands, however, the postwar government repealed the Nazi anti-sodomy statute immediately after the war. Due to the harsh cultural environment, the reconstruction of a homosexual rights movement was tentative and slow to achieve significant gains. In 1948, a group in the Netherlands established the *Cultuur-en-Ontspannings Centrum* (Culture and Recreation Center), which was the first postwar homosexual organization in Europe. It was also the first instance of what eventually became known as the **homophile movement**. Another group, *Arcadie*, in France, formed a few years later and launched its own journal. In Great Britain, the **Homosexual Law Reform Society** formed in the late 1950s.

The situation changed abruptly in Western Europe in the late 1960s and early 1970s. In 1967, the British government passed the **Sexual Offenses Act**, which decriminalized male-male sodomy but established unequal ages of consent for homosexual and heterosexual acts. This spurred reform efforts not just on the Continent, but in North America and in Britain's former colonies. The greater political radicalism of the post-**Stonewall** era imbued gay rights groups with an assertive and more confrontational style. The number of gay rights organizations increased dramatically. Older, **homophile** groups quickly found themselves under attack from activists for being out of touch and overly compliant. In the 1970s, gay life became increasingly public and gay neighborhoods were established in major urban centers, such as Paris and Madrid. In contrast, in Eastern Europe and the Soviet Union, the deep level of repression continued. The government of Nicolae Ceauşescu in Romania, in particular, used sodomy convictions in order to discredit and jail dissidents. What made this especially convenient was that, in the 1970s and 1980s, Western human rights groups were reluctant to come to the defense of those imprisoned purely on sexual offenses, rather than political ones.

Given the scope of organizing by gays and lesbians in the 1970s, the subsequent infighting among and even within the various groups was inevitable. Still, significant social and legal gains were achieved in the 1980s and 1990s, to the point that Western Europe is the most tolerant and pro-gay region in the world. A few countries passed **registered partnership** laws in the 1980s, such as Denmark and Sweden. The advances in the 1990s were even more dramatic. In 1993, the **European Court of Human Rights** ruled against Cyprus' anti-sodomy law, one of the last in the region. In the same year, Norway enacted a registered partnership law. Moreover, by this time most citizens in Western Europe simply took it for granted that gays and lesbians would be organized and vocal in defense of their rights. In the first years of the new millennium, gays and lesbians gained **same-sex marriage** rights in a number of countries, including the Netherlands and Belgium.

After the fall of the Berlin Wall and the dissolution of totalitarian regimes in Eastern Europe, many countries in the region soon liberalized their stance on homosexuality. An important factor in this process was the widespread desire in Eastern Europe to join the European Union (EU) and other multilateral European institutions. For example, in 1993, the Council of Europe advised the Romanian government that it needed to repeal its anti-sodomy law in order to be admitted. Even though polling data at the time showed that most Romanians were opposed to homosexuality, the law was repealed after three years. Similarly, in 2004, Estonia adopted an **anti-discrimination law** in order to join the EU.

The first decade of the 21st century was a period of rapid legal advances for gays and lesbians in Eastern Europe. In 2001, the Czech Republic added a domestic partnership law while Estonia equalized the age of consent. The next year, Hungary and Bulgaria equalized the age of consent; in 2003, Poland and Bulgaria added anti-discrimination laws. While larger cities in Eastern Europe have gay organizations and a relatively open nightlife for gays and lesbians, rural areas are much more conservative and intolerant. *See also* ADOPTION; CIVIL UNIONS; CLOSET, THE; DOMESTIC PARTNERSHIP; GAY BASHING; HATE CRIME LAWS; HOMOPHILE; HUMAN IMMUNODEFICIENCY VIRUS/ACQUIRED IMMUNODEFICIENCY SYNDROME; IMMIGRATION AND NATURALIZATION LAW; INTERNATIONAL LESBIAN AND GAY ASSOCIATION; JUDAISM; LATIN AMERICA; LITERATURE, LESBIAN; MEDICAL MODEL OF HOMOSEXUALITY; POLICE HARASSMENT; UNITED NATIONS.

EUROPEAN COURT OF HUMAN RIGHTS (ECHR). In 1950, the Council of **Europe** agreed to the Convention for the Protection of Human Rights and Fundamental Freedoms. At present approximately four dozen countries, primarily in Western and Central Europe, are parties to the convention. The European Court of Human Rights is designed to enforce the convention. Individuals in participating states can forward complaints to the court. One person who did so was a gay activist in Northern Ireland, Jeffrey Dudgeon, whom the police had questioned about his sexual activities. In 1981 the court ruled, in the case of *Dudgeon v. United Kingdom*, that Northern Ireland's **anti-sodomy law** violated the convention's privacy provisions. The ruling did give member states latitude to determine their age of consent. Northern Ireland decriminalized sodomy in 1982, and the ruling in *Dudgeon* helped to pressure other states to repeal their anti-sodomy laws. The court reiterated its displeasure with anti-sodomy laws in its 1993 ruling in *Modinos v. Cyprus*, which found against Cyprus' version of such a law.

Many subsequent decisions also encouraged states to change their laws. Article 14 of the convention, which prohibits discrimination, provided the basis for many of the pro-gay rulings. In the 1999 case of *Smith and Grady v. the United Kingdom*, the ECHR ruled that **Great Britain**'s ban upon military service by gays and lesbians violated the convention. The same year the ECHR ruled in a case from Portugal that a gay parent should have child visitation rights. The man had fathered a child in a previous heterosexual relationship. In a case from Poland the court ruled that the mayor of Warsaw, who later became that country's president, acted in an illegal and discriminatory manner when he banned a gay pride march. In 2003, the court ruled against unequal age of consent laws. The same year the ECHR found in favor of a gay man wanting tenancy rights in regard to a partner who had died from **human immunodeficiency virus/ acquired immunodeficiency syndrome**.

Not all of the ECHR's decisions have been in favor of gay and lesbian rights. In *Frette v. France*, a 2002 case, the ECHR ruled that a French court's decision against a gay man wishing to adopt was not in violation of the convention. Overall, however, the ECHR has been skeptical of state decisions and private actions that appear to violate the convention's discrimination or privacy provisions. *See also* SEXUAL OFFENSES ACT.

"EX-GAY" MOVEMENT. *See* REPARATIVE THERAPY.

– F –

FALWELL, JERRY, SR. (1933–2007). A leader in the **religious right** for over a quarter of a century, Jerry Falwell held strongly anti-gay views and worked aggressively against pro-gay public policy changes. In his 20s, Falwell founded the Thomas Road Baptist Church in Lynchburg, Virginia. At its peak, the church had over 20,000 members. In 1971, he founded Liberty University, a higher education institution that prides itself for having a curriculum based on a fundamentalist interpretation of **Christianity**. Falwell supported **Anita Bryant**'s 1977 campaign to overturn an **anti-discrimination law** in Florida. Two years later he founded the Moral Majority, which became a leading organization in the religious right in the 1980s. Falwell disbanded it at the end of that decade. Like many right-wing Christians, Falwell held a religious outlook that melded anti-Semitism and a dislike for minority sexualities. Falwell blamed the gay community for the **human immunodeficiency virus/acquired immunodeficiency syndrome** (HIV/AIDS) epidemic, calling it a gay plague that reflects the general moral decay of society. On his show *The Old Time Gospel Hour*, Falwell said that AIDS is God's judgment on "homosexual promiscuity." He also denounced the **Metropolitan Community Church** as well as the **United States** Supreme Court decision in *Lawrence v. Texas*, calling it the worst ruling since *Roe v. Wade*. Throughout his life, Falwell consistently described homosexuality as a choice and believed that **reparative therapy** could change one's sexual orientation. Probably his most noted anti-gay comments came in the immediate aftermath of the terrorist attacks on 11 September 2001. Falwell, appearing on Pat Robertson's *The 700 Club*, stated that gays, lesbians, pagans, abortion providers, and feminists had caused the attacks. Robertson agreed. Falwell later apologized, stating that only the terrorists had caused the attacks. Yet he reiterated his belief that the groups he had singled out for blame had caused God to stop protecting the United States from attack. *See also* JUDAISM.

FAMILY RESEARCH COUNCIL (FRC). In 1980, a number of evangelical leaders, including James Dobson of **Focus on the Family** (FOF), met in Washington, D.C., and decided to form a group that would advocate on behalf of their concept of families. The result was the Family Research Council, which started in 1983. Initially it was independent of FOF, although with very close ties. The two merged from 1988 to 1992, then again became independent while maintaining good working relations that included overlapping boards of directors. The organization has benefited from wealthy benefactors and a membership that has at times numbered in the hundreds of thousands.

Like FOF, the FRC holds a worldview and mission that are rooted in conservative, evangelical **Christianity**. Yet unlike many evangelical organizations, the FRC emphasizes the role of political connections and insider lobbying. Its leaders typically have had experience in elected office or senior appointments in the federal executive branch.

For example, Gary Bauer, who led the group throughout the 1990s, served in Ronald Reagan's White House. In addition to lobbying, the group aggressively works to bolster the intellectual credentials of the **religious right**. FRC hires or, in some cases, seeks to be identified with persons who hold doctorates and share its viewpoint and then works to get those persons on television or in print media. It supports **anti-sodomy laws** and **reparative therapy** and opposes **anti-discrimination laws** and **same-sex marriage**. The group has submitted amicus curiae briefs in key cases, such as *Lawrence v. Texas*.

FOCUS ON THE FAMILY (FOF). A leading organization in the **religious right**, Focus on the Family was founded by James Dobson in 1976. He earned a doctorate in child development and then gained a position at the University of Southern California medical school, but he left that position in the mid-1970s to devote himself to writing and speaking on family-centered issues. Shortly after establishing the group he began giving radio addresses. The organization grew dramatically over time, with a staff numbering in the dozens in the 1980s and over 1,000 in the 1990s. In the early 1990s, it moved its headquarters to a sprawling campus in Colorado Springs, Colorado, and expanded its radio network internationally. FOF delivers a number of radio programs that reach several million listeners every day. It also publishes a number of magazines and newsletters that in combined circulation reach millions.

FOF espouses a conservative Christian view of sexuality and marriage. It publishes materials that criticize those who attempt to reconcile homosexuality and **Christianity**. It defends **reparative therapy** and describes gay men as promiscuous and disease prone. FOF opposes **anti-discrimination laws**, calling them "special rights," as well as **domestic partnership** benefits. The group is particularly opposed to **same-sex marriage** and portrays such laws as a deep threat to heterosexual marriage, children, and the overall well-being of society. FOF lobbies aggressively at the federal and state levels in support of these positions. *See also* FAMILY RESEARCH COUNCIL.

FOUCAULT, MICHEL (1927–1984). A deeply influential French philosopher, Michel Foucault was a leading figure in postmodern thought and he strongly influenced **queer theory**. Foucault did not hide his homosexuality and gave interviews in French and American gay magazines, where he discussed gay and lesbian issues. He died in 1984 from a **human immunodeficiency virus/acquired immunodeficiency syndrome**–related illness.

Foucault's first book, *Madness and Civilization*, focused on the history of psychology as a human science. He wrote it in the late 1950s, while persons in the **homophile movement** were cooperating with mainstream psychologists. In contrast, Foucault launched a scathing and Nietzschean-inspired attack upon psychology. He argued that it has unfounded pretensions to objectivity that mask very real social effects of marginalization and exclusion. At a time when most psychologists described homosexuality as a form of pathology, Foucault argued that distinctions of sanity/insanity were political and capricious.

While criticism of the human sciences was a central theme throughout his writings, it was his work in the 1970s that proved the most influential. In the first volume of his *History of Sexuality*, Foucault criticized what he called the "repressive hypothesis." Instead of seeing the contemporary age as liberating a sexuality that was previously repressed, Foucault argued that we should see sexuality as socially constructed by an intricate set of power relations and resistance against those. Instead of seeing sexuality as a given and asking whether it is liberated or repressed, Foucault argued that we should instead attend to how power in modern society forms sexuality, especially through such disciplines as medicine and psychiatry, including categories of normal and abnormal.

Many scholars criticized Foucault's work from this period as portraying persons as exclusively determined by power and thereby denying any hope of meaningful resistance. The two subsequent volumes in his *History of Sexuality*, which turn to look at cultural norms and philosophic reflections about sex in **ancient Greece** and **ancient Rome**, seek in part to address that criticism. Foucault examined practices of care of the self and the attempt to reshape one's life according to aesthetic criteria, rather than moralistic ones. *See also* ADOPTION; ESSENTIALISM; FRANCE; LITERATURE, HOMOSEXUAL MALE; SOCIAL CONSTRUCTIONISM.

FRANCE. Carolingian kings, especially Charlemagne, temporarily halted the cultural and economic decline of **Europe** after the fall of **ancient Rome**. The empire that Charlemagne forged after years of war in the late eighth century encompassed most of present-day France, **Germany**, Belgium, Holland, Switzerland, and Austria. Relations between church and state were very close and a series of church councils issued decrees against sodomy. After Charlemagne's death, a leading bishop convened the Council of Paris, which issued a document endorsing the death penalty for sodomy. At roughly the same time, a monk forged a number of documents that were attributed to Charlemagne. Blaming homosexual relations for a host of ills, the documents over time gained legitimacy and often were seen as establishing legal precedents for strict punishments. A portion of the monk's forgery incorporates word-for-word language from the council's document, and it too calls for the death penalty.

In the 11th and 12th centuries, a group of poets in northern France wrote about same-sex attraction with frankness. The three most prominent figures of this movement were Marbod of Rennes, his student Baudri of Bourgueil, and Hildebert of Lavardin. Each rose to high positions in the church, with the latter two serving for years as archbishop. Influenced by Roman culture, their poetry also has a Christian didacticism and in many of their works they discuss the temptations that young men stir in them, only to reject that temptation as brought by Satan. As with many classical Roman authors, each seemed to assume the naturalness of bisexuality. They were celebrated as some of the best poets of the day. At roughly the same time, and again in northern France, anonymous authors wrote epigrams about the prevalence of homosexuality. A 13th-century writer identified a specific area of Paris as frequented by **sodomites** looking for sexual encounters.

France did not have a strong, unitary legal system in the Middle Ages. Instead, laws varied considerably from region to region. Punishment for sodomy varied, including death by hanging or burning, or castration. One of the few laws that specified punishment for female-female sex mandated genital mutilation for the first two offenses and death by burning for the third. Sometimes punishment included the confiscation of property by either secular or religious authorities, which had the effect of encouraging allegations. The Knights Templar, composed of knights who formed a monastic order dedicated to Christian control of the Holy Land, were accused of sodomy and other crimes in an effort by Philip IV of France to gain their wealth. In 1307, Philip had sealed orders sent across France demanding the arrest of all Templars. For seven years, Templars were hunted down until the group was destroyed.

The rate of prosecutions, and executions, accelerated in the 16th and 17th centuries. The authorities also executed women for passing as men and engaging in same-sex relations. Yet during this same period, some aristocratic circles were open to same-sex sexuality. The courts of **Henry III** and Louis XIII were aware of how the sovereign was attracted to men, as well as who the current favorite or favorites were. Louis XIV's brother, Philippe d'Orléans, was also quite openly homosexual and his second wife, Elisabeth Charlotte, exhaustively recorded not only his affairs, but also those of other aristocratic men. She wrote that free discussion of homosexuality was common among the aristocracy. Also during this era, the soldier, author, and seigneur de Brantôme, Pierre de Bourdeille, coined the term *lesbienne*, although it would not displace **tribade** until the 19th century. His book *The Lives of Gallant Ladies* offers, for its time, a surprisingly neutral to even positive description of female-female love, although he is sharply critical of homosexual men.

The general French perception in the 18th century was that aristocratic persons commonly succumbed to what was known as *le beau vice*. The police, however, increased their attempts to suppress homosexuality in the general population, including through entrapment and **police harassment**. Yet a gay subculture still managed a palpable, though marginal, existence. There were gay taverns in Paris, as well as known places for cruising, such as Pont Neuf and the Tuileries gardens. It is likely that this era's move away from the death penalty for sodomy helped in the preservation of this subculture. The few executions for sodomy that took place in the 18th century usually involved other attendant crimes; the last execution for just sodomy occurred in 1750. One change during this era is especially notable. The **Enlightenment** and its secular forms of reasoning had displaced the role of religion in public life, including in moral and legal affairs. Police and courts moved away from the term "**sodomite**," in preference to *infâme* or *pédéraste*, which referred to homosexuals in general. In 1791, without much fanfare, the Constituent Assembly decriminalized sodomy. A systematic codification of the laws was

enacted after Napoleon had crowned himself emperor. Called the
Code Napoléon, it maintained the legal silence about sodomy.

In the 19th century, the various governments that rose and fell
maintained the legal silence about sodomy, but police harassment
and arrests still occurred. The second empire was especially punitive.
In the late 19th and early 20th centuries, harassment and punishment
again became infrequent. The Parisian gay subculture, previously
relegated to the margins and under continuous threat, flourished.
Among the upper class, lesbian relationships were seen as fashion-
able, although there were certainly limits and women were still
universally expected to marry. Still, figures such as Colette did not
hide their same-sex relationships. American expatriates in Paris, such
as **Gertrude Stein** and Alice Toklas, also lived openly as same-sex
couples. After the liberation of France in World War II, Stein and
Toklas welcomed American soldiers into their home while still calling each other by their pet names.

The early **homophile movement**, which emerged in the 1950s,
had a French component. In 1952, the homosexual journal *Futur*
was established. Yet its circulation was very limited and it ceased
publication after just three years. In 1954, André Baudry began the
more influential journal *Arcadie* and set its editorial stance that,
like other **homophile** publications, emphasized the normality of
homosexuals and encouraged its readers to adhere to that standard.
It also denounced anti-homosexual changes in law from the previous
decade. The Vichy government, which was the rump French state
that collaborated with the **National Socialists**, had raised the age of
consent for homosexual sex to 21. The law applied to lesbian sex as
well as male-male acts. Also, in 1960, Charles de Gaulle's government passed the Mirguet Amendment, which labeled homosexuality
a "scourge" alongside prostitution and alcoholism. There was a social
group affiliated with *Arcadie*, but a real movement did not begin in
France until the late 1960s and early 1970s. In the tumult of 1968,
the *Comité d'Action Pédérastique Révolutionnaire* (Committee for
Revolutionary Homosexual Action) was formed. It was much more
confrontational in style, as was the *Front Homosexuel d'Action Révolutionnaire* (Homosexual Front for Revolutionary Action). It was
formed in 1971, but within just a few years was superseded by the
Groupe de Libération Homosexuelle (GLH, Homosexual Liberation

Group), and in particular by the pragmatic *Politique et Quotidien* (PQ, Politics and Daily Life) wing of the GLH. This shift was reflective of a general move from a Marxist-infused gay advocacy movement to one that was less ideological and more instrumental in its approach. GLH-PQ ran gay candidates in elections and built alliances with other movements, such as feminist and abortion rights groups.

In the 1980s, the gay rights movement, which then enjoyed good collaboration between lesbians and gay men, achieved some legal successes. In 1980, the higher penalties for violations of the **age of consent laws** for same-sex relations than heterosexual ones were repealed. Two years later the age of consent was equalized for same-sex and heterosexual relations. Having achieved some of its goals, the movement increasingly turned away from politics to a subculture focused upon desire and pleasure. It was at this time that the **human immunodeficiency virus/acquired immunodeficiency syndrome** epidemic struck. Although initially slow to respond, out of fear that the disease was merely a pretext for attacking gays, the gay community formed groups to distribute safe sex literature and tend to the sick. In the late 1980s, a French chapter of the **AIDS Coalition to Unleash Power** was formed. It in turn helped to infuse a renewed sense of militancy to the gay rights movement.

In 1985, the government enacted an **anti-discrimination law**. In 1999, the French government passed a **registered partnership** law that allows same-sex and opposite-sex couples to register with the government and thereby file joint tax returns, share employment benefits, and have joint property arrangements. It does not include **adoption** rights and a few other legal benefits of marriage. While the Socialist Party supports **same-sex marriage**, the major party of the right does not. Gays and lesbians are themselves divided on the issue of marriage, with some French gays taking a pro-**assimilation** stance, while others urge rejection of mainstream society and its core institutions, including marriage. **Military service** is open to gays and lesbians. In 2004, the government passed a version of a **hate crimes law** that makes anti-gay and sexist speech punishable by fines and jail time. *See also* EUROPEAN COURT OF HUMAN RIGHTS; FOUCAULT, MICHEL; LITERATURE, HOMOSEXUAL MALE; LITERATURE, LESBIAN; UNITED NATIONS; VIAU, THÉO-PHILE DE; WILDE, OSCAR.

FREDERICK II (FREDERICK THE GREAT) (1712–1786). Son of William Frederick I, the ruler of Prussia, Frederick's father subjected him to a nightmarish childhood. Frederick was an effeminate boy who loved the flute, poetry, and French culture. His father was anti-intellectual and loathed the French. He ridiculed, and occasionally beat, Frederick for his interests. As a teenager, Frederick formed several close relationships, the most important one with Hans Hermann von Katte. Katte was several years older than Frederick and they shared interests as well as a common outlook on life. They attempted to leave Prussia but were caught when a member of the escape party betrayed the group. The king ordered a trial on charges of desertion; the penalty for Katte was life in prison, but the court was not willing to judge the prince. The king overruled the court and had Katte beheaded. Frederick was made to watch the sentence being carried out.

Frederick was ordered to marry by his father, but he had neither sexual nor intellectual interest in his wife and the marriage involved no real relationship. As an adult, Frederick continued to form close and almost certainly sexual relationships with other men, such as Michael Gabriel Fredersdorf, who was a private in Frederick's army as well as someone who shared a passion for the flute. Upon ascension to the throne, in 1740, Frederick set up a court that was entirely male and had frequent homoerotic conversation. There were young military officers, as well as cultural personages, that reflected Frederick's abiding interests in ideas and the arts. The most prominent figure that Frederick brought to his court was Voltaire, who lived in Potsdam for several years and who wrote about Frederick's homosexual liaisons in his memoirs. As ruler, Frederick also lost his youthful disinterest in military affairs and became one of the best generals in his day. He displayed an uncommon courage in battle. Yet he also was ruthless and Machiavellian in his statecraft, in addition to being an absolutist in domestic policy.

Frederick was a man of the **Enlightenment**. He supported the sciences and was tolerant of dissenting ideas, including in religion. He had a deep passion for the arts and wrote several volumes of poetry as well as dozens of musical pieces. He pursued law reform. His second commission of jurists concluded its efforts after his death, but recommended a sharp reduction in the penalty for sodomy, from death to imprisonment for as little as one year. *See also* GERMANY.

FREUD, SIGMUND (1856–1939). Although he was born in Moravia, now part of the Czech Republic, Sigmund Freud spent most of his life in Vienna. He pursued training and briefly worked as a physician, but his interests turned to nervous diseases and mental pathology. One of the most innovative thinkers of the late 19th and early 20th centuries, Freud was the father of psychoanalysis.

In regard to homosexuality, the diagnostic framework of his day emphasized degeneracy theory. A few, such as **Magnus Hirschfeld**, argued that the **etiology** of homosexuality is natural and harmless congenital variation. Freud broke with those ideas and instead argued for a developmental understanding of sexuality in general. In 1905, Freud published *Three Essays on the Theory of Sexuality*, which contained substantive discussions of same-sex attraction. In particular, he criticized Hirschfeld's approach, arguing that it simply could not account for the range in feeling and behavior in same-sex attraction. Just as **Alfred Kinsey** would point out decades later, Freud sought to emphasize the sheer variation involved, from same-sex erotic experimentation in adolescence to lifelong exclusive homosexuality.

Freud implicitly defended a number of possible etiologies for homosexuality. The most influential hypothesis is Freud's theory that persons are by nature bisexual in an early developmental stage. Due to a failure to develop completely, in the psycho-sexual sense, some persons are attracted to members of their own sex, yet quite often androgynous ones. For instance, Freud took the effeminate mannerisms of many male prostitutes, or the androgynous appearance of prepubescent males to which pedophiles are attracted, as supporting evidence. Often the developmental impediments are caused by an excessively affectionate mother, perhaps combined with an absent or emotionally distant father. Yet Freud clearly saw this developmental arrest as limited in its scope and effects, since it does not affect the intellectual or moral development of a person. Freud also propounded other possible causes of homosexuality, such as psychological adaptation to same-sex seduction as a child, or a narcissistic involvement with one's own body.

Freud's overall approach, and concrete analyses, is double-edged in its implications. Against those who asserted the naturalness of heterosexuality, Freud's argument that persons by nature go through a bisexual stage, which for various reasons may then become the hallmark of the adult's sex object choice, was both radical and objectionable. Yet Freud's positing heterosexuality as fully adult, or as the proper developmental achievement, has been criticized by those who see Freud's work as contributing to the **medical model of homosexuality**. It is important to note, however, that Freud himself did not share this disparaging view of homosexuality. In an interview in 1905, Freud flatly denied that homosexuality is a sickness. In his self-analysis, Freud lingered upon what he saw as his own latent homosexual feelings toward a friend, Wilhelm Fliess. He also supported the effort to overturn **anti-sodomy laws**. Many of Freud's followers, however, emphasized the arrested development explanation for homosexuality. Freud doubted that analysis could change a person's sexual orientation and instead focused on the possibility that psychiatrists could help persons reconcile themselves to their sexuality. Yet many Freudians, seeking to overcome what they saw as a deeply flawed psychological development, participated in what is now known as **reparative therapy**. Thus, some supported electroshock or castration "therapy." Ironically, Freud had actually devoted time and effort to understanding what he saw as an irrational hatred of homosexuals. Freud's example of a scientific search for truth about sexuality, including behaviors traditionally seen as taboo or unnatural, has itself been influential, as has his placing the quest for the etiology of homosexuality within the search for causative factors within sexuality in general. *See also* EUROPE; *WISSENSCHAFTLICH-HUMANITÄRES KOMITEE*/SCIENTIFIC-HUMANITARIAN COMMITTEE.

– G –

GANYMEDE. In the mythology of **ancient Greece**, Ganymede was a beautiful youth and the son of the king of Troy. An eagle carried him off to Olympus to be a cupbearer to the gods; Zeus in particular was smitten with him. Some versions of the myth held that Zeus transformed himself into the eagle that kidnapped Ganymede. Another version has Minos as the abductor.

Ancient Greek art and other works repeatedly referred to the legend. The earliest version, from Homer, does not imply a sexual relationship between Ganymede and Zeus, yet by the time of **Plato** such relations are assumed. Virgil retold the myth in the *Aeneid*. In the Renaissance, **Michelangelo** made drawings of the youth, including his abduction in *The Rape of Ganymede*. Benvenuto Cellini made statues of Ganymede, and in England, Christopher Marlowe used the myth as one of his many classical allusions to homoeroticism. In the 20th century, W. H. Auden and others have used the tale as a source of inspiration for their work. *See also* LITERATURE, HOMOSEXUAL MALE.

GAY ACTIVISTS ALLIANCE (GAA). Within months of the founding of the **Gay Liberation Front** (GLF) in 1969, a faction split off and founded the Gay Activists Alliance. While the GLF had been modeled on New Left groups, concerned with forming alliances with other leftist causes such as women's liberation and involving a participatory meeting style, the founders of the GAA wanted to focus solely upon gay liberation. They also ran meetings according to Robert's Rules of Order. The GAA was solely a New York–based group, but its aggressive political stance, both as a means of displaying gay political influence and changing gay consciousness, proved influential.

The GAA undertook a number of actions. It engaged in "zaps," or political confrontations, forcing candidates and officeholders to take a stance on gay rights issues. Members picketed a police station and otherwise worked against **police harassment**. They also lobbied aggressively for **anti-discrimination laws**. They lost on that issue and in the process displayed the increasing factionalism between radical and reformist elements within the GAA. In 1973, several activists broke off from the GAA and formed the National Gay Task Force, later re-named as the **National Gay and Lesbian Task Force**. The GAA fell apart in 1974.

GAY BASHING. Violence or threatening violence against gays and lesbians is known as gay bashing. In contrast to formal state persecution of homosexuals, as exemplified in cases such as **McCarthyism**, gay bashing is perpetrated by private individuals. While the police may look the other way or even encourage such acts, it is also distinct from **police harassment**. In the **United States**, studies show that a majority of gays and lesbians have been assaulted, threatened with assault, or had private property damaged due to their orientation. According to federal statistics, anti-gay violence constitutes about one-eighth to one-sixth of all hate crimes in any given year, which is substantially higher than the gay proportion of the overall population.

Many countries suffer from violence against homosexuals. Although Brazil has a reputation as tolerant, beatings of homosexuals are strikingly common. In Jamaica, a number of reggae musicians have released songs with violent anti-gay lyrics. Several recent anti-gay attacks and killings have been linked to such "murder music." In the **Middle East**, families sometimes attack or threaten violence against family members who engage in same-sex relations. Anti-gay violence also occurs in **Europe**, especially in Central and Eastern Europe, such as in Croatia and **Russia**. *See also* HATE CRIME LAWS; LATIN AMERICA; SAME-SEX MARRIAGE; QUEER NATION.

GAY LIBERATION FRONT (GLF). In the weeks following the **Stonewall** riots in late June 1969, activists broke off from the New York **Mattachine Society** to form a militant group. Calling itself the Gay Liberation Front, it emphasized pride in one's homosexuality, the need to come out of **the closet**, alliance with other leftist causes, and the development of separate, gay institutions. Within months, GLF chapters formed in Chicago, Los Angeles, Berkeley, and elsewhere. It also began publishing a newspaper, *Come Out*. The GLF drew as its leaders persons with extensive experience in movement politics, in groups such as Students for a Democratic Society and the Yippies. GLF members helped to coordinate a march to commemorate the first anniversary of Stonewall, which has become the annual gay pride parade.

Just like many New Left groups, the GLF was quickly torn by factionalism. Many smaller divisions, or cells, broke off to form their own groups that catered to a specific ideology or demographic. The GLF had broken down into a loose coalition by the end of 1970, but in its brief life it had played a key role in altering the gay rights movement.

GLF chapters formed in **Great Britain** as well. Bob Mellors and Aubrey Walter met in the **United States** but returned to Britain. Dissatisfied with the **homophile movement** groups there, they established a GLF chapter in London. Hundreds were soon attending meetings; chapters formed in other cities. The British GLF was very active, engaging in demonstrations, selling various gay pride badges to encourage people to come out of the closet, and holding pride celebrations. It also formed subgroups to focus upon specific issues, such as mainstream psychiatry's portrayal of gays and lesbians as "sick." Like its United States counterpart, the British GLF was soon torn by factionalism, especially between lesbians and gay men, and between those who urged alliances with broader movements, such as trade unionism, and those who wanted an exclusive focus upon gay issues. The British GLF largely fell apart by the end of 1972, by which time it had dramatically increased the public visibility of gay liberation and ushered in a new proliferation of gay groups and ideologies. *See also* GAY ACTIVISTS ALLIANCE; NATIONAL GAY AND LESBIAN TASK FORCE; NORTH AMERICAN CONFERENCE OF HOMOPHILE ORGANIZATIONS.

GAY MARRIAGE. *See* SAME-SEX MARRIAGE.

GERMANY. The evidence concerning ancient Germanic tribes' attitudes toward homosexuality is sketchy and even contradictory. Some contemporaries, such as Quintilian, described early Germans as favoring it. Ammianus Marcellinus, writing in the fourth century C.E., described a tradition of institutionalized pederasty. Others, such as Tacitus, a senator and historian in **ancient Rome**, depicted harsh punishments and social norms against same-sex relations, especially for men taking the passive role with other men. The contemporary sociologist David Greenberg interprets the contradictory data as a reflection of tensions within ancient Germanic tribal society, in particular between warrior-hunters, who were opposed to effeminacy, and farmers, who were more open to it. It is safe to say that the evidence is mixed and fragmentary, and conclusions must be tentative. From the fifth to the ninth centuries, these seminomadic tribes became more settled and established a set corpus of law. With the sole exception of Visigothic **Spain**, these codes of law did not include punishments for homosexual sex. The various small states that constituted what is today Germany did not have **anti-sodomy laws** during the Middle Ages.

In 1532, however, Charles V of the Holy Roman Empire laid out a comprehensive criminal code that mandated death as the penalty for sodomy. Enforcement varied dramatically from German state to state and over time, even while the law remained in place for over two centuries. In 1721, Prussian police arrested a woman who had passed as a man, even to the point of serving in more than one army as well as marrying another woman. Such cases were rare and thus the legal system had difficulties deciding on a punishment. The case eventually wound its way to the ruler, King Frederick William I, who sentenced the woman to death. She was beheaded in what is likely the last execution for female sodomy in Europe. Ironically, Frederick William I was the father of **Frederick II**, who was most likely homosexual and who commissioned a group of jurists to reform Prussia's legal codes. Consequently, Prussia became the first German state to abolish the death penalty for sodomy, in 1794. Flogging and imprisonment were the reduced punishments. Later, the **Code Napoléon** led many states to abolish their anti-sodomy laws. In 1871, this liberal legal regime ended. Under Paragraph 175 of the Criminal Code of the German Empire, male same-sex sodomy was criminalized once again. Subsequent attempts to add lesbianism failed. Before 1900, each year approximately 500 men were convicted under its provisions.

Paragraph 175, as well as its predecessor law in Prussia, helped prompt the first organized homosexual law reform movement, in addition to an extensive debate about homosexuality and the law. In the waning years of the 19th century, Germany had rapidly growing cities with increasingly vibrant homosexual niches, along with a newfound range of discussions about social change. In 1897, **Magnus Hirschfeld** co-founded the *Wissenschaftlich-humanitäres Komitee* (WHK, Scientific-Humanitarian Committee). Over the next three and a half decades, it was the foremost group in the world working on behalf of homosexual rights. From 1898 to 1908, over 1,000 pamphlets debating the appropriateness of the legal regulation of sexuality were published. In 1902, a group of men established the *Gemeinschaft der Eigenen* (GE, Community of the Special). In contrast to the WHK, the GE rejected any scientific approach, appealing instead to ideals of ancient Greece, including trans-generational sex. Another difference between the two groups was the WHK's eagerness to advocate women's rights and include women as members, while the GE eschewed any female involvement. The editor of a homosexual magazine engaged in the first modern, pro-gay example of **outing**. In an effort to overturn Paragraph 175, he outed the leader of a conservative group that defended the law. The effort backfired, however. The homosexual rights movement divided over the morality and efficacy of the tactic, and sodomy prosecutions increased significantly. In 1919, Hirschfeld founded the *Institut für Sexualwissenschaft* (Institute for Sexual Science).

Germany during the Weimar era had a flourishing homosexual subculture, especially in Berlin. There were gay bars and clubs, as well as an activity center for gays in Berlin. Freedom of the press led to the establishment of more than two dozen gay periodicals. The first gay-themed movies were also made; *Different from the Others* told the tale of men blackmailed under threat of social ostracism and legal punishment for being gay. *Mädchen in Uniform* was about a lesbian love relationship between a teacher and her student and was a protest against intolerance and capricious authority. The effort to repeal Paragraph 175 slowly advanced in the 1920s. Yet it never quite succeeded and the rise of Adolf Hitler and **National Socialism** ended the early homosexual rights movement in Germany. Under Hitler, the penalties of conviction under Paragraph 175 were made more severe, the types of acts subject to penalty were broadened, tens of thousands were convicted, and the homosexual subculture was brutally suppressed. Thousands of homosexuals were sent to death camps and most perished.

After World War II, West Germany retained Paragraph 175. While the 1950s and 1960s were largely an era of silence and oppression, there were some scattered homosexual bars and organizations, though only of a social nature. Tens of thousands of men were charged and convicted during that time, and others committed suicide after being charged. While the general human rights picture in East Germany, known as the German Democratic Republic (GDR), was bleak, homosexuals were treated somewhat better than in the Soviet Union. The German Communist Party had been allied with Hirschfeld's group, and East Germany's first prime minister had, before the war, supported the abolition of Paragraph 175. In 1948, the East German state altered its version of the anti-sodomy law from the expansive and more punitive Nazi version, to the narrower, earlier version. In 1957, the GDR government announced that it would no longer enforce Paragraph 175. A bit more than a decade later, it repealed the law. Due no doubt, however, to the overall oppression in the GDR, the legal relaxation did not result in any significant flourishing of homosexual life. The West German government repealed the main provisions of its anti-sodomy law in 1969, although it made the **age of consent** apply to those under 21, substantially higher than for heterosexual sex. The age of consent was not equalized for heterosexual and homosexual acts until 1994, after the two countries were unified.

Beginning in the 1970s, a gay rights movement began to emerge in West Germany. In the GDR, the same process took place in the mid-1980s, under the influence of glasnost in the Soviet bloc at large as well as Western media. Courage, a gay rights group, was formed in 1988. The first East German film with a sympathetic portrayal of homosexuality, *Coming Out*, debuted on the same night that the Berlin Wall fell. In the 1990s, the gay rights movement began to achieve significant gains. Some German states passed **anti-discrimination laws**, including Brandenburg in 1992.

The first decade of the 21st century has seen a rapid advance in rights for gays and lesbians. Gays and lesbians are not barred from **military service**, and the policy against gays serving as officers was overturned in 2000. The German government also recognizes **registered partnerships**. The law offered a limited yet important range of rights, such as on inheritance and immigration status. It has been broadened to include adoption rights. Germany also has passed a national anti-discrimination law, providing penalties for discrimination on the basis of gender identity in the areas of employment and services. *See also* ASYLUM; ELLIS, HAVELOCK; EUROPE; FRANCE; KERTBENY, KARL MARIA; MEDICAL MODEL OF HOMOSEXUALITY; REPARATIVE THERAPY; ULRICHS, KARL HEINRICH.

GREAT BRITAIN. Some of the earliest evidence about homosexuality in the British Isles comes from Christian penitentials, which were guides used by priests to determine punishments for various sins. While they appear to have originated in Ireland, they were quickly adopted in Britain. A seventh-century penitential, by Theodore of Tarsus, who rose to be the archbishop of Canterbury, stands out for including lesbian acts as deserving of penance. Other penance handbooks from the time typically omit female-female relations.

A later scandal helped reinforce the repression of homosexuality. William the II, commonly known as William Rufus, ruled from 1087 to 1100. He never married and some writers of the day insinuated that sodomy and loose sexuality were common to his court. Anselm, the archbishop of Canterbury, asked him to convene a church council so that sodomy could be repressed. William refused, but after his death his brother, Henry I, allowed the plan to go forward and the Council of London issued a canon against sodomy in 1102. Some complained, however, that the measure did not work and was rarely enforced. Evidence supports the proposition that Henry's great-grandson, Richard I, or Richard the Lion-Hearted, was only attracted to men. Ruling in the late 12th century, he did not father any children and even publicly confessed to his sexual sins. At the same time, Richard of Devizes chronicled London's underworld, including its boys who were pretty and sexually passive. Some poems from the era also describe male prostitution in the cities.

By the end of the 13th century, some cities had enacted **anti-sodomy laws**. Although the historical record is somewhat contradictory, the best evidence is that the punishment laid out was death by fire. Actual enforcement of the law, however, was either rare or nonexistent. Yet in 16th-century Scotland, which had no anti-sodomy law, persons were executed, clearly an outcome of its fierce Calvinism. In 1533, the English Parliament passed **Act of 25 Henry VIII**, which criminalized anal intercourse, whether homosexual or heterosexual, but not sex between women. In one version or another, the law stood for centuries and became the basis for many anti-sodomy laws in Great Britain's empire. The effects of the law have been global in scale and felt for centuries. Its silence about lesbianism was reflective of Britain's general reluctance at the time to mention female same-sex love. There were a few exceptions. In the 1590s, the poet John Donne wrote "**Sappho** to Philaenis," which movingly spoke of the beauty of a woman's deep love and erotic attachment to another woman. In the 17th century, Katherine Philips wrote poetry about female same-sex affection and love, although it was not overtly erotic, in contrast to the more outspoken poems of her contemporary Aphra Behn. Margaret Lucas, a duchess, wrote a play about lesbianism, although in the final act, one of the women is revealed to actually be a man.

A new homosexual subculture clearly emerged in the late 17th and early 18th centuries, at least among males. The slang of the day talked about "molly," which meant an effeminate man. The precise origin of the term is unclear. It may have derived from the Latin term *mollis* (soft), which also denoted male sexual passivity, or from the English slang for a female prostitute, a Molly, or from the diminutive for Mary, which is also Molly. Mollies frequented specific taverns, known as "molly houses," in London. Proprietors often arranged beds in a back dormitory for assignations. Mollies would address each other by female names or titles, such as "miss." Starting in the 1690s, a group called the Society for the Reformation of Manners tried to entrap, capture, or otherwise expose mollies and other "**sodomites**." A number of the persons the society caught were put to death. The society overreached in its attempts to reform morals, in addition to being plagued with corruption, and it fell apart in the 1730s. The authorities continued to prosecute sodomy cases, although with less frequency. Assembled crowds sometimes beat to death men sentenced to the lesser penalty of the pillory. In 1816, the pillory was dropped as a penalty for sodomy.

Even though the **Enlightenment** in continental **Europe** had led to more open discussion of same-sex love and lighter criminal penalties, its influence in Great Britain, at least as far as sexuality, was scant. In the 1780s, prosecutions once again became more frequent. From 1800 to 1836, when the last sodomy execution took place in Great Britain, more than 50 were executed for that offense. Punishment in the navy was especially severe. Those convicted of sodomy were more likely to receive the death penalty than convicted mutineers; a lesser sentence was 1,000 lashes. In 1861, the penalty for sodomy was reduced from death to imprisonment, albeit potentially for life. Felony prosecutions were rare, however. An 1871 scandal at the elite British school of Eton showed that in some quarters trans-generational same-sex relationships still flourished, especially in those circles exposed to **ancient Greek** pederast writings. At the same time, London clearly had a gay male subculture with its own slang and sexual roles that crossed traditional lines. In 1885, the British Parliament passed the **Labouchère Amendment**, which made male-male oral sex punishable by up to two years in prison with hard labor. A decade later, the law was the legal basis for the prosecution of **Oscar Wilde**.

In the late 19th and early 20th centuries, writings about homosexuality became more readily available, including defenses of same-sex love by persons such as **Havelock Ellis** and **Edward Carpenter**, both of whom later played an integral part in the **British Society for the Study of Sex Psychology** (BSSP). The group worked to promote research into sexuality, advance homosexual rights, and overturn anti-sodomy laws. Public attitudes, however, did not significantly change. Even at the end of World War I, when poets such as Wilfred Owen and Siegfried Sassoon had written haunting poems about beautiful young men in the trenches and overt defenses of same-sex love were more readily available, the **Billing Case** showed that the public was still quick to link homosexuality with degeneracy and treason.

There is a dearth of evidence about a lesbian subculture until the 1920s. Although there is some data about upper-class lesbian relationships and scattered references to a few meeting places for women seeking other women prior to that, it is thin compared to the materials about men. In the 1910s and 1920s, however, several factors came together to increase the prominence of lesbianism in Britain. Some London clubs catered to a lesbian clientele. Female same-sex relationships were portrayed in novels by D. H. Lawrence (negatively) and A. T. Fitzroy (positively). Due to the increased awareness, some members of Parliament attempted to broaden the Labouchère Amendment to cover female same-sex acts, but the move failed. The single most important event was the publication, in 1928, of **Radclyffe Hall**'s novel *The Well of Loneliness*. Authorities, including the home secretary, moved to suppress the book. The ensuing obscenity trial was the most important since that of Oscar Wilde. The prosecution won and the book was not published in Britain for over two decades. Yet the book was widely available on the Continent, and the trial itself received extensive coverage.

With the help of Havelock Ellis, the World League for Sexual Reform was founded the same year that Hall published her influential novel. The group worked for the same goals as the BSSP, although internal factionalism hampered its effectiveness. Although the group disbanded in the mid-1930s, Norman Haire kept the British section of it going until the eve of World War II. After the war, Haire continued writing and organizing on behalf of the public acceptance of homosexuality and the repeal of anti-sodomy laws. He served as president of the Sex Education Society and editor of the *Journal of Sex Education*. The journal had an international readership and the society hosted well-attended public lectures. Both efforts, however, died along with Haire in 1952.

While convictions under the Labouchère Amendment and related laws rose from the late 1930s on, the postwar era witnessed the sharpest increases. Thousands of men were prosecuted each year. Police increasingly used entrapment or encouraged chain confessions in order to broaden their net. Right-wing persons in government and the defection of two Russians spies working in the British government, Guy Burgess and Donald Maclean, contributed to the atmosphere behind the increased surveillance and arrests. Yet scandals involving homosexuals also contributed to the appointment, in 1954, of a committee charged with reviewing laws pertaining to homosexuality and prostitution. The **Wolfenden Report**, issued three years later, was a key turning point in the debate over anti-sodomy laws and, less directly but more broadly, the place of homosexuals in British society. The report also led to the formation of the **Homosexual Law Reform Society**. Yet the government of the time, under Harold Macmillan, did not want to act, worrying that it would be too far out in front of public opinion. The rate of prosecutions did not decrease either.

A lesbian movement was slower to emerge, due at least in part to the more constrained economic situation of most women. Also, women did not have the same legal and surveillance apparatus aimed at them that homosexual men did, and hence lacked a natural rallying point. In 1963, Esmé Langley and Diana Chapman founded the Minorities Research Group. It started a magazine, *Arena Three*, in 1965. A faction split off to found Kenric, which functioned as a social club and support group. It purposely kept a low profile and never sought to change public attitudes or policy directly.

Public attitudes, however, did slowly change in the 1960s. Still, an opinion poll from 1966 showed a plurality opposed to the decriminalization of same-sex acts. In 1967, the government enacted the **Sexual Offenses Act**. While it was a significant advance for homosexual rights, it did not end prosecutions. In fact, for the next several years they increased. The law only legalized acts conducted in private, and it defined "public" in a very broad manner as any place a third person was likely to be present.

After the **Stonewall** riots in the United States, in 1969, British activists quickly adopted the radicalism newly present in America. Activists formed the **Gay Liberation Front** (GLF), which, in its two years of existence as a coherent group, dramatically altered the style and scope of demands of the gay rights movement. In fact, after the GLF it is more accurate to speak of a plurality of movements that overlapped and conflicted. In the 1970s, the gay community also became much more visible, with alternative media, a flourishing bar scene, and social forums as alternatives to the bar scene. Yet in contrast to what early liberationists such as the GLF wanted, the gay community became commercialized even while it was still more connected to the political movement than was typical on the Continent. Radical politics waned in influence in the late 1970s. The rise of the **human immunodeficiency virus/acquired immunodeficiency syndrome** (HIV/AIDS) epidemic changed that. Friends of the first British man to die of AIDS established the Terrence Higgins Trust, which quickly became a formidable organization. Among other things, it lobbied aggressively for more government support for AIDS victims, and research on the prevention and treatment of the disease.

A political backlash against the emerging gay community had begun even in the early 1970s, but it did not reach its fruition until the 1980s. The government, under Margaret Thatcher, pushed for a law, the Local Government Act, which contained an anti-gay provision. Known as **Clause 28**, the law was designed to stop local councils from promoting homosexuality. In 1988, it passed after extensive debate and public protest. The gay rights movement was energized by the fight, however. A number of prominent Britons came out of the closet during the battle. The politics of backlash waned after the passage of the controversial law. Thatcher's Tory successor, John

Major, supported and helped pass an **age of consent law**, although it did not equalize the age with heterosexual relations.

The first decade of the 21st century has witnessed a significant advance for British gays and lesbians, propelled by the confluence of a mature and well-organized gay rights movement and a sympathetic government under Tony Blair. In 2000, the government lifted its ban on homosexuals in **military service** and equalized the age of consent for heterosexual and homosexual relations. In 2002, it also changed laws to allow adoption by same-sex couples. The next year, Clause 28 was repealed. In 2005, a weak version of a **registered partnership** law went into effect. Support for at least a modicum of gay rights is now widely held even in the Conservative Party. Public attitudes have shifted significantly over the past several decades and mainstream acceptance and even **assimilation** of gays and lesbians are prevalent in most regions of the country. *See also* AIDS COALITION TO UNLEASH POWER; ASYLUM; CANADA; EUROPEAN COURT OF HUMAN RIGHTS; JUDIASM; POLICE HARASSMENT.

– H –

HALL, RADCLYFFE (1880–1943). Author of perhaps the most influential lesbian novel ever, *The Well of Loneliness*, Radclyffe Hall was from **Great Britain** although she often went to the Continent, especially Paris. The novel, published in 1928, is about an aristocratic young woman. Wanting a boy, her father, Sir Philip Gordon, names her Stephen. Hall portrays Stephen as lesbian by dint of nature, and the theories of the early sexologists clearly influenced Hall's thinking. **Karl Heinrich Ulrichs** is referred to in the book, as Sir Philip reads widely in an attempt to understand his unconventional daughter. Stephen grows up and has a love affair with a rather conventional, feminine woman, Mary. Ultimately, in a gesture of self-sacrifice, Stephen gives up Mary so that she can be united with a man and live a "normal" life. Under the impress of Ulrichs, **Havelock Ellis**, and others, Stephen is portrayed as masculine in build, bodily movements, and interests. Hall herself was known for her mannish appearance, which she reinforced through her choice in clothing. Like her character, Hall too was widely known by a male name, John.

The novel became the subject of a famous literary trial, which occurred just months after publication. Authors such as Virginia Woolf and E. M. Forster attended in order to be called as witnesses for the defense, which was not allowed due to an antiquated law. Hall's longtime partner, Una Troubridge, also was there. The judge ruled the book obscene. The **United States** Customs Service also moved to disallow importation of the book, but soon relented. Then the New York City police seized hundreds of copies and charged the distributor with selling obscene materials. They were able to secure a conviction but an appellate court subsequently overturned it. The book was a great success in the United States, selling tens of thousands of copies in just a few years. The work was not published in Britain until 1949, although it was widely available outside the country, secretly circulated within it, and sold very well.

Despite her novel's success, Hall was left bitter and alienated by the experience of the trial and the controversy. She returned to the Continent, although this time to live there. For a time in the 1930s, she espoused anti-Semitism and praised Fascism. *See also* BRITISH SOCIETY FOR THE STUDY OF SEX PSYCHOLOGY; LITERATURE, LESBIAN.

HATE CRIME LAWS. Over the past few decades, gay and lesbian groups have lobbied for the inclusion of sexual orientation and gender identity in hate crime laws. In general, such laws provide for enhanced penalties for those who commit crimes out of a bias against a protected class, such as members of a certain race or ethnicity. In the **United States**, a majority of states include sexual orientation as a protected class in their hate crime laws. They only apply to acts such as assault, not speech.

Some countries in **Europe** have similar laws, although groups such as the **International Lesbian and Gay Association** believe they are underutilized. Some states ban speech that has the intent of fostering hatred of minority groups, such as gays and lesbians. Countries with those laws, such as Sweden, have had difficulty in sorting out their application and whether they are in contravention of European Court of Justice rulings. *See also* FRANCE; GAY BASHING; SHEPARD, MATTHEW.

HAY, HENRY (1912–2002). One of the principal founders of the **Mattachine Society**, a leading **homophile** group of the 1950s and 1960s, Hay was a longtime Communist Party activist. His work during the Great Depression and World War II as a party and union organizer gave him a breadth of experience that proved invaluable to the homophile groups he helped form. Along with several other men in Southern California, Hay established the Mattachine Society in 1951 in order to raise the consciousness of homosexuals as an oppressed minority and thereby foster their organizing for liberation. His Marxist background deeply influenced his analysis of the plight of homosexuals in American society, especially during **McCarthyism**.

The radical leftist politics of Hay and the other founders of the Mattachine Society quickly became a liability, and in the mid-1950s Hay left the society. The House Un-American Activities Committee had him testify in 1955 about his Communist activities. After a period of withdrawal from activism, Hay helped to organize the first gay pride parade in Los Angeles, in 1966. In the late 1970s, Hay co-founded the Radical Faeries. Hay saw the Faeries as a way of overcoming the stifling dichotomy of a repressive heterosexual culture versus a marginalized gay minority that failed to offer a sense of genuine community.

Although the achievements of the homophile groups such as the Mattachine Society were often denigrated in the immediate post-**Stonewall** era, academic scholarship over the past two decades has helped to restore an appreciation of their accomplishments. Hay not only was a key organizer in gay politics, he also provided theoretical insights into gender relations in society and the effect those had on persons attracted to their own sex. He also contributed his time and effort to other groups, such as the Rainbow Coalition. *See also* HOMOPHILE MOVEMENT.

HENRY III (1551–1589). The son of Henry II and Catherine de Medici, Henry III became king of **France** at the age of 23. In that role, he surrounded himself with attractive young men, his *mignons*, and bestowed gifts and favors on them. The king had intense emotional attachments to some of these young men, and participated in orgies, most likely bisexual in nature, with them. When two of them died in a duel, Henry had a marble statue erected in their honor. Henry often wore clothes that imitated those worn by ladies of the court, as well as cosmetics and pearls, and his *mignons* soon followed his style of dress. Given the tenor of the age, it was inevitable that his behavior would become the object of public scorn and political attack. The scope of the attacks, with nearly a thousand pamphlets produced in the five years before his death, and the shrillness, accusing the king of acts well beyond sodomy, such as incest and sorcery, were extreme even for the day.

King Henry was a political moderate, although he had the misfortune of ruling during a time of zealotry and polarization. In his youth, he led attacks against Huguenots, but after coming to power, he made peace with them. He continued working to convert Protestants, however. Catholics denounced the king, who was childless, when he named a Protestant, Henry of Navarre, as the next in line. Catholic leaders urged the king to pursue harsh policies toward French Protestants, with the goal of wiping them out. Henry refused, although he did affirm that Catholicism was, for him, the one true faith for all of France. He was stabbed to death by a fanatical monk at the age of 38.

HIJRA. *See* INDIA.

HIRSCHFELD, MAGNUS (1868–1935). Working as one of the first sex researchers, Magnus Hirschfeld wrote prolifically about same-sex attraction. His approach was strongly influenced by the work of **Karl Heinrich Ulrichs**. He argued, like Ulrichs, that homosexuality is biologically determined for some members of the population. Arguing that same-sex love is thus natural, he campaigned for the repeal of **anti-sodomy laws** in **Germany**.

Hirschfeld formed a series of groups to advance the cause of legal and social reform. In 1897, he co-founded the *Wissenschaftlich-humanitäres Komitee* (WHK, Scientific-Humanitarian Committee). Over the next three and a half decades, it served as the leading group working on behalf of homosexual rights. In 1919, Hirschfeld founded the *Institut für Sexualwissenschaft* (IS, Institute for Sexual Science).

The IS provided social services, such as testing for sexually transmitted diseases, and housed a collection of anthropological and biological research. In 1921, Hirschfeld helped to found the World League for Sexual Reform (WLSR). He served as co-president along with **Havelock Ellis** and August Forel. The WLSR fought on behalf of sexual freedom in general, including the legal access to contraception and abortion, as well as the right of consenting adults to engage in homosexual relations free of legal sanction. Hirschfeld, as a prominent gay man and Jew, clearly took risks for being outspoken. On two different occasions in the 1920s, a group of anti-Semites assaulted Hirschfeld and viciously beat him.

The rise of **National Socialism** ultimately frustrated Hirschfeld's efforts. In 1933, while Hirschfeld was in Paris, Nazis ransacked the WHK and IS offices, housed in the same Berlin building. They then burned much of the material in a purge of "un-German" publications. Hirschfeld saw the book burning in newsreels. The rise of Nazism also provoked internal disputes within the WLSR over whether the group should focus narrowly on its agenda of sexual freedom, or whether that fight in turn required working against Fascism. The group disbanded in 1935, the same year Hirschfeld died. *See also* BRITISH SOCIETY FOR THE STUDY OF SEX PSYCHOLOGY; ETIOLOGY; EUROPE; FREUD, SIGMUND; OUTING; TRANS-SEXUALISM; TRANSVESTISM.

HIV/AIDS. *See* HUMAN IMMUNODEFICIENCY VIRUS/ACQUIRED IMMUNODEFICIENCY SYNDROME.

HOLOCAUST. *See* NATIONAL SOCIALISM.

HOMOPHILE. The word "homophile" was created by Jaap van Leeuwen in early 1950. Use of the term quickly spread. One factor was the dislike of the term "homosexual," given that it appeared to focus merely on the carnal aspects of same-sex attraction, rather than upon the role of emotional, romantic, and social bonds. Derived from the Greek *homo* (same) and *philia* (love of), many defenders of same-sex love in the 1950s and 1960s preferred "homophile" in part since it avoided the common negative stereotype of homosexuals as persons with insufficient control of their libidos, or otherwise as made ill by sexual pathology.

The radicalization of the homosexual rights movement after **Stonewall** contributed to the decline of the term as people turned to the words "gay" and "lesbian." "Homophile" is still occasionally used, however. The Church of England has recently used it in the old-fashioned sense as a synonym for homosexual. Some within the gay community use it to refer to a straight person who has close friendships with gays and lesbians. *See also* CANADA; DAUGHTERS OF BILITIS; FRANCE; HAY, HENRY; HOMOPHILE MOVEMENT; NORTH AMERICAN CONFERENCE OF HOMOPHILE ORGANIZATIONS; UNITED STATES.

HOMOPHILE MOVEMENT. The principal homophile organizations were established in the 1950s. The earliest, however, was founded in the Netherlands. The "Amsterdam Social Club" began in 1946 and it in turn formed the nucleus of a larger group, the *Cultuur-En-Ontspannings Centrum* (COC, Culture and Recreation Center). Both groups published their own journals, served as forums for discussions and social gatherings, and campaigned for equal rights. This Dutch movement was responsible for the popularization of the term *homofiel*, or **homophile**. In 1951, the COC founded the International Committee for Sexual Equality in an attempt to foster coordination between various national homophile groups. For more than a decade after its founding, the COC stood as the best-organized homophile group in the world.

In the **United States**, the **Mattachine Society** began in 1950 as a radical organization, but quickly altered its leadership. The **Daughters of Bilitis**, founded in 1955, often focused on the difficulties lesbians faced in terms of social acceptance, but did not defend far-reaching efforts to change society. Instead, these two groups, as was the case with most other homophile organizations, argued that heterosexuals and homosexuals are just alike, except in their sexual and emotional attractions. The political and legal context in which these groups started was especially difficult, given that **McCarthyism** and norms of conformity deeply influenced the contemporary social milieu. Homophile groups thus turned to experts within mainstream society as their best chance for acceptance. This strategy, however, largely resulted in disappointment. The key exception was **Evelyn Hooker**, who recruited subjects from the Mattachine Society and raised profound questions within psychiatry about the homosexuality as pathology paradigm.

In **France**, André Baudry began the journal *Arcadie* in 1953. The broader homophile group behind it was also known as Arcadie. It too shared in the general homophile emphasis on education, social gatherings, and the provision of support services to its membership. Given the legality of same-sex sodomy in France, its political agenda focused on having an equal **age of consent** for both heterosexual and homosexual activity.

The 1950s were difficult for the homophile movement. While in many cases they were able to offer meaningful support and social services, their political agenda languished. With the partial exception of the Dutch component of the movement, the groups remained small; members were afraid of exposure and potential members stayed away out of fear. The 1960s, however, saw a much greater degree of success. The creation of the birth control pill helped to set off a sexual revolution in the West, which partially disentangled sexual pleasure from reproduction. England, Wales, and a couple of American states all decriminalized sodomy in the 1960s. In the United States, one factor was the rise of the civil rights movement and the activism that inspired among homophile groups. Some chapters of the Mattachine Society, for example, began taking on local police who engaged in entrapment and **police harassment**. They also helped to organize the first public demonstrations in the United States by homosexuals demanding equal rights.

Even though many homophile activists became more assertive and confrontational as the 1960s progressed, after **Stonewall** they were quickly outflanked by more militant activists. Internal disagreement also wracked many homophile groups. Most dissolved in the 1970s. One notable exception is the Dutch group COC. It continues to play an important part in lobbying for legal changes in the Netherlands, such as the enactment in 1992 and 1993 of **anti-discrimination laws**. Today called the *Nederlandse Vereniging tot Integratie van Homoseksualiteit*, or Netherlands Association for the Integration of Homosexuality, it is the world's oldest gay and lesbian rights group. *See also* AUSTRALIA; CANADA; EUROPE; FOUCAULT, MICHEL; GAY LIBERATION FRONT; HAY, HENRY; KAMENY, FRANK; LITERATURE, LESBIAN; NORTH AMERICAN CONFERENCE OF HOMOPHILE ORGANIZATIONS; SAME-SEX MARRIAGE; SOCIETY FOR INDIVIDUAL RIGHTS.

HOMOPHOBIA. First coined in the 1960s in the **United States**, the term "homophobia" refers to a fear or hatred of homosexuality and gays and lesbians in general. The term is used in a way that emphasizes the "phobia" aspect of the term, in the sense of an extreme or irrational aversion to gays and lesbians. Therefore, those who favor social and legal equality for homosexuals are more likely to use the term, since from their point of view there is nothing wrong with homosexuality and thus fear of it is irrational. Most of those who evince hatred or fear of gays and lesbians, such as some on the **religious right**, believe that their dislike and abhorrence are reasonable and thus do not count as a phobia.

Like many who defend social disapproval for entire groups or subcultures, such as anti-Semites, homophobes typically rely on stereotypes. For instance, they portray gay men as effeminate and promiscuous and lesbians as mannish. Homophobes often make outrageous claims against the suspect group. Just like some on the religious right have portrayed the global economy as secretly manipulated by Jews, some of the same persons have claimed that gays and lesbians either secretly desire the downfall of civilization or will cause its downfall though immorality.

Many have argued that homosexuals too have sometimes manifested homophobia. Many persons deeply in **the closet** have denounced homosexuality in the strongest terms, including from the pulpit or the floor of the U.S. Senate. In such cases, it seems likely that the negative view of homosexuality in society has been internalized, leading to deep inner psychological turmoil and denial. One argument made by proponents of **coming out**, such as Michelangelo Signorile, is that coming out helps to destroy homophobia within oneself as well as in society at large. *See also* ASSIMILATION; JUDAISM; QUEER; QUEER NATION.

HOMOSEXUAL LAW REFORM SOCIETY (HLRS). After the publication of the **Wolfenden Report** in 1957, A. E. Dyson and others founded the Homosexual Law Reform Society to lobby for the enactment of its recommendation that homosexual sex be legalized. One of the events that helped to launch the HLRS was a letter to the *Times* (of London) arguing in support of the Wolfenden Report's recommendations and criticizing Parliament for its failure to promptly enact them. Thirty-three prominent figures—including former Prime Minister Attlee; philosophers A. J. Ayer, Isaiah Berlin, and Bertrand Russell; writers C. Day Lewis, J. B. Priestly, and Stephen Spender; and several bishops—signed it.

The HLRS engaged in educational activities in order to overcome demeaning stereotypes. There were university debates, public meetings, and letter-writing campaigns. Antony Grey, the secretary for the group in the 1960s, once caused some disgruntlement at a Rotary dinner. He was asked what homosexuals were really like and he replied, "Rather like a Rotary Club" (quoted in Bedell 2007). The HLRS also published a newsletter, occasional pamphlets, and a regular journal, *Man and Society*, which focused on sexuality and legal reform.

In 1967, **Great Britain**'s Parliament passed the **Sexual Offenses Act**, which decriminalized homosexual sex in England and Wales. With its major political objective achieved, the HLRS soon began suffering from declining membership. In 1970, it changed its name to Sexual Law Reform Society. For the next two decades, it focused on providing counseling services and support. It also lobbied to extend the decriminalization to Scotland and Northern Ireland, as well as having the legal age of consent be the same for homosexuals as for heterosexuals. *See also* EUROPE.

HOOKER, EVELYN (1907–1996). As a psychologist at University of California Los Angeles (UCLA) in the 1950s, Hooker undertook a series of clinical studies of homosexual men to evaluate scientifically the common perception that persons attracted to their own sex were pathological. She found that such men did not fit a specific psychological profile, nor were they disproportionately likely to be pathological. She also presented ethnographic data, as well as sociological analysis, of the homosexual male milieu she observed. Her work, produced from the mid-1950s through the late 1960s, provoked substantial controversy in the medical and scientific fields. It put in question the orthodox view that homosexuals were mentally ill and needed **reparative therapy**. Other researchers pursued similar studies which, when combined with her work and that of **Alfred Kinsey**, gave scientific support for the **American Psychiatric Association**'s de-listing of homosexuality as a mental disorder in 1973. She resigned from UCLA in 1970 and went into private practice. In 1991, the American Psychological Association formally recognized her as having given distinguished contributions to the field. *See also* HOMOPHILE MOVEMENT; MEDICAL MODEL OF HOMOSEXUALITY.

HUMAN IMMUNODEFICIENCY VIRUS/ACQUIRED IMMUNODEFICIENCY SYNDROME (HIV/AIDS). One of the worst pandemics in the world today, HIV/AIDS has caused immense suffering around the world. The demographic profile of those most affected varies considerably by region. It has also provoked significant sociocultural changes.

HIV, the retrovirus that ultimately manifests itself as AIDS, attacks the immune system. Without treatment, the virus lowers the body's ability to ward off opportunistic infections. A person is classified as having AIDS once he or she has one or more of those infections and has a T cell (a type of immune system cell) count below a specific level. Diagnosis may also happen when a person falls prey to one of approximately two dozen illnesses that are particularly common among HIV-positive persons. There are several different types of HIV virus that, while closely related, have different levels of virulence. The virus multiplies at a very high rate and has a high level of mutation. That, in turn, has unfortunate implications for the control and cure of the disease, as does the fact that the disease has an incubation period lasting several years. It is most often spread through sex, although there are other means of transmission, such as from an infected mother to her child, the use of infected blood products, and intravenous drug use with tainted needles. Globally, most cases have been spread through heterosexual intercourse. Sub-Saharan Africa has been most affected, with some areas having infection rates among adults topping 30 percent. Anal sex is a more effective means for viral transmission than vaginal intercourse. Oral sex is also a vector of transmission, although that is believed to be a much more difficult route for the virus.

The detection of HIV/AIDS in the early 1980s was due to the sudden rise in previously rare diseases, such as a form of pneumonia, *Pneumocystis carinii*, caused by a specific type of fungus, and Kaposi's sarcoma, a form of skin cancer. Many persons are host to *Pneumocystis* for their lifetime, yet it is harmless and latent. Only someone with a failing immune system is susceptible to the full-blown illness. In general, as a person's T cells fall in number, illnesses become more common and virulent. This ultimately results in death, usually one to two years after the onset of AIDS.

The timing of the emergence of the disease in the 1970s and early 1980s was especially tragic because in several countries, such as the **United States** and **France**, gay men had just achieved a good degree of sexual freedom. In places such as California, bathhouses had proliferated and some men practiced unsafe sex with a number of partners. It was an ideal environment for the rapid spread of the disease. Furthermore, since the gay rights movement had been fighting for decades for the decriminalization of homosexual sex, many fought against the effort to close the bathhouses, and even resisted the identification of male-male anal sex as the prevalent means of transmission in some populations. It seemed like an attack on the very things the movement had fought for, rather than as a public health response. The resulting fight between the medical community and gay activists slowed the enactment of policy changes, such as the closing of baths.

Despite a subsection of the gay community's actions on issues such as bathhouse closure, the initial reactions to HIV/AIDS in the United States only came from that community and medical agencies, such as the Centers for Disease Control and Prevention (CDC). **Larry Kramer** helped to found Gay Men's Health Crisis, in 1981, which quickly became a large and influential community-based organization. In **Great Britain**, a circle of friends established the Terrence Higgins Trust, an AIDS support group. Most governments at any level did not respond effectively for several years. Among those countries where gay men have been the primary victims of AIDS, those in northern **Europe** were generally the quickest to respond. Ronald Reagan's administration was perhaps the slowest of any developed country; its attitude has often been characterized as one of malign neglect. In contrast, grassroots efforts in the gay community itself led to marked changes in sexual behaviors. Unsafe sex became much less common, although studies showed that public awareness campaigns were less effective among men of color and those who did not self-identify as gay.

In the United States, it took about eight years for the first 100,000 cases to be diagnosed. It took only a bit over two years for the next 100,000. In the 1990s, HIV/AIDS became the leading killer of men aged 25–44 in the United States. It caused an immense amount of suffering in the gay community, a level of catastrophe that was unimaginable yet all too real, and for many was virtually unbearable. The rate of HIV infection among gay men was higher in the United States than in Europe, but there too the scope of the tragedy was immense. Leading figures in the arts, fashion, and academic worlds had their lives cut short, including Rock Hudson and **Michel Foucault**. The trauma caused varied reactions, ranging from men trying celibacy to others knowingly engaging in risky behaviors in response to losing so many friends and loved ones. The gay community responded with candlelight vigils, the AIDS quilt project, and other memorials. Leading persons in the arts also created works that spoke to the crisis. Many of these are clearly of profound artistic significance, such as Larry Kramer's *The Normal Heart* and Tony Kushner's *Angels in America*.

Fighting AIDS became the unifying theme of the disparate gay rights movements in the developed world from the early 1980s well into the next decade. The perennial tension between lesbian and gay male activists weakened (even though the former were at greatly reduced risk for the disease). In part, this was because activists rightly saw the lack of reaction of the Reagan administration and other governments, and murmurings about quarantine from the right wing, as hostility to homosexuality in general. A renewed sense of radicalism appeared, manifested in groups such as the **AIDS Coalition to Unleash Power (ACT UP)**. Such groups worked aggressively for more funding for HIV/AIDS research, different drug research protocols, and better support services for those affected. Also, there was a clear disconnect between activists and the medical/scientific communities. The latter typically saw the first years as a time of solid scientific progress, with the disease and transmission mechanisms rather quickly identified. The relevant antibodies were also deduced, leading to a blood test to detect infection in 1985. AZT, the first drug to control the virus' replication, also became available soon after. Yet virtually everyone in the gay community was frustrated by the pace. Whole circles of friends were cut down in their youth. The frustration continued under President Clinton, since he had promised a crash program of massive funding for the prevention and treatment of HIV/AIDS, yet failed to deliver.

In 1996, scientists developed an anti-retroviral "cocktail" of three drugs. By inhibiting the virus' replication it often sharply reduces the prevalence of the virus in the body. It has made it possible for many of those infected to live relatively normal lives. Some persons suffer significant side effects from the medication, and the medication is expensive, which has caused difficulty in making it widely available. There is also concern about the virus mutating in ways that ultimately defeat this drug therapy. Globally, the rate of new infections appears to have peaked in the late 1990s and is now declining. Unsafe behavior among young gay men, however, has led to increased rates of infection in some neighborhoods in the United States. In 2007, the CDC reported that HIV/AIDS diagnoses had increased 11 percent from 2001 to 2005 among men who have sex with men. In that group, the prevalence among black men is twice that of their white counterparts.

Some epidemiologists now speak of the graying of the AIDS epidemic in the developed West. AZT and the subsequent development of a much more effective drug cocktail have made it so that a generation of long-term AIDS survivors is now reaching late middle age or senior citizen status. According to the CDC, the number of AIDS victims 50 and older nearly doubled from 2001 to 2005. Unfortunately, long-term AIDS survivors seem disproportionately likely to suffer from chronic illnesses that typically afflict the aged, such as osteoporosis, diabetes, and cardiovascular disease. While scientific studies to establish the validity of this perception have only begun, many doctors believe that the toll that HIV/AIDS takes on the immune system along with the side effects of the drug cocktail taken to treat it result in significant long-term complications. *See also* ANTI-DISCRIMINATION LAWS; ASIA; ASSIMILATION; FALWELL,

JERRY, SR.; HUMAN RIGHTS CAMPAIGN; IMMIGRATION AND NATURALIZATION LAW; LITERATURE, HOMOSEXUAL MALE; MIDDLE EAST; NATIONAL GAY AND LESBIAN TASK FORCE; RELIGIOUS RIGHT; SAME-SEX MARRIAGE.

HUMAN RIGHTS CAMPAIGN (HRC). A group of activists, including Steve Endean, founded the Human Rights Campaign in 1980. It primarily works as a political action committee (PAC) and lobbying organization. The HRC has a very large membership and is a comparatively well-funded PAC. It contributes to gay-friendly candidates for public office and lobbies on issues such as **anti-discrimination laws**, **same-sex marriage**, and **human immunodeficiency virus/ acquired immunodeficiency syndrome** funding. It has also contributed funding in high-profile legal cases, such as *Romer v. Evans*, and works on behalf of equality in **military service**. The HRC is one of the most important mainstream gay and lesbian political organizations in the **United States**.

– I –

IMMIGRATION AND NATURALIZATION LAW. The strict control of borders, immigration, and naturalization is a product of the modern state. The scientific investigation of sexuality and the resulting **medical model of homosexuality** led many states to attempt to prevent immigration by inverts and others considered sexual degenerates. Thus, at least in the developed world, immigration exclusions specifically targeting homosexuals are largely a product of the late 19th and early 20th centuries.

In the **United States**, an 1891 immigration law barred those guilty of "moral turpitude." The commissioner general of immigration, in 1909, spoke of the need to keep out anarchists, criminals, and sexual degenerates. Application of the law often depended on socioeconomic status; the federal government often debarred or deported poor persons who admitted to same-sex relations, while wealthier persons, clergymen, and others of status typically were not. Congress made the anti-homosexual thrust of U.S. immigration law more formal with the McCarran-Walter Act of 1952. While not mentioning homosexuality, it did mandate the exclusion of "persons afflicted with psychopathic personality," which members of Congress had been assured covered homosexuals (quoted in Eskridge 1999, 69). Even though the law, reflecting its roots in **McCarthyism**, was meant to tighten restrictions, fewer homosexuals were debarred or deported under it than previously. Congress amended the law, in 1965, by adding "sexual deviation" in order to clarify that homosexuals were barred.

The broader dynamics supporting anti-homosexual immigration exclusions diminished in the late 1960s and 1970s. The decriminalization of sodomy in many U.S. states and European countries made it harder to argue for exclusions, since the sexual expression involved was no longer criminal. Broadened notions of privacy and acceptable behavior also put immigration restrictions in question. In 1976, the Immigration and Naturalization Service (INS) announced that admission of homosexuality would no longer be grounds for denying naturalization. The policy remained in effect for immigration, but the INS did not actively enforce the policy in the 1980s. Congress repealed the exclusion in 1990. In 1994, a Board of Immigration Appeals case recognized sexual orientation as a possible basis for **asylum**. Attorney General Janet Reno directed the Justice Department to see the case as setting precedent. The United States, however, does have a strict ban upon immigration by those who are **human immunodeficiency virus/acquired immunodeficiency syndrome** (HIV/AIDS) positive. Senator Patrick Leahy introduced a bill, the Permanent Partners Immigration Act, into Congress. It would recognize same-sex couples for the purpose of immigration and naturalization rights, but it has not yet passed.

Much of **Europe** has gone further than the United States. Same-sex spouses or registered partners have immigration and naturalization rights in those countries that have either **same-sex marriage**, such as the Netherlands, or **registered partnerships**, such as Finland and Sweden. The same is not true in the United States, since only a few states recognize same-sex marriages and civil unions. In **Africa**, only South Africa recognizes same-sex relationships for the purposes of immigration and naturalization. In **Latin America**, only Brazil does so, as the result of a court decision in 2003. **Australia** and New Zealand accord standing to same-sex relationships for immigration and naturalization. No country in **Asia** recognizes such relationships for immigration purposes. As of 2008, only 12 countries prohibit the entry of HIV/AIDS-positive persons, including Libya, Iraq, and **Russia**. *See also BOUTILIER V. IMMIGRATION AND NATURALIZATION SERVICE*; CIVIL UNIONS.

INDIA. Given the sheer size of India and its vast array of subcultures, it is difficult to generalize about cultural attitudes and norms. Moreover, its political boundaries and its cultural influence, which are not always aligned, have shifted over time. Still, it is fair to say that there is little mention of homosexuality in historic Indian and Hindu texts. There are some notable exceptions. The Buddhist monastic code, dating back to the third century B.C.E., does prohibit homosexual (and heterosexual) sex among monks. The Kama Sutra devotes a chapter to fellatio, including a description of how eunuchs perform the act. Other erotic texts also have positive references to homosexual sex. In contrast, ancient codes of behavior prescribed penalties for homosexual sex acts. The *Manusmriti*, or Code of Manu, was the most prominent of these. It called for a purification ritual for a man who swallowed semen. A man from a high caste who engaged in an "unnatural offense" with another man had to purify himself by bathing with his clothes on, which was a minor penalty since the norm was to bathe in rivers and lakes while clothed. In general, the code did not demand the same standard from persons of lower castes, so no penalties apply to homosexual sex for them. The medieval takeover of northern India by Muslim conquerors brought greater restrictions on sexuality. A counterinfluence, however, was the rise in popularity of Tantrism among Hindus, since it sees sexuality as potentially liberating and embraces the switching of gender roles.

Early British and Dutch traders gave salacious reports of Indian sexual practices and the frequency of pederasty, especially among Muslims, though these are not entirely reliable. The British asserted direct rule after 1857 and imposed their **anti-sodomy laws** as a matter of course. In 1861, the government changed the law to reduce the penalty for sodomy from death by hanging to life imprisonment. This law was carried over after independence and became Section 377 of the Indian Penal Code. Its wording is vague, leading to varied interpretations. In contrast to many other countries, however, India has had a high evidentiary standard for convictions and thus prosecutions have been very rare. While there is a movement in India to repeal Section 377, the absence of any convictions under the law for over two decades has likely made that movement less powerful than it otherwise would have been. There are isolated reports of **police harassment** of gays and lesbians, condom distributors, and others, which are then justified in the name of the law. Nobel laureate Amartya Sen and author Vikram Seth, who wrote novels such as *The Golden Gate* and *A Suitable Boy*, have spoken out in favor of repeal.

South Asia, including Bangladesh and Pakistan, also has *hijras*. They are commonly seen as a third sex, neither male nor female. Most were born male, although there are some female *hijras*. Some of the men have undergone surgery to remove the penis, scrotum, and testes. Reports on the numbers of *hijra* vary wildly, but there are certainly tens of thousands, even hundreds of thousands, in India alone. The specific aspects of a *hijra*'s life are deeply affected by the diverse ethnic and linguistic tapestry of South Asia. Most Indian *hijras* are devotees of the mother goddess Bahuchara Mata. Many work as performers, such as dancers and singers. They perform at weddings and the birth ceremonies for boys, sometimes uninvited but expecting payment. Others work as prostitutes. It is common for *hijras* to live together in small communities. In some communities, they are seen as feminine males. *Hijras* take the passive role in homosexual sex. The men who take the active role with them are not seen as gay, since gender choice is not often equated with sexual identity. Some of these pairings between men and *hijras* are long term, although they lack the social legitimacy of heterosexual marriages. *Hijras* are subjected to discrimination and occasionally violence. In 2008, a new talk show hosted by a *hijra* had its debut in India. The audience numbered in the tens of millions.

Gay rights, including same-sex marriage, do not have much support in India. For example, the leadership of the Sikh community is very hostile. In cities, however, it is becoming possible for homosexual Indians to live a life of anonymity away from the demands of family and caste. Life for persons attracted to their own gender is generally more difficult in rural areas. *See also* ACT OF 25 HENRY VIII; ASIA.

INQUISITION. The rise of the Inquisition occurred in the 12th and 13th centuries. Building on previous efforts against heretics, Pope

Gregory IX formally established the papal Inquisition in 1233. Pope Innocent IV, in 1252, permitted the use of torture to extract confessions and otherwise ensure compliance with the authorities conducting a trial. While the main object of the Inquisition was to repress religious heresy, persons who engaged in homosexual sex were also a target. In 1242, the city of Perugia, in what today is central Italy, amended its laws to organize a group of dozens of men to find **sodomites**. In 1255, in Bologna, the head of a local Dominican Order urged a local group of laypersons, the Society of the Blessed Mary, to ferret out sodomites. The city eventually formalized this tactic in law, charging the Society to continue it efforts.

It was in **Spain**, however, that the fiercest version of the Inquisition took hold. In the 15th century, a pronounced fear and even hysteria about religious heresy became common among Catholics. Suspicions were rife about Muslims, Jews, and foreigners. In response, the royal authority, with the permission of the Pope, established the Inquisition in Spain. In 1505, King Ferdinand decreed that inquisitors could prosecute sodomy, although the Inquisition governing body held just a few years later that secular courts should handle the cases. In 1524, the Pope gave Spanish inquisitors the authority to prosecute sodomites. By the late 16th century, some jurisdictions were prosecuting more sodomy cases than heresy. By the time the Spanish Inquisition dropped the death penalty for sodomy, in 1633, the church and other authorities had executed hundreds for male-male sexual activity. Those who had been tortured, exiled, subjected to lashes, or otherwise punished short of death also numbered in the hundreds, if not over 1,000.

The situation for lesbian relations was more complex. Sometimes church authorities took those cases and other times not. The number of women prosecuted for sodomy, however, was clearly much lower. The authorities in some locales did not view acts lacking penetration as sexual.

The Inquisition even prosecuted those who merely questioned whether sodomy was a sin. The authorities publicly whipped and imprisoned for a year a mendicant whose sole offense was that he defended homosexual love as potentially just and pure. Even though the death penalty ended in the 17th century, Spanish inquisitors continued to pursue sodomy cases. Some of the sentences they handed out, such as 10 years in the galleys, were nearly equivalent to death, given the high mortality rate in Spanish galleys. The Spanish Inquisition finally ended in the early 19th century. The Inquisition in Portugal began in 1536. Just as in Spain, one of the central targets was recently converted Jews who were suspected of being insincere converts and still continuing Jewish traditions and ceremonies in secret. *Sodomitigos*, or "sodomites," were the second most frequent target. While the laws in Portugal were as severe as in Spain, authorities used the death penalty less frequently. Thousands of persons were accused of sodomy. The Holy Office had hundreds arrested and tried, and 30 ultimately were burned at the stake. Penalties short of death, however, still meant horrific punishments. Inquisitors subjected persons to hundreds of lashings, confiscated their property, and took away the civil rights of their relatives. Initially, lesbianism was considered a crime, but in 1646 the Holy Office narrowed the definition of sodomy to exclude female homosexuality. Secular law still considered lesbianism a crime, however, and hence the practical effect of this exclusion was limited. Portugal too ended its Inquisition in the early 19th century. *See also* CHRISTIANITY; EUROPE; ITALY; JUDAISM; LATIN AMERICA.

INTERNATIONAL LESBIAN AND GAY ASSOCIATION (ILGA). Originally named the International Gay Association, the ILGA was founded in 1978. Although its origins were in **Europe**, arising out of discussions between Dutch and British gay rights groups, ILGA now has chapters on every continent and in more than 90 countries. It publishes reports on topics such as anti-gay laws across the world. It lobbies international organizations such as the **United Nations**. ILGA helped to convince Amnesty International to classify those imprisoned for their sexual orientation as prisoners of conscience, and encouraged the World Health Organization to delete homosexuality from its list of mental illnesses. It organizes conferences and petitions, and also works through the media. ILGA is the oldest global gay rights group. *See also* HATE CRIME LAWS; JAPAN.

ISLAM. The central religious text in Islam, the **Koran**, has a broadly negative approach to same-sex sexuality, although it does not call for specific punishments and the severity of the sin is left uncertain. Stories about Mohammed, who the tradition believes had the Koran revealed to him by an angel, depict him as lenient toward homosexuality. After Mohammed's death, his followers gathered together statements they attributed to him, known as the hadith. The statements pertaining to homosexuality are severe, and one even calls for those caught in homosexual sex acts to be put to death. Islamic scholars consider some of the hadith reliable, while others clearly refer to events or issues that only arose well after his death and hence are considered later inventions attached to Mohammed's name in order to give them greater legitimacy. Portions of the hadith dealing with homosexuality fall within the latter category, and thus Islamic scholars and traditions differ with one another as to their weight. Some of the more fundamentalist traditions take these controversial hadith at face value and therefore support the inclusion of the death penalty for gays and lesbians in sharia, or Islamic law. Others, however, note the lack of a specified penalty in the Koran and the dubiousness of the anti-gay hadith, and thus take a more tolerant approach.

Historically, there has been substantial variation in Muslim societies' regulation of same-sex sexuality. Some made a distinction based on whether those caught were married or not, with harsher penalties, including death, for the former since their actions were adulterous. Since standards of evidence have usually been high, requiring the testimony of trusted individuals or repeated confession, the frequency of convictions has been low. Other societies have taken the approach that while same-sex sexuality is sinful, as long as those engaging in it show discretion, there is little point in trying to regulate private behavior where efforts are made to not disrupt general social norms. The rise of Islamic fundamentalism in the 20th century has hardened attitudes against homosexuality in the Muslim world, particularly in the **Middle East**. *See also* LITERATURE, HOMOSEXUAL MALE; UNITED NATIONS.

ITALY. After the fall of **ancient Rome**, the land that comprises present-day Italy was subjected to numerous invasions from disparate peoples, many of which left their mark as far as cultural and political arrangements. The Germanic invasions, such as by the Visigoths and the Lombards, did not lead to **anti-sodomy laws**. Instead, the rediscovery of, and intense interest in, the **Justinian Code** in the 12th and 13th centuries is what caused the re-adoption of the harsh penalties from almost a millennium earlier. The church moved the same direction. The Third Lateran Council, held in Rome in 1179, decreed that priests found guilty of sodomy were to be defrocked and sent to monasteries. Convicted laypersons were to be excommunicated. Given the close church-state relations of the day, in some areas this could amount to a death sentence. It was only a few decades later that the **Inquisition** was established in Italy and subsequently took hold elsewhere, especially in **Spain**.

A number of Italian city-states enacted anti-sodomy laws in the 14th century, with some prescribing death, such as Bologna, Florence, Rome, and Venice. Others, such as Milan, passed anti-sodomy laws with the death penalty in the 15th century. Given that there has often been a gap between the passing of a law and its enforcement, it is worth noting that Venetian authorities in the 15th century were especially repressive. Hundreds were decapitated or burned to death. Children were tortured to extract confessions. In the 16th century, Venice lowered its penalties to exile, fines, or other non-lethal punishments. The situation in Florence was very complicated. Although the city passed an anti-sodomy law with death by burning as the punishment, it was typically applied only against those who had engaged in homosexual rape. It then moved to a system of fines. Florence, during the Renaissance, appears to have had a flourishing subculture of male-male love and frequent bisexuality. A reputation developed and spread across Europe. In Germany, sodomites were referred to as *Florenzen*.

In the 17th and 18th centuries, authorities had less recourse to the death penalty. In 1761, Cesare Beccaria published a short treatise on criminal law. It was an outstanding example of **Enlightenment** thinking. Beccaria denounced the use of torture in general, but also specifically in relation to sodomy cases. His work, subsequently popularized by figures such as Voltaire, helped to spark a wave of legal reform. Until Italy's unification in 1861, there was significant variation in the legal status of homosexuality, as well as its social understanding. Some areas had repressive statutes, while others had none. After unification, Sardinia's repressive laws were adopted nationwide, but were later repealed with the adoption of a new penal code in 1889.

Given Italy's fragmented political history, its deep cultural variation is unsurprising. For centuries, in southern Italy, rigidly prescribed roles for men broke those who engaged in homosexual sex into either the active partner, who was seen as fully "male," and those who played the passive role. It was only the latter who were seen as violating gender roles. Persecution was generally reserved for them. Yet some homosexual communities formed and were more or less tolerated. The cultural understanding in northern Italy has, historically, been more closely aligned to that of northern Europe, where the dichotomy of active versus passive is much less relevant and instead the most salient division is between those who are attracted to members of their own sex and those who are not.

While the legal silence about homosexuality has remained ever since the penal code reforms of 1889, the authorities during Italy's Fascist era did persecute homosexuals. After 1938, some were incarcerated while others were sentenced to internal exile. After World War II, the status quo ante of no criminalization yet no social toleration continued. In the late 1960s, the Unitary Front of Revolutionary Italian Homosexuals, or FUORI, was formed. This group, whose acronym means "out," was the first prominent gay rights group in the country. After several years, however, it suffered from divisions between those who wanted to ally with broader political and civil rights movements and those who did not. In 1982, FUORI fell apart. Yet in the 1980s, local gay groups forged a larger umbrella group, Arcigay, that made connections with left-wing parties. In late 1989, a related lesbian group was formed. It was originally named Arcigay Donna, but later renamed Arcigay Arcilesbia. With over 150,000 members, Arcigay is one of the largest gay and lesbian groups in the world.

There is no prohibition on gay and lesbian **military service**. Some regions have passed **anti-discrimination laws**, but there is no national law yet and some groups, such as the Catholic Church, oppose it. Italy does not have **same-sex marriage**. The leading center-left party has committed itself to a weak version of a **civil union** law, but Parliament has yet to pass any. *See also* ETIOLOGY; LEONARDO DA VINCI; MICHELANGELO; SOTADIC ZONE.

– J –

JAMES VI AND I (1566–1625). Son of Mary, Queen of Scots, James became James VI of Scotland when his mother was forced to abdicate. He ascended to the English throne, as James I, in 1603. During his time on the throne, he was often caught up in the religious and political conflict between Protestants and Catholics. His commissioning of the King James Version of the **Bible** is an important part of his legacy.

James often made public displays of affection with his male favorites. It was a pattern he began as a teenager and continued throughout his life. Members of the court noted that his comportment with his beloved, whomever it happened to be at that time, was so untoward that it was as if James had mistaken a man for a woman. Even though the English of the time were especially reluctant to discuss same-sex love, the king's "lascivious" kissing of other men made speculation of his homosexuality a frequent topic at court. James, like several other homosexual or bisexual royals, bestowed titles and great wealth upon his male favorites. One of them, Robert Carr of Scotland, was named earl of Somerset and thereby gained a seat in the House of Lords. He thus became the first Scotsman to serve there.

Even though England had an **anti-sodomy law** at the time, as the sovereign James was politically immune to such prosecution. He did not, however, show any leniency on this issue to his subjects. He ordered his chancellor to be especially strict in sodomy cases. James also wrote a book on kingship and in it he singled out sodomy as a particularly horrible crime, equating it to murder.

JAPAN. Japan was deeply influenced by the cultural traditions of **ancient China**, especially with the introduction of Buddhism in the mid-sixth century. Thus, the positive norms and understandings about male same-sex love in China helped shape Japanese perceptions. The lack of any anti-homosexual religious tradition also made Japan open to such views.

The Buddhist figure Kūkai is credited with bringing the tradition of male love to Japan, in 806, after his religious studies in China. In the 11th and 12th centuries, Buddhist monks developed a tradition of love affairs between monks and their acolytes that had its own terms, rituals, and stereotypical behaviors. Centuries later, the Jesuit missionary Francis Xavier was appalled at the homosexual relationships he witnessed at a Zen monastery, complaining that not only were the relationships public, but also that the monks had no feelings of shame at their behavior. Yet the value attached to same-sex love ultimately spread to aristocratic, artistic, and military circles. Elevnth-century courtiers wrote in their diaries, in explicit terms, about their assignations with men. Japanese erotic art from the same period also has many examples of explicit depictions of male-male love. A love affair between a shogun and young actor deeply influenced the evolution of *Nō* drama. *Nō* had ignoble origins, coming out of folk dances and acrobatics, but in 1374 a young actor named Zeami performed for a shogun, Yoshimitsu. Entranced by the youth's beauty and talent, the shogun befriended him and supported his artistic endeavors. Zeami went on to write many classics of *Nō*, and Yoshimitsu began a tradition of shogun patronage of that form of drama.

Samurai in medieval Japan developed idealized same-sex relationships analogous to those in **ancient Greece**. The older male was not supposed to be simply after physical gratification; instead, he was supposed to be concerned about the education of the younger, in both the intellectual and moral senses. The lover was even to help his beloved learn proper etiquette. Likewise, a noble younger man was to select a suitor based on the nobility of his soul. It was also thought that having lovers fight together in battle would spur them to greater acts of courage. Just like in ancient Greece, however, reality often fell short of this ideal. There are many stories of deception and political intrigue involving male-male lovers.

The frequency of this sort of love relationship is startling to many modern readers. For instance, of the over two dozen shoguns who ruled Japan from the 14th into the 19th centuries, probably more than half had male lovers. Toward the end of the shogun era, a burgeoning middle class adopted this samurai tradition, although often in a more base fashion. Male prostitution became more common, and some quarters in larger cities had dozens of boys and young men employed in brothels. Erotic woodblock prints also became popular during this time, many of which depict women engaged in lesbian sex acts. The history of lesbianism in Japan, however, is very obscure and there are few references to it in pre-modern society. One exception is **Ihara**

Saikaku's novel *Life of an Amorous Woman*, in which the heroine has an affair with the head of an all-female household. During the Meiji era of the late 19th and early 20th centuries, Japan's leaders sought to modernize and catch up with the social and technological developments in the West. Political elites adopted the West's negative attitudes about homosexuality. In 1873, male homosexual sex was criminalized, although the penalty of 90 days in jail was dramatically less than that in many Western countries. The government repealed the law a decade later. In general, the attempt to repress homosexual relationships and sexuality was unsuccessful, probably in part because there was no strong religious or cultural tradition that saw homosexuality as a threat.

For much of the 20th century, homosexuality was largely invisible in Japanese society. Moreover, mainstream society strongly emphasized the need for conformity. This silence made it so that there is no **anti-sodomy law**, although some local governments have made the age of consent higher for homosexual than heterosexual sex. Political parties, both inside and outside the mainstream, mostly continue to avoid the issue. There were some homoerotic cultural undercurrents, however. The novelist Yukio Mishima, who was homosexual, wrote works that overtly described male same-sex attraction and sadomasochistic desires. He was a prolific author who published close to two dozen works before he killed himself, in 1970.

The relative media silence ended abruptly in the 1990s, however. Kakefuda Hiroko, a lesbian author, was one of the pioneers in this transformation. Gay and lesbian groups, which had existed largely underground since the 1950s, also gained prominence and a newfound assertiveness. Notable examples of Japanese gay and lesbian groups are Occur, the Japanese chapter of the **International Lesbian and Gay Association** (JILGA), and Gay Front Kansai. JILGA organized Japan's first-ever gay pride march, which took place in Tokyo in 1994. Hundreds participated in the first march, but the numbers have increased significantly since then.

There is no formal ban on **military service** for gays and lesbians. **Same-sex marriage** is not recognized. The prospects for change in marriage laws in the short term are rather dim, given the continued emphasis on conformity and the political leadership's reluctance to address issues of homosexuality. There is little to no repression of homosexuality, though. Gay bars are numerous and open discussion of homosexuality is at a level that would have been unthinkable as recently as the 1980s. *See also* ASIA; LITERATURE, HOMO-SEXUAL MALE.

JENNINGS, DALE (1917–2000). One of the founders of the **Mattachine Society** in 1950–1951, Jennings was a writer previously active in the defense of the civil liberties of Japanese Americans. In 1952, police arrested Jennings and charged him with lewd behavior. He in turn alleged **police harassment** and entrapment. The society decided to fight the police charge and publicly come to his defense. They formed the Citizens Committee to Outlaw Entrapment, distributed fliers, and asked for contributions for his legal defense. The trial concluded with a hung jury and the charge was dismissed. The committee's efforts dramatically increased the prominence and membership in the society. By 1953, the society estimated that it had more than 2,000 members and began to publish a magazine, *ONE*, that while formally independent from the Mattachines, was primarily directed by members of the society. Jennings served as its first editor. In that capacity, Jennings wrote extensively in defense of the rights of homosexuals, as well as against the view that persons attracted to people of their own gender are mentally ill. When the Mattachine Society subsequently changed leadership, dropped its leftist roots, and opted for a moderate and low-key political approach, Jennings was sharply critical in the pages of the magazine. One of his screenplays was made into a John Wayne movie, *The Cowboys*.

JUDAISM. Since the **Torah** is fundamental to the Judaic tradition, that text's denunciations of same-sex sexuality carried over into rabbinical commentary and religious practice. Early Judaic scholars accepted the prohibition on male same-sex relations in Leviticus, even while they did not interpret Sodom's sin as homosexuality. The Jewish Diaspora's encounter with a Hellenistic world that was much more accepting of same-sex relations did not alter its views. In fact, one of the most prominent theologians and jurists of the Greco-Roman era, Philo of Alexandria, vehemently defended the death sentence for men who engage in same-sex relations. Early Torah commentators largely ignored female same-sex relations. While the call for capital punishment had little significance for formal state law, in that the Jewish people lost their independence in the first century of the Common Era, Jewish communities usually had some autonomy and often had the power to banish members who violated norms. Medieval commentaries upon the Torah and Talmud continued the tradition of hostility to same-sex relations. The most prominent medieval Jewish philosopher, Maimonides, addressed the issue in the 12th century. He condemned female same-sex relations as obscene, but did not equate it with male same-sex relations, where he defended the traditional penalty of death.

Historically, Jews have often been subjected to persecution by the same persons and governments that persecuted those who engaged in same-sex relations. Medieval **Christianity**, for example, espoused intolerance toward Jews and **sodomites**. This mind-set found its culmination in the **Inquisition** in which those two groups formed the vast majority of those interrogated, tortured, and killed. More recently, especially in **Europe**, the advent of nationalism again spurred waves of repression against the two groups. **National Socialism**, for instance, targeted Jews and homosexuals. Millions of the former and thousands of the latter died in concentration camps. These religious and nationalist persecutions have been similar in that the agents of repression espouse a creed of religious or national homogeneity. Those who differ are seen as a threat, especially those who may reasonably hope to "pass" among the majority. The same ideals of national and religious purity are espoused today, with the same results. In the **Middle East**, many governments denounce homosexuality as a foreign, decadent expression of sexuality. The same regimes, such as Iran's, similarly denounce Israel and Judaism in anti-Semitic terms. Some public figures in the West likewise invoke an idealized image of the past and then denounce those who, they allege, threaten it. In the **United States**, Pat Buchanan and **Jerry Falwell** combined overt **homophobia** with covert anti-Semitism.

The Jewish people regained state control in 1948 with the establishment of Israel. Previously under British control for several decades, the new state inherited **Great Britain**'s **anti-sodomy law**. Authorities did not prosecute consensual same-sex acts conducted in private, however. In 1988, the Israeli government repealed the law. Since the 1970s, the country has had a small gay rights movement.

The Knesset, Israel's parliament, passed an **anti-discrimination law** in 1989. Out gays and lesbians must, like other Israeli citizens, engage in **military service**.

In the West today, Judaism is divided into three primary movements. Orthodox Jews take the Torah to be the literal word of God. As such, they have a very strict version of what it means to be observant. This branch is the most hostile to same-sex sexuality due to the passages from Leviticus. Conservative and Reform Jews interpret the Torah as divinely inspired, yet not literally God's word since it is also the handiwork of man. This gives greater latitude in observance, although Conservative Jews place much weight on Jewish tradition. As the most culturally liberal branch, Reform Judaism has been the most open to homosexuality, at least since the 1970s. There are gay-affirming Reform synagogues, sometimes led by openly gay rabbis. All three branches, however, have often worked together to support equal civil rights for gays and lesbians. Many Orthodox rabbis have supported the repeal of anti-sodomy laws. *See also* SPAIN.

– K –

KAMENY, FRANK (1925–). Kameny brought a degree of assertiveness to the **homophile movement** that it had previously lacked. He was a consistent and outspoken advocate for equal treatment for gays and lesbians, fighting to repeal the ban upon gay and lesbian employment by the federal government, as well as for the repeal of **anti-sodomy laws**. He also proved himself to be an effective organizer.

Kameny received his Ph.D. in astronomy from Harvard in 1956. The next year the **United States** Army hired him as a civilian employee, but just a few months later he was fired after a background check revealed that he had been arrested on a lewd conduct charge just weeks after having received his Ph.D. The Civil Service Commission then banned him from all federal employment. Kameny fought the commission's ruling. His suit, *Kameny v. Brucker*, was fought all the way to the federal appellate courts. When Kameny lost there, he appealed to the U.S. Supreme Court, but it declined to hear the case.

In 1961, Kameny founded the Washington, D.C., chapter of the **Mattachine Society**. Unlike leaders in other chapters, Kameny made sure the Washington one was forceful, consistent, and engaged in activism along the lines of the civil rights movement. His educational achievements likewise made him less deferential to experts in psychiatry and medicine. The Washington chapter appealed to members of Congress and senior bureaucrats for meetings about various anti-gay policies. The chapter also played a key role in getting the American Civil Liberties Union (ACLU) to revisit its 1957 policy statement that anti-sodomy laws are constitutional. Kameny also helped persuade the ACLU to fight the ban on gays and lesbians in federal government work.

In 1963, Kameny was instrumental in the founding of the East Coast Homophile Organizations (ECHO), which tied together four **homophile** groups in an effort to consolidate the more militant wing of the homophile movement. Within a couple of years, ECHO was mounting picket demonstrations in front of several federal agencies, including the Civil Service Commission. Kameny's forceful advocacy of a civil rights approach persuaded some influential members of the **Daughters of Bilitis** (DOB) to drop their reliance on experts and political quietism, even though picketing was controversial within the DOB. Kameny also played a key role in the establishment of the **North American Conference of Homophile Organizations** (NACHO) in 1966. He coined the phrase "Gay is good" that NACHO adopted as its official slogan, in a gesture showing its complete repudiation of the medical model of homosexuality as pathology.

For decades afterward, Kameny continued his work on behalf of gay rights. In the 1970s, he worked to overturn the **American Psychiatric Association**'s listing of homosexuality as a mental disorder. He also continued to organize gay rights groups, including helping to found the **National Gay and Lesbian Task Force**. Well into the 1990s, Kameny advised U.S. soldiers about how to confront the ban on **military service**. While many contemporary gay activists have disdain for the homophile movement, Kameny is almost universally recognized as a gay rights pioneer.

KERTBENY, KARL MARIA (1824–1882). Born in Vienna and raised in Budapest, Karl Maria Kertbeny was a journalist and prolific author. In the 1860s, he wrote and anonymously published pamphlets opposing **Germany**'s **anti-sodomy law**. He laid out two basic lines of argument. The first was that anti-sodomy laws violate basic human rights; private, consensual sex should not be subjected to governmental regulation. Second, he argued that sexual attraction was inborn and therefore same-sex eroticism was natural, rather than a mark of moral failure or sin. He coined the term "homosexuality" (*homosexualität*). According to Kertbeny, as a young man he had a homosexual friend who was blackmailed and, as a result, committed suicide. Kertbeny thus resolved to fight the injustice of anti-homosexual persecution. *See also* ELLIS, HAVELOCK.

KINSEY, ALFRED (1894–1956). Kinsey was a longtime professor of zoology at Indiana University who specialized in entomology, particularly in gall wasps. In the 1930s, he began collecting data on individuals' personal sexual histories. He gained significant grant support for his work in the 1940s, primarily from a foundation supported by the Rockefellers. In 1948, he published, in collaboration with two other authors, a comprehensive presentation and analysis of his data, *Sexual Behavior in the Human Male*. It was followed by a volume in 1953, *Sexual Behavior in the Human Female*. Together they are known as the Kinsey Reports.

Their publication provoked great interest and controversy, with the latter involving both political and methodological disagreements. One of Kinsey's most significant findings concerned the frequency of homosexual experiences. From the onset of adolescence, Kinsey found that 37 percent of men had had an orgasmic homosexual experience; for women the percentage was 13 percent. In the three years prior to the interview, 8 percent of men had been exclusively homosexual, while 4 percent had been solely homosexual for their entire lives. The proportions for women were analogous, though somewhat lower. Kinsey and his co-authors also argued that sexual orientation was more diverse than a simple heterosexual/homosexual dichotomy. He developed a taxonomy, now called the Kinsey Scale, that ranged from zero for exclusive heterosexuality to six for exclusive homosexuality. Since he also asserted that in many cases this is changeable over a person's lifetime, Kinsey placed in question the notion of set orientations and the alleged naturalness of heterosexuality. Kinsey did little to hide the fact that part of his social and political agenda was to show the innate variety of sexual expression, and thus allow greater room for persons to express their sexuality without negative consequences. This included support for repealing **anti-sodomy laws**.

The foundation that had been his primary source of funding withdrew its funds in 1954, due to political pressure. Kinsey himself was attacked in the press and by evangelists such as Billy Graham. He died prematurely in 1956. One of the central long-term impacts of Kinsey is that he helped to open the door for public discussion of sexuality. *See also* CLOSET, THE; FREUD, SIGMUND; HOOKER, EVELYN; MCCARTHYISM; MEDICAL MODEL OF HOMOSEXUALITY.

KORAN. The primary holy text of the Muslim faith has a mildly negative view of same-sex sexuality. One koranic verse speaks of rebuking men who commit an "unchastity" with one another (in the fourth sura, or chapter). Still, repentance is sufficient to avoid any penalty, and homosexuality is not one of the acts that are specifically proscribed with a corresponding penalty (the *hadd*). There seems to be a broadly negative depiction of same-sex sexuality, however, that is conveyed primarily in discussions of Lut (or Lot, as he is called in the **Bible**). The interpretation of these passages is disputed though. In contrast to the biblical presentation of the story of Lot, which occurs in just one place (Genesis), the one in the Koran is spread across 7 of the 112 suras. There is room for doubt that the central point of the story of Lut is to condemn homosexuality. For example, some take the issue of hospitality as critical and point out that Lut argues to the townspeople that he has an obligation to shelter his guests. Others focus on the nonconsensual nature of the situation; the people of Sodom and Gomorrah want to rape Lut's guests. There is a sura that refers to men turning away from their wives and desiring Lut's guests. It is sharply critical of this turning away, but the point here could be that sex outside of one's marriage is adultery, which is one of the *hadd*. *See also* ASIA; ISLAM; MIDDLE EAST; SPAIN.

KRAMER, LARRY (1935–). A writer and activist, Larry Kramer has at turns been loathed and lauded by many, including in the gay activist, medical, and literary communities. His 1978 novel, *Faggots*, proved controversial due to its moralistic tone. Some in the gay male community saw it as anti-sex and an example of self-loathing. Nevertheless, it sold well and many regarded it highly. In 1981, Kramer was one of the first to sound the tocsin about **human immunodeficiency virus/acquired immunodeficiency syndrome** (HIV/ AIDS). Some took Kramer's warnings as another example of an alleged anti-sex attitude. In 1982, Kramer took the lead in founding the Gay Men's Heath Crisis (GMHC), a New York–based group that provides health and support services for those who are HIV-positive. It quickly proved to be an influential grassroots model that was emulated in other communities across the **United States**. The founding of a group like the GMHC is an element in Kramer's play *The Normal Heart*. Kramer was dissatisfied with the GMHC, however, arguing that it was too politically weak and not radical enough. He left its board in 1983. In 1987, he helped to found the more radical **AIDS Coalition to Unleash Power** (ACT UP). More recently, Kramer has helped to steer ACT UP in the direction of alliances with other liberal and leftist causes, such as universal health care.

– L –

LABOUCHÈRE AMENDMENT. In 1885, the government of **Great Britain** passed the Criminal Law Amendment Act. Section 11 of the law broadened Britain's **anti-sodomy law**. Whereas under the previous legal regime, established by **Act of 25 Henry VIII**, only male-male anal sex was criminal, the 1885 law made male-male oral sex punishable by two years in prison, with the possibility of hard labor. Section 11 is commonly known as the Labouchère Amendment after its chief legislative sponsor, Henry Labouchère. It was also frequently referred to as the "Blackmailer's Charter," since it made homosexual men much more susceptible to the practice. The law was the basis for the prosecution of **Oscar Wilde**. An effort to extend the law to lesbian sex failed in the 1920s. The British government repealed the law in 1967, with the **Sexual Offenses Act**. *See also* AUSTRALIA.

LATIN AMERICA. There are extensive reports by early chroniclers and conquistadors of same-sex sexuality among the indigenous peoples they encountered. In addition, there are later accounts of the same by anthropologists, including in tribes still in existence. Among some tribes in the northwest Amazon there is substantial sexual play among unmarried men, such as caressing and fondling of genitalia. These tribes, such as the Barasana and the Yanamamo, do distinguish between such behavior, which they often see as rather light-hearted play, and more serious same-sex sexuality. While the former is widely accepted and may even occur in public, the latter is not. Other tribes, such as the Tapirape of the southern Amazon, had men who allowed others to have anal sex with them. While some of those men were married, others adopted female names and gender roles. Some tribes report the same adoption of cross-gender roles, including same-sex marriage, among women. Some Andean coastal areas had temple prostitutes available for same-sex relations. Among the Araucanians of southern South America, there were shamans who adopted female gender roles and engaged in same-sex relations with men. Certainly not all peoples had tolerant or accepting attitudes toward same-sex relations. At the time of European conquest, the Aztecs and the Incas were hostile to same-sex relations. The Aztecs may have executed some for homosexual relations.

Given that early explorers and conquerors came from late medieval **Europe**, they brought with them an anti-sodomy framework often strongly influenced by **natural law** theory. These early travelers found the attitudes toward, and sometimes even open displays of, same-sex sexuality to be shocking, such as what they saw among the Mayans. Europeans wrote about the frequency and shamelessness of homosexuality and the adoption of cross-gender roles in accounts that were then widely circulated in Spain. The extirpation of this sin then became one of the justifications for the colonization of the New World, with all of its attendant brutality. In the 16th century, Vasco Nuñez de Balboa had 40 men whom he believed guilty of sodomy attacked by dogs in Panama; a Spanish magistrate in Peru burned to death many accused of sodomy; an archbishop in Mexico had them flogged. This repression continued into the 18th century, with executions, flogging, and other punishments, although the rate of prosecutions fell significantly in Mexico. The Portuguese exported the **Inquisition** to Brazil. In contrast to some areas of inquisitorial rule, in Brazil women were also accused and punished. The abolition of the Inquisition in the early 19th century, along with the influence of the **Code Napoléon**, led to the abolition of **anti-sodomy laws** in many areas, including Brazil. Yet the colonizers continued to disapprove of same-sex relations. The legalization of sodomy had the effect of reducing the amount of evidence available to historians and thus homosexuality in 19th-century Latin America is an especially opaque era.

Many in modern Latin America see same-sex relations through a framework that emphasizes an active-passive dichotomy. There are, however, significant complicating factors involved, including the social construction of gender and patriarchy, important regional variations, age-differentiated roles in some areas, and class distinctions. The historical legacy is important, given that contemporary Latin American culture is largely the product of the melding of Iberian culture with indigenous cultures through conflict and adaptation, miscegenation, and other factors. The formation of the resulting mestizo culture, in regard to homosexuality in particular, is difficult to trace due to scant evidence from the colonial era. Yet there are glimmers. In 1658, a group of alleged **sodomites** was arrested in Mexico City and Puebla. Out of the more than 100 caught up in the scandal, 14 were burned to death. Evidence collected during interrogations suggests the existence of a subculture of sodomites in at least those urban areas, complete with slang speech. Age-differentiated sexuality apparently was the norm at the time, with older men being the penetrative partner. Gender construction also played a role, with the men giving female nicknames to their partners, including those of famous prostitutes. This intertwining of gender role with sexual function has been a recurring pattern in much of Latin America.

Modern constructions of sexual identity, which clearly were forged in Europe in the latter half of the 19th century, likely came about later in Latin America and did not spread as comprehensively across the subcultures of society. Yet in legal and scientific circles, the rise of the **medical model of homosexuality** clearly occurred in the first decades of the 20th century. European discussions of sexuality strongly influenced the discourse in Latin America. For instance, lesbians were depicted as beings whose sexuality upset normal social roles, went against nature due to a degenerate physiognomy, and exhibited an unhealthy psychology. As the active-passive dichotomy came to play an important role in the construction of male homosexuality, the active or penetrative role generally was seen as having less social stigma. For instance, in early 20th-century sodomy cases tried against Brazilian sailors, those accused of taking the penetrative role often did not try to hide their actions but instead excused it as the result of alcohol or some other fleeting cause. Those accused of passivity were more likely to conceal their actions and also argued that they had defended their honor by resisting. Few were discharged.

In modern and contemporary societies, the active role in same-sex relations has not had mainstream legitimacy. As long as such activity remains in the shadows, however, and is spoken of euphemistically, it is not generally seen as too problematic. Active men who are troubled by their actions are often able to avoid cognitive dissonance by feminizing their partners: they are not queer, they can say to themselves; they are just using a man as a woman. This allows such men to more easily maintain a sense of self as having the appropriate gender role and a heterosexual social identity. The role of the penetrated partner, or *puto* (bitch or queer), is doubly stigmatized. Not only does he, from the perspective of mainstream society, engage in questionable sexual actions, he surrenders his masculinity. In societies with a strong ethic of machismo, such willful abandonment of one's maleness is troubling.

Lesbianism has been even more closeted. While compulsory heterosexuality was the norm, and in most places still is, many men in practice were bisexual. In contrast, since female sexuality is repressed in patriarchal societies, lesbians have fewer opportunities to freely associate and establish safe private spaces. Rural areas in particular have been particularly effective at informal policing of residents' sexuality.

Modern Latin American states have varied substantially in their tolerance or repression of same-sex sexuality. The most punitive regimes have typically been either far to the left or to the right. In 1959, the Communist revolution in Cuba ended the lively but seedy Havana nightlife, which had cruising areas and bars for those attracted to their own sex. Fidel Castro's regime denounced homosexuality and established Committees for the Defense of the Revolution, which patrolled neighborhoods and invaded private space. In the mid-1960s, the regime even briefly established internment camps that largely housed homosexual men and political prisoners. Conditions improved in the later 1970s and 1980s. The regime's pursuit of equality between the sexes indirectly helped lesbians in particular. The Cuban government subsequently repealed its anti-sodomy laws.

On the right, a military dictatorship took power in Argentina in 1976. Since the rather weak gay movement that had begun to emerge in the country under the preceding civilian rule had allied itself with the left, the dictatorship's crackdown upon potential dissidents included many gays. Since the regime viewed women as being of little importance, it rarely targeted lesbians. The regime quashed the gay movement, arrested men who frequented cruising areas, and closed down gay bars. The military government stepped down in the early 1980s. The gay rights movement re-established itself soon after civilian rule was once again achieved. In 1984, the country's foremost gay rights organization was established, *Comunidad Homosexual Argentina*.

Although Brazil's military government in the late 1960s and early 1970s was not as brutal as Argentina's, it too suppressed homosexual groups and a previously vibrant gay press. When the regime decided to pursue liberalization in the late 1970s, a homosexual movement quickly re-asserted itself although it did not achieve a critical mass until the late 1980s. It did so in spite of rampant violence against gays and lesbians.

The gay rights movement that strengthened and achieved public visibility in the 1980s and 1990s has had some notable successes. In 1992, President Carlos Menem of Argentina signed a decree mandating equal legal protections for gays and lesbians. In 2002, Buenos Aires began recognizing **civil unions**. It also has become more gay friendly in its approach to tourism, with gay-themed soccer matches, hotels, and performances by drag queens. In 2007, Uruguay began recognizing same-sex and opposite-sex civil unions, if the couple can show five years of cohabitation. One influence behind these changes is globalization. The greater penetration of global media and the increased frequency of international tourism have helped to erode homophobic attitudes among many, although the Catholic Church has opposed most reform efforts. One way in which this is reflected is the more widespread use of the term "gay." *See also* GAY BASHING; IMMIGRATION AND NATURALIZATION LAW; LITERATURE, LESBIAN; SPAIN; UNITED NATIONS.

LAWRENCE V. TEXAS* (2003).** In 2003, the **United States** Supreme Court ruled that the right to privacy included the right to engage in consensual sodomy in private, whether opposite-sex or same-sex in nature. The Court thereby invalidated not just the Texas **anti-sodomy law** that was at issue, but all U.S. anti-sodomy laws. The ruling overturned ***Bowers v. Hardwick, its 1986 decision that upheld the constitutionality of a Georgia anti-sodomy law.

One of the most remarkable aspects of the decision was that Justice Anthony Kennedy's majority opinion did not approach homosexuality in a reductive fashion, focusing solely on sexual behavior. The majority's decision in *Bowers* had discussed heterosexuality in the context of relationships and family but homosexuality only through narrowest sexual terms. In contrast, Kennedy's decision equated homosexuality with heterosexuality and placed intimate physical acts of both types in a larger perspective of expressions of emotional intimacy. Justice Antonin Scalia's dissent noted this and stated that the majority decision laid the groundwork for a later ruling in favor of a right to **same-sex marriage**, which he opposes. *See also* FALWELL, JERRY, SR.; FAMILY RESEARCH COUNCIL; NATURAL LAW; POLICE HARASSMENT; *ROMER V. EVANS*.

LEONARDO DA VINCI (1452–1519). Born into illegitimacy in Tuscany, Leonardo was raised by his grandparents. In his early 20s, he was twice accused of homosexual sodomy. After investigations, the authorities dropped the charges. He became famous for his paintings, such as his fresco *The Last Supper* and the *Mona Lisa*, and for his extensive and far-ranging scientific and architectural pursuits. Leonardo was an accomplished anatomist. He also served as a military engineer for Cesare Borgia (who in turn strongly influenced Niccolò Machiavelli) and Louis XII. Along with **Michelangelo**, he embodied the pinnacle of Renaissance cultural achievements.

Leonardo was a private man and even recorded personal notes in mirror writing (that is, it can only be read by using a mirror). His arrest at a young age undoubtedly contributed to his reticence and secretiveness. It is known that Leonardo was devoted to a young assistant whom he nicknamed Salai and whom he took into his house when the boy was 10. Salai was his companion for over a quarter of a century and Leonardo, who never married, left him a portion of his estate. Later in life, Leonardo became devoted to a teenaged aristocrat. This man inherited the bulk of Leonardo's estate, as well as his voluminous writing and sketches. *See also* ITALY.

LESBIAN CONTINUUM. In 1980, the poet, essayist, and Stanford University professor Adrienne Rich published an influential essay, "Compulsory Heterosexuality and Lesbian Existence." Addressed simultaneously to the feminist movement and a broader audience, Rich argues that lesbian existence properly understood is different from male homosexuality. Female-female relationships that are non-erotic but still have deep emotional resonance are part of a "lesbian continuum." She develops this argument in part to show heterosexuality as a political institution maintained by an ideological superstructure, media portrayals, and social norms. She also wants to overcome divisions between feminist and lesbian movements, implying that heterosexual feminists could see themselves in some sense as lesbians and overtly arguing that lesbianism should be seen as a source of knowledge and insight into the power relations in a patriarchal society that mandates heterosexuality in order to control women. Others, such as the important lesbian historian Lillian Faderman, have adopted similar positions, contending that non-sexual yet deeply committed female-female relationships should be seen as "lesbian."

Some have been critical of the idea of a lesbian continuum. For them, Rich's position takes the sexual component out of female homosexuality. From this viewpoint, she is intent upon wedding feminism and lesbianism, rather than exploring the affectionate and erotic aspects of female same-sex desire apart from its political implications. *See also* BOSTON MARRIAGE; LITERATURE, LESBIAN.

LITERATURE, HOMOSEXUAL MALE. The history and scope of male same-sex-oriented literature are immense. They extend more than two and a half millennia and across a broad range of cultures. Authors have explored homoerotic themes in every literary genre, including poetry, novels, plays, and philosophical treatises.

In **ancient Greece**, lyric poetry as far back as the seventh century B.C.E. discussed homosexuality. As far as work that is extant, the two most significant authors are Theognis and Pindar. While the work ascribed to Theognis may have been the product of more than one person, it is a classic treatment of the practice of **pederasty** as a form of ennobling a youth's character. The author(s) dedicates many of the poems to a youth, Cyrnus, and counsels him in social and moral norms appropriate to a future aristocrat. Pindar wrote many poems about the beauty of young athletes and the benefits of a pederastic relationship for young men. A number of Hellenistic poets wrote poetry with homosexual themes. Callimachus, from North Africa, wrote about his attraction to selective youths; Theocritus of Syracuse also explored pederasty and was an early bucolic poet. The work of a number of Athenian and Hellenistic authors shows that the older man–younger boy cultural ideal was likely not always adhered to in practice.

In **ancient Rome**, references to the passive or penetrated role in male-male sex acts were commonly made as accusations. There are some exceptions to this norm of portraying male-male relations as the expression of power and force, rather than affection, and the generally negative treatment of homosexual relations. Albius Tibullus primarily wrote verse about heterosexual love, but he wrote a series of poems about his affection for a boy, Marathus. Most notably, a section of Virgil's most famous work, the *Aeneid*, focuses on the same-sex relationship between Nisus and the youth Euryalus.

While historical accounts of same-sex love in **ancient China** go back to at least the sixth century B.C.E., literary discussions do not appear until centuries later. In the third century C.E., two of the Seven Sages of the Bamboo Grove, a renowned group of nonconformist writers, had a love affair. Xi Kang and Ruan Ji were both bohemian poets and the latter wrote about same-sex love. Bo Xingjian authored an eighth-century work that combined science and literary aspects in its frank although often metaphorical discussions of sexuality. It is sometimes translated as *Poetical Essay on the Supreme Joy of the Sexual Union of Yin and Yang and Heaven and Earth*, and sections of it discuss same-sex love both in Chinese history and as a personal attribute and quality of character.

For centuries, the Islamic world had a tradition of literary writing praising same-sex affection. Given **Islam**'s complicated but ultimately negative view of homosexual attraction and acts, much of the poetry and stories conjoin praise of a youth's beauty with protestations of the chastity of the affection. The scope of the tradition is immense, spanning from Muslim areas of India to Afghanistan, Persia, Turkey during the reign of the Ottomans, Baghdad and Damascus, across to North Africa. The greatest flowering of Islamic homoerotic writing, particularly in poetry, was in **Spain** from the 9th century to the 15th. A smaller tradition of Hebrew homoerotic poetry also flourished during this period.

Pre-Meiji **Japan**'s literature is rife with stories about same-sex love. In a story from the eighth century, two male courtiers loved each other deeply and were buried in the same tomb. There were expressions of homosexual love in poetry. In the most famous literary work of early Japan, *The Tale of Genji*, there is a scene in which Prince Genji is turned down by a woman he has pursued so he turns to her younger brother and seduces him instead. Lady Murasaki wrote this sprawling epic in the early 11th century. After the introduction of Zen Buddhism in the 13th century, monks wrote poems and stories that told of love between men, especially between monks and their acolytes. The poets wrote in Chinese, however, reflecting the deep influence of that culture on Japan. The master-apprentice theme carried over into tales of samurai and the young warriors who studied under them, mostly from the 15th through the 17th centuries.

The conversion of much of the West to **Christianity** made the literary expression of same-sex love more difficult. From the time of the conversion of the Roman Empire to Christianity up to the 20th century, literary discussions of homosexuality in the West are typically negative or are often coded if they are more ambiguous or supportive. In the late 11th and 12th centuries, a small group of poets often wrote in frankly sensual terms. Yet the authors, such as Marbod of Rennes, either adopted a critical tone toward such same-sex desire or used literary devices to distance themselves from what their work clearly implied. Writers who overtly and sympathetically described same-sex relations were few. Often they paid a high price for their candor, as was the case with the 17th-century French poet **Théophile de Viau**. More typical are works like Christopher Marlowe's poetry and play *Edward II*, with their allusions to classical figures known for their same-sex loves, and scenes suggestive of homosexual desire. Similarly, Shakespeare's sonnets clearly express a deep, consuming passion for a younger man, but in language that is dense and sometimes ambiguous. Pornographic literature, however, was more forthright in its exploration of homosexuality. Some prominent figures authored such works, such as the Frenchman Mirabeau, whose novels depicted male and female homosexual acts. The Marquis de Sade is perhaps the most important person in the tradition of European pornographic literature. His works often depict male-male sexuality, although often as part of a larger tableau wherein the characters are bisexual or, more accurately, omnisexual with unfettered desire.

The French government's passage of the **Code Napoléon** in the early 19th century partially liberated literature in that country as far as its portrayal of same-sex relations. Honoré de Balzac had a homosexual character, Vautrin, recur in several of his novels, such as *Le Père Goriot*. Subsequently, Théophile Gautier and Gustave Flaubert also portrayed homoerotic situations and relationships. The former, in his novel *Mademoiselle de Maupin*, lays out a proto–**social constructionist** understanding of gender and sexuality. In the latter 19th century, Paul Verlaine wrote overtly homoerotic poetry, some of which was co-authored with Arthur Rimbaud. The two had a tumultuous love affair. In contrast, 19th-century British literature notably lacks in overtly homosexual characters, even though there are many with ambiguous gender and sexuality. Even **Oscar Wilde** used literary devices to render his gay themes oblique. In the **United States**, **Walt Whitman**'s *Leaves of Grass* celebrated the "love of comrades," the beauty of the human form, and sensuality, in a combination that some found scandalous and others liberating. Yet the lack of clear homosexual identity or role in his cultural milieu made the poetry merely provocative rather than overtly homoerotic, probably even to Whitman himself.

One exceptional literary work, Marcel Proust's *À la recherche du temps perdu* (often translated as *Remembrance of Things Past*), has the exploration of the psychology of same-sex attraction as one of its central themes. Its volumes were originally published from 1913 to 1927. Many find the novel homophobic, although others find its treatment more evenhanded, especially given the historical context in which Proust was writing. Jean Cocteau also portrayed homosexuals as narcissistic and same-sex attraction as frequently involving a troubled mother-son relationship.

Literary treatments in the West during the post–World War II era are marked by a different tone, with homosexual characters often shown in a more positive light and sometimes protesting against mistreatment. Gore Vidal's *The City and the Pillar* has a character argue passionately for **coming out**, then admitting that he does not have the courage to do so in his own life. James Baldwin was one of the most influential black authors in the postwar era. His novel *Giovanni's Room* contains a protagonist who is deeply ambivalent about his homosexuality, which almost certainly reflects Baldwin's own perspective. Yet its warmth and plea for persons to embrace love, regardless of the sex of the one they love, ultimately makes the novel a moving piece of gay literature, especially in the United States during **McCarthyism**. In an earlier story, "**Outing**," Baldwin portrays two boys realizing their homosexuality.

In contrast, the rise of totalitarian governments ended some homosexual literary traditions. In **China**, the Communist government repressed homosexuality in general and it viewed literary works as a way to advance ideological goals. To this day, public discussion of homosexuality, including in literary works, risks censorship. In contrast, a number of writers in Taiwan have published works since the 1980s that involve homosexual themes.

Russia had a brief flowering of homosexual literature in the early 20th century, such as with the work of Mikhail Kuzmin. As in China, the Communist Party that took over Russia promised sexual liberation but then harshly repressed same-sex behavior. In the 1970s, a few writers began testing the limits by circulating their gay-themed work among friends and associates. One such poet, Gennady Trifonov, spent years in jail for this. The opening up of Russian society in the 1980s and 1990s permitted the republication of Kuzmin's work and those of samizdat gay writers, such as Yevgeny Kharitonov. A new generation of gay authors has appeared on the Russian literary scene over the past decade, although they often downplay overt homosexuality and publish in marginal presses. Nikolas Koro is one example. Also, expatriate Russians play a large role in Russian gay literature.

In the United States, the 1970s witnessed a proliferation of gay fiction that was marked by a greater range of styles and often had significant literary merit. Andrew Holleran's *Dancer from the Dance* portrayed denizens of discos and Fire Island; similarly, **Larry Kramer**'s *Faggots* described a gay scene where sex was easy to find but love was not. Vladimir Nabokov singled out Edmund White, author of *Nocturnes for the King of Naples*, as a great American prose craftsman. All three novels were published in 1978.

The **human immunodeficiency virus/acquired immunodeficiency syndrome** (HIV/AIDS) epidemic altered gay literature profoundly beginning in the 1980s, especially in the developed world since it was there that the disease disproportionately struck men who have sex with men. Much of the significant literary output of the past quarter century by gay authors has touched on AIDS. While the disease has inspired a lot of literature that is marred by self-pity or stereotyping, such as gay men as sexual predators, the best works are deeply moving and capable of speaking to traumatized gay communities while also addressing a heterosexual world that has drifted between indifference and hostility in the face of the crisis. In the United States, the plays of Tony Kushner and Larry Kramer stand out, as does Paul Monette's memoir *Borrowed Time*. In **France**, Hervé Guibert's novel *À l'ami qui ne m'a pas sauvé la vie* (*To the Friend Who Did Not Save My Life*) has a character who is a thinly veiled **Michel Foucault** during his final days of fighting the disease. The British poet Thom Gunn has written about AIDS, such as in *The Man with Night Sweats*.

Some contemporary writers have chosen not to write about HIV/AIDS. Instead, they explore the pre-AIDS era, such as Allen Gurganus or Felice Picano's *Like People in History*. Others write lighter, more comic pieces. David Sedaris is one example, although his work is not really literary in nature. *See also* GANYMEDE; PLATO.

LITERATURE, LESBIAN. While not as vast as male same-sex-oriented literature, the history and breadth of female same-sex-oriented literature are still large, extending from **Sappho** in **ancient Greece** to an explosion of recent novels, poetry, plays, and memoirs. In contrast to **homosexual (male) literature**, writings about lesbianism have often been written by the opposite sex. Such male-authored works typically mean to either titillate, denigrate, or sometimes both. It was not until the 20th century that lesbians gained enough independence and prominence to craft a literary tradition that consistently affirmed their status and identity, although there was an earlier European tradition that affirmed female-female friendship and love.

Aside from Sappho, the only other female poet from ancient Greece that wrote verse implying same-sex relations was Nossis. Writing during the Hellenistic period, she often focused on female beauty and spoke of herself as a devotee of Sappho, although her extant poems are not overtly lesbian. Some male authors in **ancient Rome** wrote about lesbianism, sometimes referring to the female initiator as a "**tribade**," but the descriptions were typically negative. A few extant literary works from medieval **Europe** refer to female-female love. Some romances have women falling in love with a woman passing as a man, although the relationship ends with the discovery of the disguised woman's true identity or with divine intercession that turns her into a man. There is also a 13th-century French love poem from one woman, Bieris de Romans, to another, a "Lady Maria."

In 16th-century **France**, the libertine tradition portrayed female-female love as an amusing prelude to heterosexual lovemaking, or a nonthreatening and temporary diversion from it. Yet such tolerance did not extend broadly in French society. Montaigne, in his *Travel Journal*, tells of a woman who cross-dressed, married another woman, and then was discovered. She was executed for her crime.

During the Renaissance, Europe had many regions where passionate same-sex friendship was idealized, although typically such relationships were understood as non-sexual in nature. Although first written about among men, 17th-century France and England provide multiple examples of romantic friendship in literature. The poetry of Katherine Philips is the most notable. In Germany, Bettina von Armin's mid-19th century novel *Die Günderode* also had a passionate friendship at its center. Some authors in the **United States** also explored works in this vein in the 1800s, such as Sarah Orne Jewett. The tradition of female-female romantic friendship continued as a literary and social ideal well into the late 19th century in the West.

In 17th-century **China**, increased population density on the coasts and greater affluence caused a growth in literary output. While most authors ignored female-female relations, there was a group of upper-class women who wrote autobiographical poetry that referred to intense feelings for female friends, as well as appreciation of their physical beauty. This poetry used classical styles of verse and integrated traditional heterosexual romantic expressions into their praises of same-sex affections and love. In the same century in **Latin America**, a nun named Sor Juana Inés de la Cruz dedicated her love poems to other women. Her brief work "Divina Lysi mía" ("My Divine Lysi") is a moving, passionate poem to a beautiful woman by whom the author wishes to be possessed.

Some of the most famous 19th-century French novelists put lesbian characters into their novels. Balzac, anticipating a device later used by Virginia Woolf and Ursula LeGuin, has a character changing gender in his *Seraphita*. George Sand, in *Gabriel*, explores similar territory. Emile Zola has lesbian and bisexual characters in several of his novels. Guy de Maupassant has lesbian couples in a short story that is notable for its sympathetic treatment of same-sex attraction. In poetry, Baudelaire and Verlaine also discuss lesbianism, the former quite critically. Verlaine himself was homosexual and that likely contributed to his accepting portrayal of female same-sex love and attraction. Similarly, one of the foremost 19th-century U.S. novelists, Henry James, provided what is likely the most forthright treatment of lesbianism from that era in *The Bostonians*.

In the 20th century, many countries repressed same-sex-oriented literature. Sometimes the repression was formal, legal, and systematic, which prevented even coded expressions of same-sex relationships or eroticism. For decades, that was the case in China and the Soviet Union, even though in the latter case the gifted novelist Vasily Grossman discussed lesbian relationships in *Forever Flowing*. In the past two decades, Taiwan has witnessed the growth of a lesbian writers' movement, with Hong Ling, Chen Xue, and Qiu Miaojin as the leading figures.

In some of the West, however, lesbian literature flowered as the 20th century progressed. The women's movement, increased political clout with the advent of the vote, greater access to education and thus higher literacy levels, and some degree of economic independence all contributed to the growth of lesbian fiction by female authors. For decades, however, the portrayal of lesbians, even by female authors, often continued the preceding centuries' norms by presenting joyless women who are tortured by their attraction to other women. Perhaps the most famous lesbian novel of the first half of the 20th century, **Radclyffe Hall**'s *The Well of Loneliness*, has a main character, a woman named Stephen, who is largely unhappy and ultimately gives up her true love so that the object of her affections can find happiness in the arms of a man.

In contrast to the negative portrayal in British and, later, American fiction, Paris attracted a group of writers in the first decades of the 20th century that put forward various portraits of lesbian relationships. Key figures in that group were **Gertrude Stein**, Natalie Barney, Colette, Renée Vivien (Pauline Mary Tarn), and Djuna Barnes. Stein's work is still often read today and it helped to usher in modernist writing, but Barnes' novels also have literary merit and she described this circle of artists in *The Ladies' Almanack*. Another expatriate American lesbian writer, H. D., contributed to the modernist movement in poetry. In Germany, the late 19th- and early 20th-century homosexual rights movement influenced some lesbian authors. Aimée Duc, in her turn-of-the-century novel *Sin des frauen? (Are These Women?)*, presented a positive lesbian, feminist identity. Lesbian literature flowered during the Weimar Republic, led by authors such as Christa Winsloe, Maria Saeur von Peteani, and Anna Elisabet Weirauch. The rise of **National Socialism**, however, ended the homosexual rights movement in Germany and set the nascent lesbian literary movement back. For decades, female authors there approached lesbian themes elliptically.

In postwar America, lesbianism was most frequently addressed in cheap and sensationalist pulp fiction. Often written to arouse male readers, the stories contained recurring elements designed to condemn the very sexuality upon which they focused. At the end of novels, marriage converted women to heterosexuality, or tragic events exposed the folly of female-female love. Still, magazines founded by **homophile movement** groups published stories with happy endings. In **Canada**, the author Jane Rule published novels that avoided cheap sensationalism in favor of realistic characters, including lesbians who embodied positive morals. Although Rule continued to write for decades, her 1964 work *Desert of the Heart* is still regarded as the pinnacle of her achievement. It was made into a movie in the 1980s.

The post-**Stonewall** era ushered in a newfound candor and self-affirmation in lesbian literature. In the United States, Rita Mae Brown's *Rubyfruit Jungle* was a mainstream success in the 1970s. Audre Lorde, a black feminist poet, wrote openly about her homosexuality and criticized the mainstream feminist movement for marginalizing women of color. The development of gay and lesbian studies, and lesbian literary criticism, led to the rediscovery of previous authors and the appropriation of them as lesbian-feminist authors. The work of historians and critics such as Lillian Faderman has permanently changed how figures such as Jewett and Stein are read. While the growth of a lesbian segment in the American publishing industry was slower than that for gay male fiction, it is now well established. Genre fiction, such as detective novels, romance, science fiction, and erotica, does especially well.

Just as the post-Stonewall movement was international in scope, so too were the changes in lesbian literature. Starting in the 1970s, lesbian poets in Latin America explored love and eroticism openly and have generally played a more prominent role than fiction authors have. Leading figures include Cristina Peri Rossi from Uruguay, Magaly Alabau of Cuba, and Sabina Berman of Mexico. Just as in the United States, the fast rise of lesbian and feminist theory and criticism in France and Germany strongly influenced literary fashion in the 1970s and 1980s. Monique Wittig and Hélène Cixous, both French theorists and literary authors, were leading figures. Sarah Waters, a British novelist, authored a number of well-regarded historical novels. In 2002, she published *Fingersmith*, which was shortlisted for the Booker prize. The post-Stonewall era has also seen the growth of an infrastructure aiding lesbian literature, with bookstores and literary magazines supporting and publishing authors. France's first lesbian publishing company was founded in 1985, Finland's in 1992. *See also* LESBIAN CONTINUUM; NAVRATILOVA, MARTINA.

LOG CABIN REPUBLICANS. Founded in California in the late 1970s, the Log Cabin Republicans is composed of Republicans who lobby their party to support equal rights for gays and lesbians. The group has gained prominence since the mid-1990s and presidential candidate treatment of the group has come to stand as a barometer of their support for gay rights in general. Senator Bob Dole, when running for president, returned the group's donation. During his 2008 campaign, Senator John McCain met privately with representatives from the group. In general, the influence of the anti-gay **religious right** strongly outweighs that of the Log Cabin Republicans in the party. The group's name is a reference to the first Republican president, Abraham Lincoln, who was born in a log cabin.

– M –

MANUAL V. DAY **(1962).** In 1960, **United States** postal censors seized hundreds of copies of three magazines that were ostensibly for bodybuilders, but mainly featured pictures of scantily clad, muscular young men. The seizure of *MANual*, *Trim*, and *Grecian Guild Pictorial* ultimately resulted in *Manual Enterprises Inc. v. J. Edward Day, postmaster general of the United States*. The authorities secured a conviction, but the defense appealed all the way to the Supreme Court. There the majority ruled in favor of the defense. The majority did not stand behind a single opinion; instead, there were three different rationales, and only one signed majority opinion. Justice John Harlan's concurring opinion affirmed a single standard of obscenity. He argued that whether photographs or text were aimed at promoting homosexual or heterosexual desire should be irrelevant, from a constitutional perspective. The Court's decision led to *MANual* becoming more explicit in its photographs and more overtly homosexual. More significantly, the decision helped to spur those interested in publishing homosexual-themed material in general.

MARRIAGE. *See* SAME-SEX MARRIAGE.

MATTACHINE SOCIETY. Formed in the early 1950s in Southern California, the Mattachine Society was the first and most prominent group in the **homophile movement**. According to its principal founder, **Henry Hay**, the name of the group came from a medieval French society of unmarried men who performed dances while wearing masks. Hay chose the name to emphasize that homosexuals were forced, in effect, to wear masks, yet were capable of community building. Their initial goals were striking, especially considering the social and political context of the time. The founders of the Mattachine Society, several of which had Communist backgrounds, sought to raise the consciousness of homosexual men as an oppressed group.

Hay and others believed that such awareness would spur homosexual men to organize to fight oppression. Their central political objective was to repeal **anti-sodomy laws**, since in their view as long as those were on the books, homosexuals would always be oppressed in their sexuality and would continue to be second-class citizens.

The initial structure envisioned for the Mattachine Society was similar to that of other underground, radical leftist groups: individual cells, with only one or two members of each cell knowing anyone else from another cell, with a top-down hierarchy imposed upon the entire structure. The founders of the society believed this secretive approach was necessary due to what they saw as the rise of Fascism in the **United States** during **McCarthyism**.

In 1952, police charged one of the founders, **Dale Jennings**, with lewd conduct. The Mattachine Society fought the charge, alleging entrapment and **police harassment**, and in the process increased the society's prominence and membership significantly. New chapters were established and the group expanded into northern California. By 1953 the society estimated that it had more than 2,000 members and began to publish a magazine, *ONE*, that, while formally independent from the Mattachines, was primarily directed by members of the society. By this point, the Communist background of most of the founders was an increasing liability, both for the group and the individual leaders. Therefore, in 1953, the society held a convention that abolished the secretive structure and the founders relinquished control. A new set of leaders emerged and the society quickly changed direction away from a leftist analysis of society, a focus upon collective action, and the fight against police harassment. Instead, they emphasized the similarities between homosexuals and heterosexuals, and they believed that scientific and medical experts would help integrate them into society. The initial effect of this move to a moderate and even quiescent politics was a decline in membership. In the mid-1950s, however, the slide in numbers halted and the group began publishing its own magazine, the *Mattachine Review*, and established chapters in New York and Chicago.

The society consistently suffered from tensions in its relations with the **Daughters of Bilitis**, the leading female homosexual group of the time. Relations between the two almost entirely broke down in the early 1960s. At the same time, conflict within the society itself led to the dissolution of the national structure in 1961. That, in turn, led to the collapse of the Denver and Boston chapters.

In November 1961, **Frank Kameny** founded the Washington, D.C., chapter. Kameny had fought the federal government for several years over his dismissal in 1957 as a civilian employee of the U.S. Army. He was dismissive of the traditional Mattachine approach of education, non-confrontation, and reliance on experts. The Washington chapter engaged in letter-writing campaigns and lobbying, as well as supporting litigation to overturn the ban against employment of homosexuals by the federal government. They also worked to change the American Civil Liberties Union (ACLU) stand on homosexuality. In 1957, the ACLU laid out as policy that anti-sodomy laws and the ban on federal employment of homosexuals were constitutional. In 1964, the ACLU repudiated its stance on anti-sodomy laws, arguing that private consensual sex acts are not under the state's legitimate purview. The Washington chapter's activist approach slowly spread through other chapters, though not without substantial resistance from the old guard. The gay rights movement radicalized in the wake of **Stonewall**, however, and the Mattachine Society fell apart soon afterward. *See also* GAY LIBERATION FRONT; *ONE, INC. V. OLESEN*; SOCIETY FOR INDIVIDUAL RIGHTS.

MCCARTHYISM. In early 1950, a State Department official testified before the **United States** Congress that many government workers fired for moral turpitude were homosexual. The subsequent media and right-wing outcry led to a formal Senate investigation into the role homosexuals play in government. The investigation culminated in a report issued at the end of 1950, entitled "Employment of Homosexuals and Other Sex Perverts in Government."

The authors of the report argued that the federal government should not employ homosexuals. They put forward two lines of argument to justify this: homosexuals, they alleged, are morally weak, and the general social stigma attached to homosexuality made them uniquely prey to blackmailing. The authors also, surprisingly, used data from **Alfred Kinsey**'s report on sexuality. Since the Kinsey Report showed that homosexual sex is more prevalent than previously thought, and since homosexual men and women do not necessarily conform to the popular imagination's stereotypes of behavior and body type, the threat is much more widespread than previously believed.

The persecution of homosexual men and women continued throughout the McCarthy era. A variety of right-wing media figures denounced homosexuals as a threat to American morals and security. Dwight Eisenhower revised Harry Truman's loyalty program for federal employees to include "sexual perversion" as sufficient grounds for termination. Thousands of persons were either fired or, due to background checks, never hired because of their homosexuality. State governments and the military also increased their surveillance and termination efforts. In 1975, the Civil Service Commission stated that it would no longer enforce the ban against gays and lesbians in federal employment. *See also* CANADA; GAY BASHING; HAY, HENRY; HOMOPHILE MOVEMENT; IMMIGRATION AND NATURALIZATION LAW; LITERATURE, HOMOSEXUAL MALE; MATTACHINE SOCIETY; POLICE HARASSMENT; *WASHINGTON CONFIDENTIAL.*

MEDICAL MODEL OF HOMOSEXUALITY. In contrast to the medieval era, which understood illness and sexual behavior through a theological framework, the modern era has groped for more naturalistic explanations. The medical model of homosexuality posits that same-sex attraction is a form of mental illness, rather than a sin. Proponents of this view have disagreed over the causes of homosexuality, whether "**reparative therapy**" is a genuine option, and if so, what form(s) of therapy work best.

During the **Enlightenment**, some medical writers focused on the dangers of masturbation. In a treatise published in 1766, Samuel Tissot argued that masturbation, especially among women, caused same-sex attraction. Tissot and others' writings proved influential for decades. In the middle of the 19th century, attention turned from masturbation to congenital accounts of the **etiology** of homosexuality. **Karl Heinrich Ulrichs** argued that in utero developmental factors caused homosexuality, thereby rejecting the central point of the medical model, arguing that same-sex love was benign and natural for those congenitally disposed to it.

Medical and legal discussions of homosexuality reflected the growing influence of the Darwinian account of evolution in the late

19th century. Richard von Krafft-Ebing, author of the influential *Psychopathia Sexualis*, saw homosexuality primarily as gender role reversal and argued that it signified "degeneracy," a backward movement in evolution. This speculation about homosexuality, heredity, and mental illness was widespread. From the 1880s well into the 20th century, medical figures from across **Europe**, including **Russia**, to the **United States** and **Latin America** argued against one another within this common framework. A number of authors contended that since, in their view, homosexuality is congenital, it was inappropriate to criminalize it. Krafft-Ebing, for instance, argued that while same-sex attraction was a form of pathology, **Germany** still should repeal Paragraph 175, its **anti-sodomy law**. Yet this focus on heredity and homosexuality was congenial to eugenicist thinking as well. Some argued that reproduction by degenerates needed to be prevented and therefore forced sterilization was appropriate. The eugenics movement led a number of countries, such as Denmark, and many U.S. states, such as Michigan, to castrate thousands of persons, including homosexuals. The most extreme form of this line of thinking culminated in calls for genocide. The leaders of the German **National Socialist** movement pursued such an agenda, but medical and cultural figures in the United States and elsewhere made similar statements.

After World War II, the focus turned to psychological explanations and possible treatments for same-sex attraction. Even though **Sigmund Freud**, the father of psychoanalysis, did not consider homosexuality an illness, many of his followers did. Three of the most influential psychiatrists arguing that homosexuality is pathological were Sandor Rado, Irving Bieber, and Charles Socarides. For them, same-sex attraction reflects an unconscious fear of the opposite sex. They argued that problematic family dynamics lay behind such attractions: An overly attached and "seductive" mother, combined with a distant father, causes homosexuality in men. A domineering and guilt-inducing mother, again in conjunction with a distant father, causes lesbianism. Socarides, in particular, argued that homosexuality results from the worst forms of mental pathology, such as paranoid schizophrenia. Psychiatrists who accepted this line of thinking that homosexuality is sickness contended that analysis could often cure the pathology. Some claimed that they were able to make more than one-half of their gay patients straight.

The modern countermovement against the medical model of homosexuality gained force in the 1940s and 1950s, largely propelled by the work of **Alfred Kinsey** and **Evelyn Hooker**. The view that homosexuality is not an expression of mental illness became the majority perspective among American psychiatrists by the late 1960s and 1970s. Mainstream scientists and medical practitioners in the contemporary developed world have largely abandoned the medical model. In contrast, defenders of reparative therapy, often backed by groups associated with the **religious right**, finance studies that purport to show that homosexuality is a curable illness. Many researchers, however, have raised serious questions about the methodology used in those studies. *See also* AMERICAN PSYCHIATRIC ASSOCIATION; ELLIS, HAVELOCK; IMMIGRATION AND NATURALIZATION LAW; SODOMITE; *WISSENSCHAFTLICH-HUMANITÄRES KOMITEE*/ SCIENTIFIC-HUMANITARIAN COMMITTEE.

METROPOLITAN COMMUNITY CHURCH (MCC). In 1968, the Reverend Troy Perry founded the Metropolitan Community Church in Los Angeles. His Pentecostal church had defrocked Perry years earlier due to his homosexuality. His goal in establishing the MCC was to have a church that was open and affirming of gays and lesbians. Others soon established chapters around the country. The MCC now has hundreds of congregations spread across more than a score of countries. The church grants local communities of worship a large degree of autonomy, as long as each abides by core theological tenets in Christianity, sexual equality, and inclusion of gays and lesbians. A good number of MCC pastors are gays and lesbians. MCC churches frequently conduct **same-sex marriage** ceremonies. *See also* CHRISTIANITY; FALWELL, JERRY, SR.

MICHELANGELO (1475–1564). Raised in Florence, Michelangelo was one of the greatest artists of the Renaissance, alongside Botticelli and **Leonardo da Vinci**. Some of his sculptures are universally recognized as masterpieces, such as the *Pietà* and the *David*. He was also a remarkable painter, his work including the famous ceiling on the Sistine Chapel.

Michelangelo had a strong attraction to young men. A wealth of letters and poems attest to that, although it must also be noted that he frequently proclaimed the chastity of his relationships. In his artist's studio, he employed male youths, some of which likely served as models for nudes that can be seen in some of his works, including in the Sistine Chapel. In 1532, he met a young nobleman, Tommaso de' Cavalieri, and formed a deep bond that lasted for the rest of Michelangelo's life. There has been substantial debate over whether Michelangelo consummated this or any other emotional and erotic attachment. Some contend that given the strongly anti-homosexual currents within the Florence of his day, as well as his devout Catholicism, it is unlikely that Michelangelo had physical relations with the young men whose beauty and character he deeply admired. Others believe that he did, but likely stopped such relations in his middle age. Yet in a letter written by Cavalieri to Michelangelo, when the latter was in his 50s, Cavalieri says that he could never make love to anyone but Michelangelo. *See also* GANYMEDE; ITALY; SOCIAL CONSTRUCTIONISM.

MIDDLE EAST. There are few references to homosexuality in the ancient Middle East prior to the spread of Hellenistic influences to the region in the third and fourth centuries B.C.E. The exceptions include the laws of Middle Assyria (13th century B.C.E. in Mesopotamia) that had severe punishments for men who raped their social equals or who falsely accused another man of taking the passive role in homosexual sex. The laws of Zoroastrianism in ancient Persia were punitive toward homosexual sex. After the time of Alexander the Great, however, the scope of references broadens considerably. Under the laws of **ancient Rome**, homosexuality was legal until the sixth century C.E.

The **Koran**, composed in the seventh century, does mention and condemn homosexuality, but not at length or with any specific penalty. The hadith, which are the sayings attributed to the prophet Mohammed and collected (or forged) after his death, are much stronger in their statements against homosexuality. The hadith even recommend death by stoning for those caught in same-sex sex acts. Still, a literature that was full of discussions of same-sex love flourished in the Middle East for centuries. From the eighth century onward, there are lyric poems and odes to male and female homosexual relations and desires. The understanding of sexuality and the structuring of roles are similar to that in **ancient Greece**. For example, there is no word for, or concept similar to, the current dichotomy of heterosexual/homosexual. Many poets wrote from the perspective of someone who is attracted to both sexes, or discussed such a person. The idealized male same-sex relationship involved an older man and a younger male on the verge of getting his beard.

The sharp contrast between an **Islamic** legal tradition with strictures against sex acts outside of marriage, especially in regard to anal sex between men, and the sheer wealth of literature that praises same-sex love obviously creates difficulties in cultural interpretation. Some scholars argue that what was stigmatized was the passive role in male same-sex encounters. This contention often emphasizes the role of status in Arab society. Others argue that while homoerotic affection was pervasive and unproblematic, corresponding sex acts were seen as immoral. Many poems do proclaim the chastity of the relationship, even while noting the beauty of the beloved's physique or eyes. What is certain is that Arab travelers to Europe, all the way into the 19th century, found it remarkable that Europeans did not engage in same-sex courtship.

In the contemporary Middle East, the situation is difficult for persons attracted to those of the same sex. Public opinion generally sees same-sex sexuality as un-Islamic and unnatural. It is also often perceived as a specifically Western type of perversion and hence as something to be attacked in the name of "Arab purity" or "Islamic values." The regional norm is to force women who are attracted to women to enter into a heterosexual marriage; some families do the same to homosexual men. Even discussion of homosexuality is uncommon. In contrast to the dominant understanding in the West today, the Arab world is not typically concerned with sexual identity. Sex acts with persons of the same gender are problematic and the notion that some persons have a "gay" identity is uncommon. Instead, homosexuality is more often seen as an intentionally perverse choice, or as the result of mental illness. Often even those who are attracted to persons of the same sex do not self-identify as gay or lesbian.

Israel and Lebanon, especially Beirut, are more open and tolerant, relative to other Middle Eastern countries. In Israel, openly gay and lesbian citizens serve in the military. In 2008, Israel's attorney general ruled that gay couples could jointly adopt children. Lebanon has the only gay rights group that is active in an Arab country. Helem, or "dream" in Arabic, is an acronym for *Himaya Lubnaniyya lil-Mithliyyin* (Lebanese Protection for Homosexuals). It advocates for equal rights, including for the repeal of Lebanon's **anti-sodomy laws**, as well as providing health and **human immunodeficiency virus/acquired immunodeficiency syndrome** (HIV/AIDS) information. Helem has connections abroad, from which it draws financial and technical support.

Other Middle Eastern countries are generally more repressive of homosexuality, especially in the public sphere. For example, in 2004 a Human Rights Watch report documented an Egyptian crackdown on homosexual men. Egyptian authorities jailed, harassed, and even tortured scores of men. The authorities then released them without charges. In 2008, a similar crackdown on HIV-positive men was reported. While there has not been a similar campaign against lesbians, it is still an intolerant and lonely situation for them. Other countries in the region are also deeply repressive toward those who engage in same-sex sexual acts. In Saudi Arabia, sodomy is punishable by death, although the law is infrequently used. Jailings and **police harassment**, however, are more common. In such places, however, there is still an underground scene complete with parties, coded behavior in public, and cautious Internet chat rooms. Iran stands out as one of the worst countries in its treatment of lesbians. Female same-sex relations are punishable by the death penalty. There are multiple reports of such executions being performed, though these are often difficult to confirm. *See also* AGE OF CONSENT LAWS; CLOSET, THE; GAY BASHING; JUDAISM; MILITARY SERVICE; SAME-SEX MARRIAGE.

MILITARY SERVICE. In pre-Christian **Europe**, men who desired other men often served in the militaries of various city-states, including as leaders or prominent heroes. The foremost example of this is undoubtedly the **Sacred Band of Thebes**. Elis, in **ancient Greece**, would post lover and beloved side by side in units. It is also reasonable to infer from the historical evidence that there was a significant degree of homoeroticism in the ancient Spartan military. Centuries later in feudal **Japan**, homoeroticism functioned in an analogous manner among samurai. The (probably idealized) cultural norm was that an older samurai and an apprentice warrior were, as lovers, to spur one another to greater feats of courage and honor. Furthermore, the samurai was to aid in the education of his beloved apprentice.

In Christian Europe, however, the situation was markedly different. Generally, European states and principalities criminalized same-sex sex acts, which had the effect of preventing men who openly desired other men from serving, or at least from being open with their desires. It was only after the rise to prominence of the idea of homosexuals as a category or type that militaries acted to ban a whole class of persons. For instance, prior to World War II the **United States** military did not ban homosexuals. It simply had an **anti-sodomy law**. In World War II, however, the United States attempted to screen homosexual men from service. In October 1944, the military began trying to screen for lesbians.

Over the past two decades, many Western nations have changed policy and now allow gays and lesbians to serve in the military. **Great Britain**, for example, lifted its ban in 2000. All the Scandinavian countries allow gays to serve, as well as **Spain**, Switzerland, **Canada**, Israel, and others. The United States adopted the **"Don't Ask, Don't Tell"** policy in 1993, but in practice it has not functioned to lift the ban upon military service. In the **Middle East**, **China**, and much of **Africa**, gays and lesbians are banned from the military outright, or sodomy in general is punishable by jail or death. *See also* ASIA; FRANCE; GERMANY; HUMAN RIGHTS CAMPAIGN; ITALY; JUDAISM; KAMENY, FRANK; OUTING.

MILK, HARVEY (1930–1978). After living on the East Coast, Harvey Milk moved to San Francisco in the early 1970s. There he started a small business and began running for elected office. In 1977, he was elected to the San Francisco Board of Supervisors and thus became one of the first openly gay individuals elected to public office in the **United States**. The board, the equivalent of a city council, had begun electing representatives by district and Milk won a plurality of the vote in the Castro, the city's increasingly gay neighborhood. As a supervisor, Milk successfully pushed an **anti-discrimination law** that protected gays and lesbians in housing and employment. He also took a leading role in the fight against Proposition 6 (the **Briggs Initiative**), a statewide ballot proposition that would have banned out gays and lesbians from employment as teachers in public schools in California. Although polls showed early support for Proposition 6, Briggs' measure was ultimately defeated by a good margin.

Soon after the board passed the anti-discrimination measure, another supervisor, Dan White, entered city hall armed with a gun. He shot and killed the mayor and Milk, largely out of a sense of revenge. White was subsequently convicted on the lesser charge of voluntary manslaughter rather than murder, which set off riots at city hall and in the Castro. Milk had only served 11 months on the board. White later committed suicide.

Milk's reputation has only grown since his death. The 1984 film *The Times of Harvey Milk* won an Academy Award for best documentary. Milk's assassination and the ensuing trial were also the basis for a Broadway play and, in 1998, an opera. A New York City school designed as a safe zone for gay and lesbian youth was named in honor of Milk. In 2008, Gus Van Sant directed a film about Milk, with Sean Penn playing the gay rights activist.

MINE MARRIAGES. In the first half of the 20th century, older men in mines in southern **Africa** would sometimes take adolescent and post-adolescent boys as their "wives." In some locales, this form of relationship endured even longer. The relationship in many ways was mutually beneficial. The boy received protection in a rough environment in addition to some financial benefit, such as gifts. The man in turn had someone to help with domestic chores and sexual satisfaction. Sex usually involved intercrural sex, where the older man would place his penis between the boy's thighs, a form of sexual activity common to some tribes among adolescents too young to marry. The roles mirrored expectations about opposite-sex relations, as well as the age-structured nature of traditional tribes such as the Bantu. The boy was to remain clean shaven and otherwise try to look feminine, even to the point of sewing clothes in a way that gave the impression of breasts. Also, the older man exclusively had the sexually active role. Upon coming of age, perhaps in his mid-20s, the boy would announce that he was leaving the relationship and often would in turn seek a wife for himself. The social mores of the mines dictated that it was improper to deny the request. These relationships enjoyed widespread respect in the mines. Even white managers recognized them; couples frequently approached church ministers to perform marriage ceremonies.

Partners in mine marriages did not see themselves as homosexual in the modern sense, however. They did not self-identify as a distinct group defined by a specific sexual attraction. Also, anal sex between men brought disdain from other mine workers, as it generally did in Africa. Older partners in mine marriages sometimes had wives back in towns or rural villages; one still had to fulfill the social obligation to marry and have children.

MORAL MAJORITY. *See* FALWELL, JERRY, SR.; RELIGIOUS RIGHT.

– N –

***NATIONAL COALITION FOR GAY AND LESBIAN EQUALITY V. MINISTER OF JUSTICE* (1998).** In 1957, the apartheid government of South **Africa** passed an **anti-sodomy law**, the **Sexual Offenses Act**. The post-apartheid constitution of 1996 was the first in the world to include sexual orientation as a status protected against discrimination, whether by the government or private individuals. After the act went into effect, a broad coalition of gay and lesbian groups filed suit to invalidate all of South Africa's unnatural acts and anti-sodomy laws. The suit led to the case of *National Coalition for Gay and Lesbian Equality v. Minister of Justice*. In a unanimous decision, the Constitutional Court of South Africa agreed with the gay and lesbian coalition and struck down the Sexual Offenses Act and other contested laws. The court argued along two lines. First, the constitution has strong language in its human rights section that establishes equal citizenship, including in terms of sexual orientation. The anti-sodomy laws established unequal citizenship and thus were invalid. Second, the court also held that a right to privacy and general autonomy also forbade state interference in this private domain.

NATIONAL GAY AND LESBIAN TASK FORCE (NGLTF). In 1973, activists who split off from the **Gay Activists Alliance** formed a group that they initially called the National Gay Task Force. The group quickly epitomized the mainstream gay politics of the day, with heavy influence from the civil rights movement and a desire for a more institutionalized structure than liberationist groups, such as the **Gay Liberation Front**. By the end of the decade, the group had 10,000 members, most of which were white, middle-class males. In 1986, it changed its name to the National Gay and Lesbian Task Force. It is the oldest **United States** gay rights organization still in existence.

The NGLTF today is active across a broad spectrum of issues. It has lobbyists in Washington, D.C., files amicus curiae briefs in court cases important to gay and lesbian issues, and trains activists to work at the local level. The NGLTF works on behalf of passage, at all levels of government, of **anti-discrimination laws**, as well as **same-sex marriage** rights. It has a research arm, which provides analyses of everything from election results to public policy changes. It works against the "ex-gay" movement and is openly skeptical of **reparative therapy**. The NGLTF fights abstinence-only programs, arguing that they are ineffective at combating the spread of **human immunodeficiency virus/acquired immunodeficiency syndrome**. NGLTF also has broadened its mandate to include issues of racial and economic justice, in part as a means of working to forge a broader coalition of like-minded groups. *See also* KAMENY, FRANK.

NATIONAL SOCIALISM. The rise of Adolf Hitler to power in January 1933 immediately had a negative impact on homosexuals in **Germany**. In May of that year, Nazi storm troopers raided and trashed the building in Berlin that housed the *Wissenschaftlich-humanitäres Komitee* (Scientific-Humanitarian Committee), the Institute for Sexual Science, and the World League for Sexual Reform. These were three of the leading groups in the struggle to repeal Germany's **anti-sodomy law**. They also fought for women's rights and related causes. The Nazis then burned confiscated materials in a large public demonstration. What had once been an active and broad-based reform movement in Weimar Germany quickly ended.

Several leading Nazis were rumored to be homosexual. One of them, Ernst Roehm, led a faction that was believed to threaten Hitler's hold on power. Roehm was purged and later killed as part of the "Night of the Long Knives," which was Hitler's move on 29

June 1934 to rid his party of potential enemies to himself. Roehm's homosexuality was offered to the public as a rationale for his downfall, even though the motives were purely political. This public vilification of homosexuals as enemies of the state further strengthened homophobic attitudes. Furthermore, Heinrich Himmler, a man deeply hostile to homosexuality, consolidated his power in the wake of the Night of the Long Knives. In 1935, the Nazi Party made the provisions of the anti-sodomy law, Paragraph 175, even more severe and began a systematic attempt to repress all public expressions of homosexuality. The party systematically crushed the gay nightlife in Berlin and elsewhere that had developed during the Weimar regime. Estimates vary, but the Nazi regime arrested and convicted approximately 50,000 homosexuals, mostly men.

Researchers estimate that by the time the Nazi regime ended in 1945, it had placed 10,000 to 15,000 homosexuals in the concentration camps. They were identified by wearing a pink triangle, and most perished. There is evidence that homosexuals in the death camps had even lower chances of survival than did Jews. In 2000, the German government established a reparations fund to compensate victims of the Holocaust, including homosexuals. A Berlin monument to Jewish victims of the Holocaust was inaugurated in 2005; the government inaugurated a monument for homosexual victims in 2008. *See also* FRANCE; HIRSCHFELD, MAGNUS; JUDAISM; LITERATURE, LESBIAN; MEDICAL MODEL OF HOMOSEXUALITY; OUTING; REPARATIVE THERAPY.

NATURAL LAW. In contemporary Anglo-American countries, natural law theory provides the most common intellectual defense for the unequal legal and social treatment of gays and lesbians, which is one reason why it is a controversial theory. Although natural law has its roots in some of the philosophical works from **ancient Greece**, most notably those of **Plato** and **Aristotle**, **Thomas Aquinas** gave it its classic formulation. Today academics such as John Finnis and Robert George have resurrected and popularized the theory. Mainstream contemporary proponents of this position argue for anti-gay laws and public attitudes in order to discourage homosexuality.

Traditional natural law theory assumes a theistic account of the source of morality. That is, one cannot be an atheist or agnostic yet also accept traditional natural law theory. Yet natural law theory also holds that human practical reason shows that certain things are valuable in themselves, such as life, procreation, knowledge, and society, among others. General rules of right action follow from these goods. For example, natural law theorists emphasize monogamous, companionate marriage. Given natural law theory's deep roots in the Catholic tradition, it is unsurprising that they also argue that such married couples should aspire to reproduction and often criticize abortion and contraception.

Aquinas argued that only sex in the context of a loving marital union could be moral, and furthermore it had to be intercourse of a "generative" kind. That is, only heterosexual vaginal intercourse is morally permissible. He provided no real argument for this view. Contemporary natural law theorists provide a couple of different lines of defense for this argument. The first is that sex acts that involve homosexuality, heterosexual sodomy, or the use of contraception frustrate the purpose of the sex organs, which is reproduction. This argument, often called the "perverted faculty argument," is perhaps implicit in Aquinas. It has come under sharp attack, however, and the best recent defenders of the natural law approach are trying to move beyond it.

The second line of argument relies on an account of the human good that has marriage and personal integration as core components. Personal integration, in this view, is the idea that humans, as agents, need to have integration between their intentions as agents and their embodied selves. On this account, sodomy is the immoral use of another's body as a means to sensual gratification, which thus causes "dis-integration" of the self. To the counterargument that not all instances of sodomy involve the mere use of another (or one's self), natural law theorists respond that a marriage open to procreation is the only permissible context in which to express sexuality. A happy marriage is, for natural law theorists, one of the highest human goods, along with the children such a marriage may produce. In order to justify their opposition to homosexual sex, natural law theorists must emphasize procreation. If, for example, they were to place love and mutual support for human flourishing at the center, it is clear that many same-sex couples would meet this standard. Hence, by the lights of natural theory itself, their sex acts would be morally just.

When pressed on these arguments, natural law theorists appear to waver. When defending their exclusion of same-sex couples from even the possibility of moral sex, they put forward an account of sexuality that seems crudely reductive, emphasizing procreation to the point where literally a male orgasm anywhere except in the vagina of one's loving spouse is impermissible. Then, when accused of being reductive, they move back to a broader ideal of marriage as an essential companionate relationship with affection and mutual support.

Natural law theory, at present, has made significant concessions to mainstream contemporary political thought and practice. For example, most such theorists maintain that they accept the separation of church and state. In contrast to its medieval formulation, natural law theorists today for the most part accept the need for limited government and do not believe that the state has an interest in attempting to prevent all moral wrongdoing. Still, they do argue against homosexuality and against **anti-discrimination laws** based on sexual orientation. They also defend **anti-sodomy laws**. John Finnis, for example, served as an expert witness in *Romer v. Evans*, and other natural law theorists submitted amicus curiae briefs to the U.S. Supreme Court in the case of *Lawrence v. Texas*. See also ANCIENT ROME; EUROPE; LATIN AMERICA; RELIGIOUS RIGHT; WOLFENDEN REPORT.

NAVRATILOVA, MARTINA (1956–). One of the greatest tennis players of the 20th century, Martina Navratilova did not hide her sexual orientation while she was a player. She wrote about her feelings toward other women in her 1986 autobiography. She also had an extended relationship with Rita Mae Brown, author of *Rubyfruit Jungle* and other works that explored lesbian relationships and themes. In the early 1990s, as her singles tennis career was waning, she became an increasingly outspoken advocate for gay rights. She campaigned against a Colorado constitutional amendment that had repealed the **anti-discrimination laws** of Denver, Boulder, and Aspen. She came out of retirement in 2000 and had a second successful tennis career as a doubles player. *See also* AMENDMENT 2; LITERATURE, LESBIAN; *ROMER V. EVANS*.

NEWPORT NAVAL SCANDAL. In 1919, **United States** naval investigators uncovered a circle of homosexuals connected with the

Newport Naval Training Station in Rhode Island. The investigation was not a complete success. Based on the common **police harassment** tool of entrapment, agents would approach men, fondle them, and then receive oral sex from them. Yet this approach was problematic in court, since the agents had engaged in illegal sex and arguably initiated it. As a result, one of the key suspects, Reverend Samuel Kent, a YMCA chaplain, was twice acquitted. Yet the investigation prompted changes in U.S. military policy. In 1921, Congress altered the Articles of War to criminalize same-sex oral sex. The same year, the U.S. Army for the first time adopted rules to screen out, or discharge, all "degenerates." The army rule specifically included sexual perversion as a form of degeneration.

The trial records also reveal much about the norms and self-understandings of the "inverts" the navy investigated, as well as mainstream views. The inverts adopted female gender roles, taking women's names, dressing in gowns and dresses, and otherwise acting in exaggerated feminine ways. The agents involved did not object to having sex with men, since they perceived themselves as playing the "male" role in the act. Yet others, including members of a U.S. Senate subcommittee, were deeply troubled by this. In contrast to a gender-role-inflected interpretation, they used a schema that perceived same-sex acts as unnatural.

NORTH AMERICAN CONFERENCE OF HOMOPHILE OR-GANIZATIONS (NACHO). Leaders of various groups in the **homophile movement**, such as **Frank Kameny**, formed the North American Conference of Homophile Organizations in 1966. NACHO had a legal defense fund that took up cases involving the rights of gay military personnel, among other issues. It also produced two legal reports, "The Challenge and Progress of Homosexual Law Reform" and "Homosexuals and Employment."

NACHO served as a vehicle for the more militant wing of the late **homophile** movement. It organized simultaneous demonstrations in several cities in order to maximize its chances for press coverage. It helped establish homophile groups in cities where none had previously existed. At its first meeting in 1966, only 15 groups were represented. Three years later the number had jumped to 50. In 1970, however, factionalism between those sympathetic to the **Gay Liberation Front** and

other New Left groups, versus those who wanted to retain NACHO's
exclusive focus on traditional homophile concerns tore apart NACHO.
The group dissolved within a year.

– O –

***ONE, INC. V. OLESEN* (1958).** Founded in 1953 by persons affiliated
with the **Mattachine Society**, *ONE* was a small magazine devoted
to discussions of and information about homosexuality. In 1954 the
magazine reported a circulation of 5,000, although the readership
was undoubtedly larger due to copies being passed between friends.
The letters to the editor clearly show that there were at least some
readers across the **United States**, even though most subscribers were
in Southern California. Although the contents were tame, the postmaster general in 1954 declared the publication obscene and banned
its distribution via the postal service. ONE, Inc. was able to find a
lawyer to represent it and filed suit. In 1956 a federal judge upheld
the postmaster general's action and a federal appellate court agreed
the following year. Yet in 1958 the U.S. Supreme Court, without
even hearing oral arguments, overturned the lower courts' decisions
and unanimously ruled in the plaintiffs' favor with a one-sentence,
unsigned ruling. It was the Court's first-ever ruling on any issue directly involving homosexuality.

OUTING. The practice of "outing" a person refers to the exposure of
a person's sexual orientation. A person can choose to come "out" of
the closet, or one can be involuntarily outed, sometimes in order to
achieve a political goal. In societies where same-sex orientation is
socially marginalized or carries legal risks, outing or the threat of
outing is an effective tactic for blackmail or otherwise harming a person's social status and legitimacy. While the term is quite recent, the
practice is very old. Outings were a part of the religious conflict between Catholics and Protestants in the 16th century. Calvinists took
joy in exposing Pope Julius III, named as head of the Roman Catholic
Church in 1551, as a "**sodomite**," in particular for the affection he
lavished upon a boy, Innocenzo. Julius named Innocenzo a cardinal

at the age of 15, despite his questionable character and inexperience. Catholics returned the favor by outing, perhaps inaccurately, John Calvin's chief aid, Théodore de Bèze. Polemicists on each side made charges and countercharges against various high Catholic and Protestant leaders, many of which were most likely false. A more recent, and non-Western, example is the Japanese singer Sagara Naomi, who was outed in the 1970s.

One outgrowth of the gay liberation movement has been the development of outing as a political strategy. The early homosexual rights movement, centered in **Germany** in the early 20th century, had debates about exposing public figures as homosexuals. The ***Wissenschaftlich-humanitäres Komitee*** (Scientific-Humanitarian Committee), led by **Magnus Hirschfeld**, decided not to use the tactic. Hirschfeld himself, however, later became embroiled in an outing controversy. A contemporary of Hirschfeld's, Adolf Brand, defended outing in instances where closeted homosexual political figures defended anti-gay policies. He published names in a magazine he edited, including the **National Socialist** Ernst Roehm. Gay and lesbian activists have outed a variety of political and media figures over the past quarter of a century. In the 1980s, **AIDS Coalition to Unleash Power** (ACT UP) demonstrators carried placards that named closeted homosexuals. A series of outings of prominent figures in the early 1990s, such as Malcolm Forbes and Senator Mark Hatfield, made the tactic a subject of broad and heated controversy.

Previously, outing was a strategy used by those who condemned same-sex attraction in order to de-legitimate the accused. Gay and lesbians activists, however, use outing to advance a number of goals. Probably the least controversial form of it is to expose closeted gays and lesbians who pursue or defend policies that are harmful to gay rights. For example, Assistant Secretary of Defense Pete Williams was outed in 1991. As perhaps the foremost spokesperson for the **United States** military during the first Gulf war, Williams defended the ban upon gays and lesbians in the military. Those who defended Williams' outing argued that his access to the most sensitive information possible showed that gays and lesbians are not in fact a security threat, as claimed by many who defend the ban on **military service**. Another goal of outing those who could be called anti-gay gays is to help ensure that closeted, powerful political figures do not pursue policies antithetical to gay and lesbian interests. Doing so makes them more likely to be outed.

Others, such as Michelangelo Signorile, argue that gays and lesbians should pursue a more expansive outing strategy. Any public figure whose homosexuality is relevant to the story at hand should be outed. Of course, the pivotal terms in this formulation—"public figure" and "relevant"—are flexible and even ambiguous. A member of Congress is clearly a public figure, and exposing allegations of sexual harassment of male aides would count as "relevant" to the story, since it speaks so directly to the issue. Yet other examples, such as a minor official in a rural county, are much more problematic. Signorile, a forceful advocate of outing, admits that the tactic has sometimes degenerated into a blunt instrument of attack and even blackmail. Still, its proponents believe that overall, outing has spurred significant changes, such as in how Hollywood portrays gays and lesbians, in part by making closeted gays reconsider their involvement in anti-gay projects. Thus, while not every instance of outing is defensible, the overall strategy has led to substantial improvements in the lives of millions. *See also* COMING OUT; LITERATURE, HOMOSEXUAL MALE; QUEER NATION.

– P –

PARENTS AND FRIENDS OF LESBIANS AND GAYS (PFLAG). Established in 1981, Parents and Friends of Lesbians and Gays is a gay-straight alliance that works as a support network. It has hundreds of community chapters across the **United States**, including in small and mid-sized cities, and thus serves as a frequent resource for heterosexuals seeking to come to terms with a close friend or relative coming out of the closet. PFLAG also has chapters in other countries.

PFLAG also engages in educational outreach efforts and political activity. Local chapters and the national organization have lobbied in support of **anti-discrimination laws**. It also lobbied, unsuccessfully, against the passage of the **Defense of Marriage Act**.

PEDERASTY. A term derived from the ancient Greek words for "boy" (*paida*) and "to desire" (*eran*, the verb form of eros), pederasty in **ancient Greece** was the socially idealized practice of men engaging in relationships with boys. The relationships were not necessarily consummated or even sexual in nature, although many were, and were ideally to be directed at the improvement of the boy's character. There is some debate over the age range that "boy" referred to, although from mid-teens to perhaps early 20s is a reasonable estimate. Pederasty is distinct from pedophilia (also from the ancient Greek, meaning the love of boys), in that the latter is thoroughly sexual in nature and directed at children. While many ancient Greeks praised pederasty, pedophilia was unacceptable and those caught were punished. The first extant use of the word *paiderastia* is in **Plato**'s *Symposium*. *See also* LITERATURE, HOMOSEXUAL MALE; SOCIAL CONSTRUCTIONISM.

PLATO (427?–347 B.C.E.). One of the greatest philosophers, Plato wrote extensively about eros (love/desire). Across the approximately two dozen dialogues he composed, Plato touched on a broad range of concerns that are still of central importance in philosophy today, and thus he stands as the central figure at the beginning of the Western philosophical tradition. The primary dialogues where Plato explored same-sex eros are the *Symposium* and the *Phaedrus*, and to a lesser extent the *Republic* and the *Laws*.

Plato's *Symposium* is a beautiful and moving dialogue set at an all-male drinking party at which some same-sex partners are in attendance. Various persons take turns giving speeches in praise of eros, and much of the focus is upon homosexual male desire. The speech by Pausanias is representative of mainstream views of sexuality in **ancient Greece**. He presents the ideal of the older man pursuing a younger male, who in turn may yield to the older man but—he hopes—out of more noble motives of friendship and education. Aristophanes offers a myth wherein humanity used to be comprised of persons with four legs and four arms. There were three sexes: hermaphrodite, male, and female. The gods were threatened by the pride and strength of men, so Zeus (himself pictured in ancient Greek mythology as having had a same-sex relationship with **Ganymede**) cut them in half. Persons now go around longing for their other half. With hermaphrodites separated into male and females halves, the three sexes have been reduced to two. Thus male-male, female-female, and male-female couplings are all instances of persons simply trying to re-create their former wholeness. The character of Socrates gives a speech that focuses on eros as a search for the good and beautiful. In men this initially takes the form of desire for a particular person, often a younger male. Yet persons of a nobler soul eventually come to realize that the desire should go above the transitory beauty of a certain person; one should ultimately desire eternal, metaphysical goods.

Later Platonic dialogues, including the *Phaedrus* and the *Republic*, show a deep skepticism about the appetites, including sexuality. They distract humans from philosophic activity and corrupt their reason. Thus even though the *Phaedrus* still includes the argument that the beauty and goodness of individual persons can launch a quest that culminates in a philosophic life, erotic passion is suspect and fraught with danger. Plato, however, does not single out same-sex passion as unusually dangerous. If anything, the desire that men feel for one another is more likely to be noble and result in a transcendence of the purely physical. The *Laws*, composed toward the end of Plato's life, takes a much more negative view of the appetites and sensual pleasure. The principal speaker, the Athenian, argues for a law that would ban all extramarital intercourse. If anything, the older Plato views same-sex intercourse as especially problematic since it is the most likely source of the strongest passions. *See also* ARISTOTLE; CODE OF JUSTINIAN; LITERATURE, HOMOSEXUAL MALE; NATURAL LAW; PEDERASTY; SACRED BAND OF THEBES.

POLICE HARASSMENT. Gays and lesbians around the world have frequently been subjected to entrapment, threats, arbitrary stops and searches, repeated raids on bars and other gathering spaces, and other forms of police harassment. In the **United States**, the widespread adoption of vagrancy and lewdness laws after the 1880s led to increased arrest rates. Undercover officers often posed as inverts to entrap men. Same-sex kissing in a public locale, such as a bar, was interpreted as "lewd and lascivious" behavior, as was propositioning someone. Surveillance and harassment intensified under **McCarthy-**

ism. During the 1950s, the police arrested over 1,000 homosexuals each year in Washington, D.C., alone. In Philadelphia the numbers were, if anything, even higher. More remote locales, such as Boise, Idaho, also had intermittent anti-homosexual campaigns by the authorities. Many police forces reorganized in order to establish vice or morals squads that then pursued members of homosexual subcultures for consensual crimes. The Institute for Sex Research, through survey data, found that 20 percent of their respondents had encountered problems with the police. Harassment by the police set the stage for the **Stonewall** riot in 1969.

The situation was similar in **Great Britain** during the middle of the 20th century. After World War II, British authorities dramatically stepped up efforts against homosexuals. Before the war a few hundred men a year were prosecuted for consensual homosexual sodomy; in the 1950s the number soared to more than 2,000 a year. One police tactic involved "chain" prosecutions where immunity would be offered to a defendant on condition that he name several others. The historian Neil Miller reports that 4 percent of all male prisoners in Britain were jailed due to consensual homosexual sex crimes.

In the United States, the situation has improved. Since **anti-sodomy laws** provide one important rationale for police action against gays and lesbians, the repeal of such laws at the state level in the 1970s through the 1990s made it more difficult, at least in some locales, to justify such action. The Supreme Court's decision in *Lawrence v. Texas* (2003) nullified all remaining anti-sodomy laws. Other factors have also contributed to the reduction of police harassment. For instance, even though the American Civil Liberties Union in 1957 specifically refused to take a stance against anti-sodomy laws and did not come to the defense of homosexuals, it later changed its position and has served as an advocate for many accused. Also, the greater social acceptance of gays and lesbians has contributed to the reduction, but not elimination, of police harassment. Similar improvement has occurred in much of **Europe** as well.

Other regions, however, have not seen a corresponding improvement. In the **Middle East**, for example, the police in Egypt and the Palestinian West Bank often resort to entrapment. Persons accused of breaking the regional equivalent of anti-sodomy laws sometimes face demeaning treatment and physical violence by authorities. Iranian police have used Internet chat rooms to entrap gay men. Moreover, there is evidence that authorities in Iran have selectively targeted men of Arabic descent as a way of casting aspersions upon a cultural minority. The penalty there for sodomy is death. *See also* AFRICA; ASIA; AUSTRALIA; CANADA; CHINA; CODE OF JUSTINIAN; ENLIGHTENMENT, THE; FRANCE; GAY ACTIVISTS ALLIANCE; GAY BASHING; HOMOPHILE MOVEMENT; INDIA; JENNINGS, DALE; KAMENY, FRANK; MATTACHINE SOCIETY; NEWPORT NAVAL SCANDAL; RUSSIA; SOCIETY FOR INDIVIDUAL RIGHTS; SPAIN; WOLFENDEN REPORT.

– Q –

QUEER. Although the word "queer" has been around for centuries, referring primarily to things regarded as odd or disreputable, it was not until the late 19th century that people began applying the term to homosexuals. In the early 20th century, some homosexual men in the **United States** used the term to distinguish themselves from effeminate same-sex lovers, whom they called "fairies." "Queer" remained a common pejorative term for homosexuals well into the 1960s.

In the 1980s and 1990s, some gays and lesbians took on the term "queer" as a badge of honor. The group **Queer Nation** was central to this process. Initially this was controversial, with some conservative gays denouncing the move as feeding into the stereotypes of homophobes who see gays as radically different and degenerate. The author Bruce Bawer was one of the central proponents of this view, arguing simultaneously against **homophobia** and the gay appropriation of the word "queer," as well as against **queer theory**. Others, such as David Halperin, a leading theorist of **social constructionism**, argued that "queer" had great promise as a term signifying what is radically different from mainstream sexuality. Queer in a non-pejorative sense has become a mainstream term, as shown by television show titles such as *Queer as Folk* and *Queer Eye for the Straight Guy*.

QUEER NATION. Started in 1990 by members of **AIDS Coalition to Unleash Power** (ACT UP), the goal behind the founding of **Queer** Nation was to establish a group dedicated to fighting **homophobia**,

gay bashing, and **the closet**. Author and activist Michelangelo Signorile was one of the founders. Queer Nation grew quickly and had dozens of chapters across the **United States** by the end of 1991. The group was controversial, due to its attempt to re-appropriate the term "queer," its support for **outing**, and in-your-face demonstration tactics. Group members shouted, "We're here, we're queer, get used to it!" or "We're here, we're queer, we're fabulous!" They held "kiss-ins" in public settings, where gays and lesbians would make out in malls, bars, and other locales. The group had no formal hierarchy and instead had a consensual decision-making system. Internal divisions often proved intractable and hampered chapters' ability to act. Queer Nation fell apart by the mid-1990s.

QUEER THEORY. With the rise of the gay liberation movement in the post-**Stonewall** era, various activists and academics began to put forward an overtly gay or lesbian perspective in politics, philosophy, and literary theory. Various theorists developed queer theory in the late 1980s and early 1990s, although there are obviously important antecedents which make it difficult to date precisely. It has been influential in academia, particularly in the humanities, although whether this is a good thing is a matter of controversy. There are a number of ways in which queer theory differs from earlier liberation theory. This can be seen by looking at the term "queer" itself. In contrast to gay or lesbian, "queer," it is argued, does not refer to an essence, whether of a sexual nature or not. Instead, it is purely relational, standing as an undefined term that gets its meaning precisely by being that which is outside the norm, however that norm itself may be defined. By lacking any essence, queer does not marginalize those whose sexuality is outside of any gay or lesbian norm, such as sadomasochists, bisexuals, or transsexuals. Since specific conceptualizations of sexuality are avoided, it allows more freedom in self-identification for, say, black lesbians to identify as much or more with their race (or any other trait, such as involvement in a sadomasochism subculture) than with lesbianism. Finally, it incorporates the insights of **Michel Foucault** and others about the difficulties in ascribing any essence or non-historical aspect to identity.

The central claim of queer theorists is that the categories through which identity is understood are all social constructs rather than given to us by nature. This position opens a number of analytical possibilities. For example, queer theorists examine how fundamental notions of gender and sex, which seem so natural and self-evident to persons in the modern West, are in fact constructed and reinforced through everyday actions, and that this occurs in ways that privilege heterosexuality. This is a central theme in the work of Judith Butler. Others examine how language and especially divisions between what is said and what is not said, corresponding to the dichotomy between closeted and "out," structure modern thought. They argue that when we look at dichotomies such as natural/unnatural or masculine/feminine, we find in the background an implicit reliance on a very recent, and arbitrary, understanding of the sexual world as split into two species. Another critical perspective opened up by a queer approach, although certainly implicit in what has just been referred to, is especially important. Since most anti-gay and anti-lesbian arguments rely on the alleged naturalness of heterosexuality, queer theorists attempt to show how these categories are themselves entirely social constructs.

Queer theory has been criticized in a myriad of ways. Theorists who are sympathetic to gay liberation and view it as a project of radical social change provide one set of charges. An initial criticism is that precisely because "queer" does not refer to any specific sexual status or gender object choice, it robs gays and lesbians of the distinctiveness of what makes them marginal. It desexualizes identity, when the issue is precisely about a sexual identity. A related criticism is that queer theory cannot make crucial distinctions, since it refuses any essence or reference to standard ideas of normality. For example, queer theorists usually argue that one of the advantages of the term "queer" is that it includes transsexuals, sadomasochists, and others with marginalized sexualities. Critics ask how far this extends. For instance, while some queer theorists specifically disallow pedophilia as permissible, others overtly refuse to rule out pedophiles as "queer." Furthermore, it is unclear what philosophic resources the theory has to rule out pedophilia or more extreme forms of sadomasochism. Another criticism is that queer theory, in part because it typically has recourse to a very technical jargon, is written by a narrow elite for that narrow elite. It is therefore incapable of motivating or informing a broad-based movement.

Those who reject the desirability of radical social change also criticize queer theory. For example, centrist and conservative gays and lesbians have criticized a queer approach by arguing that it will be counterproductive. If "queer" keeps its connotation of something perverse and at odds with mainstream society, which is precisely what most queer theorists want, it would seem only to validate the attacks on gays and lesbians made by social conservatives and fundamentalist religious groups.

– R –

REGISTERED PARTNERSHIP. A form of legal recognition of same-sex relationships that is common in northern **Europe**, registered partnership has almost the same scope as marriage. For instance, partners have inheritance rights, health and employee benefits, and the legal right to make decisions in the event that one's partner is incapacitated or dies. Registered partners are treated like married persons under the tax code, which usually lowers their tax liability. It also allows for **immigration and naturalization** rights. These partnerships are not internationally recognized, however. Thus while abroad, couples are legal strangers unless they are in a country that specifically recognizes such partnerships.

Denmark was the first country to adopt this type of law, doing so in 1989. Its version initially did not provide for **adoption** rights, though that was partially liberalized in 1999. All the other Nordic countries (Finland, Iceland, Norway, and Sweden) have also enacted registered partnership laws. The Nordic countries recognize partnerships entered into in one another's countries. The Netherlands also enacted a registered partnership law in 2008. Norway changed from the legal recognition of partnerships to full **same-sex marriage**, including adoption rights, the same year.

Germany and **France** have laws that are similar to registered partnerships, although they are not as far reaching. In France, the *pactes civil de solidarité* (PACS) recognize either same or opposite-sex couples that submit the appropriate form. The government passed it in 1999, although only after a heated and divisive public debate. It provides many of the central legal benefits (and liabilities) of marriage, though far from all. For instance, it excludes joint custody and **adoption** rights. PACS has an easy exit system. Germany has a *nichteheliche Lebensgemeinschaft* (life partnership) legal option. Again, many of the most frequently needed legal benefits are included, such as hospital visitation and immigration and naturalization rights, as well as joint tenancy and inheritance rights. In contrast to PACS, which allows partners to choose joint taxation status after three years of union, the German law excludes partners from favorable tax treatment, and most other state financial benefits. Adoption rights also are not included. *See also* CIVIL UNIONS; DOMESTIC PARTNERSHIP; GREAT BRITAIN.

RELIGIOUS RIGHT. More influential in the **United States** than in other countries, the rise of the religious right came out of the politicization of Protestant **Christianity** in the 1960s and 1970s. The rise of the gay rights movement (or movements, given its internal diversity), abortion rights, and other social controversies mobilized religious and political conservatives. Many mainline and evangelical Christians felt they could no longer remain outside the political world. Sociological factors, such as higher labor mobility and divorce rates and economic dislocation, likely contributed to the growth in fundamentalism as well, out of a search for certainty in a world marked by the dissolution of traditional structures.

The religious right has significant internal diversity as far as its beliefs, methods, and goals. In general, however, members of the movement are deeply concerned with what they view as sexual immorality, which are all forms of sexual expression outside of traditional, opposite-sex marriage. Their strident opposition to abortion thus overlaps with their denunciation of homosexuality, since they see both as arising from immoral, hedonistic sexuality. The most intellectually sophisticated defenders of the movement often rely upon **natural law** theory, as can be seen in the amicus curiae briefs that **Focus on the Family** and other groups have filed in cases such as *Lawrence v. Texas*. While not all of the movement is focused on homosexuality, it has been the leading force in anti-gay politics in the United States over the past three decades.

In the wake of early successes by gay activists in the 1970s, such as the repeal of some **anti-sodomy laws** and enactment of **anti-discrimination laws**, social and religious conservatives increasingly focused on gay issues. In 1977, **Anita Bryant** led an early, successful campaign against a Dade County anti-discrimination law. The movement adopted the language of "pro-family" at roughly the same time. In 1979, **Jerry Falwell** founded the Moral Majority. Persons formed local groups and chapters as well and lobbied for changes in sex education and school curricula, the retention of state anti-sodomy laws, and for other anti-gay policies. In the 1980s, Ronald Reagan's administration allied itself with the religious right and hence refused to respond to the **human immunodeficiency virus/acquired immunodeficiency syndrome** epidemic. The administration went so far as to compel its surgeon general, C. Everett Koop, not to give speeches or answer reporters' questions about the disease. Koop eventually balked, however, and he issued a landmark report in 1986 that detailed means of transmission and the need for condom use and sex education. The religious right was appalled.

Members of the religious right were behind a 1992 Colorado ballot initiative to overturn three cities' anti-discrimination laws. The initiative passed but the U.S. Supreme Court subsequently struck down the constitutional amendment, ruling it contravened the federal Constitution. Leading groups in the religious right, such as Focus on the Family, embraced **reparative therapy** in the late 1990s. Focus on the Family and others use testimonials from "ex-gays" to argue that homosexuality is not a fixed trait, unlike race or ethnicity, and therefore is not deserving of civil rights protections. The rise of **same-sex marriage** has alarmed most evangelicals, since to them it combines sexual immorality with an assault upon the traditional family. Some leaders of the religious right go so far as to state that opposite-sex marriage is the very foundation of society and that same-sex marriage, if widely allowed, will doom civilization. In 2004, anti–same-sex marriage initiatives and referenda were on the ballot in 11 states. They passed in every state and helped to get members of the religious right to the polls. In 2008, similar initiatives in California, Florida, and elsewhere again passed. Arkansas voters passed an initiative that banned same-sex couples from **adopting** children or serving as foster parents.

Since persons in the movement are typically certain that they are right and their opponents are not only wrong, but are even defending things that are evil, they are prone to actions and statements that many find offensive and are often politically counterproductive. For instance, Jerry Falwell blamed gays, feminists, and abortion providers for the terrorist attacks on September 11. A Kansas evangelical group, led by Fred Phelps, has picketed the funerals of soldiers killed in Iraq, blaming those deaths on the United States' tolerance of homosexuality. His group also picketed the funeral of **Matthew Shepard**. *See also* BRIGGS INITIATIVE; EMPLOYMENT NON-DISCRIMINATION ACT; FAMILY RESEARCH COUNCIL; HOMOPHOBIA; LOG CABIN REPUBLICANS; MEDICAL MODEL OF HOMOSEXUALITY; REPARATIVE THERAPY.

REPARATIVE THERAPY. A broad name for a wide-ranging and often contradictory set of putative "cures" for homosexuality, "reparative therapy" is still defended by some although it is now well outside the medical mainstream. Historically, the "therapies" included castration, electroshocks, and lobotomies. Lesbians were sometimes subjected to hysterectomies or hormone injections. The idea that homosexuality is a disease and is, like many other diseases, capable of being cured dates back to the origins of the **medical model of homosexuality**. Prior to the development of a largely scientific, or at least pseudo-scientific, framework, the theological perspective was dominant and saw those attracted to their own sex as **sodomites**. That is, they were one specific type of sinner, rather than a person with an illness. In the 19th century, a number of psychologists and sexologists developed a medical-scientific analysis. Although they differed in their terms and arguments, at their root was a contention that natural causes, perhaps congenital, led to homosexuality. While some of these investigators, such as **Karl Heinrich Ulrichs**, were sympathetic to same-sex attraction and argued that it was simply a form of normal human variation, many others contended it was a type of pathology. For them, the question thus became one of how it is to be cured.

Some, including doctors, argued that the sickness was so deep as to be incurable. For those who saw homosexuality as threatening, this line of thinking culminated in support for genocide. For instance, Dr.

William Robinson, an American, suggested in 1914 that the elimination of homosexuals would benefit society. The proponents of **National Socialism** in **Germany** also saw homosexuality as a form of "degeneracy" that needed to be removed from the general population. Thousands of homosexuals perished in the Holocaust.

Others have argued that homosexuality is more amenable to change. Given the diversity in proposed etiologies for homosexuality, however, it is unsurprising that the range of proposed therapies to make persons heterosexual is equally broad. In the early 20th century, some argued that "congestion" of the prostate or ovaries caused homosexuality. The resulting therapy sometimes included the surgical removal of the offending organ. Other early prescriptions, aside from the extreme measures listed above, included hydrotherapy, change in diet, or improved hygiene. Doctors also tried aversion therapy, which usually involved showing the patient pictures of someone of the same sex whom the patient found sexually attractive. The patient was then subjected to electric shocks and induced nausea. After the rise to prominence of **Sigmund Freud** and other psychoanalysts, the "talking cure" became a common form of treatment among the wealthy. Yet during the 1960s and 1970s, the medical establishment changed its views on homosexuality. Led by **Evelyn Hooker** and a few other researchers, journals began publishing studies showing that homosexuals were psychologically normal. In 1973, the **American Psychiatric Association** removed homosexuality from its comprehensive listing of mental illnesses.

As the mainstream medical community has moved away from reparative therapy, some fringe groups, often associated with the **religious right**, have sought to keep it alive. One part of their strategy has been to put forward research showing that homosexuality is an illness and amenable to treatment. The quality of the research, however, is suspect and the vast preponderance of evidence is that homosexuality is not a mental illness. In 2006, the American Psychological Association stated that there was no scientifically grounded reason to believe that sexual orientation can be changed, but that the views propounded by reparative therapy advocates foster prejudice and discrimination. There is little if any evidence showing that reparative therapy is effective in changing a person's sexual orientation, although there is some data that shows it is harmful. The persons who seek out such treatment today are usually from deeply religious backgrounds and experience profound guilt about their homosexuality. The types of therapy have moderated and now consist of various sorts of talking cures. There is also training in appropriate gender roles, such as throwing footballs for men.

The current reparative therapy movement is akin to its intellectual forebears in that it is based on the assumption that homosexuals are sick, in need of medical treatment, and can be cured. The battle over such therapy thus connects to the larger cultural debate over lesbian and gay rights. Reparative therapy advocates and fundamentalist leaders seek to prove that homosexuality is not an immutable trait and therefore should not be seen socially, or legally, as akin to race or ethnicity. *See also* CHRISTIANITY; FALWELL, JERRY, SR.; FAMILY RESEARCH COUNCIL; FOCUS ON THE FAMILY; NATIONAL GAY AND LESBIAN TASK FORCE; RUSSIA.

***ROMER V. EVANS* (1996).** In 1992, the voters of Colorado passed an initiative, **Amendment 2**, that repealed **anti-discrimination laws** in Denver, Boulder, and Aspen, and forbade any level of government from enacting such laws in the future. Within days, the three affected cities and others filed suit against the law. The suit named Governor Roy Romer as one of the defendants. A lower court issued an injunction against the law so it would not go into effect until the legal issues were resolved. The case ultimately went before the **United States** Supreme Court.

The Court struck down the law. The majority decision, written by Justice Anthony Kennedy, emphasized how Amendment 2 went well beyond striking down three cities' ordinances. Instead, it would prevent one class of persons, gays and lesbians, from seeking redress in legislative bodies in the state. Kennedy argued that there was no rational basis for such a sweeping action. The motive must have been anti-gay animus. The law singled out a class of citizens for an unequal or inferior legal status, which is constitutionally impermissible. Coming a decade after *Bowers v. Hardwick*, *Evans* marked a turn away from the strident condemnation of homosexuality in that ruling's majority and concurring decisions. The new direction culminated in *Lawrence v. Texas*, where again the majority struck down a law targeting gays and lesbians. Justice Kennedy also wrote the majority opinion in that case. *See also* HUMAN RIGHTS CAMPAIGN; NATURAL LAW; NAVRATILOVA, MARTINA.

RUSSIA. One of the earliest references to homosexuality in the Russian tradition is by an anonymous author describing the events surrounding the murder in the 11th century of two princes from Kievan Rus', the first Russian state. In the story, *The Legend of Boris and Gleb*, when the assassins kill Boris, his servant, George, proclaims his love for his master and asks to die with him. The assassins then oblige the servant and kill him too, in this widely distributed retelling. The Slavic version of Eastern Orthodox **Christianity** was introduced during the Kievan Rus' empire, and thus a theological climate hostile to homosexuality eventually became the norm. Despite this, however, after the Mongol invasion of the 13th century had waned and Moscow had emerged as the new seat of political and cultural power, homosexuality seems to have been quite common. For example, the ruler to emerge after Ivan the Great, Grand Prince Vasily II (r. 1505–1533), was exclusively homosexual. In the 16th century, Western travelers to Russia remarked upon the frequency of homosexuality among both the peasantry and the nobility. Many leaders of the church, however, denounced such relations.

In the late 17th and early 18th centuries, Peter the Great and apparently a niece of his, the Empress Anna Ioannovna, were bisexual. Peter sought to modernize Russia, especially along Western lines. One of the ideas imported from the West was the need to repress homosexuality. In the wake of his reign, social hostility to homosexuality increased, although there was no **anti-sodomy law** until 1832, enacted during the reign of Tsar Nicolas I. It applied only to anal sex between men and it was not frequently enforced. In 1861, Tsar Alexander II abolished serfdom and pursued other reforms, which in turn allowed a greater openness for homosexuals in Russian society. A number of prominent figures in late 19th-century Russian society, especially in the literary world, were homosexual or bisexual. When the homosexual novelist and publisher Prince Vladimir Meshchersky was caught having sex with a soldier on palace grounds, Tsar Alexander III ordered the witnesses silenced. Composer Peter Ilyich Tchaikovsky, poet Alexei Apukhtin, early feminist and editor Anna Yevreinova, and poet and translator Polyxena Soloviova were other

examples of homosexuals in the artistic demimonde. During the same
era, there is evidence of gay bars and bathhouses in Moscow and St.
Petersburg.

The 1905 Revolution led to further reforms and eased censorship.
The next year, Mikhail Kuzmin published his novel *Wings*, which
was ardently pro-homosexual. The novel was largely autobiographical and was popular enough to go through several reprintings up
through the 1920s. In 1907, Lydia Zinovieva-Annibal published
Thirty-Three Freaks, which was a deeply felt exploration of lesbian
relationships and affection. These works were prominent enough
that literary critics from both the right and left criticized them in
print. The ballet dancer Vaslav Nijinsky, who was bisexual, also rose
to fame during this period. Many widely recognized figures were
known to be homosexual, yet did not suffer in reputation or influence as a result. The rise to power of the Bolsheviks, however, ended
this openness. Even though they abolished the old Russian law codes
that had criminalized male-male sodomy, the Bolsheviks declared
homosexuality a mental disorder that required treatment. They also
reduced and, in the 1930s, ended the publication freedom that overtly
homosexual authors had enjoyed. By the 1920s, persons attracted to
members of their own sex usually had to marry in order to pursue a
viable career. For example, Soviet authorities forced the prominent
Russian filmmaker Sergei Eisenstein into a heterosexual marriage in
order to continue his career.

In 1933, the Soviet state enacted an anti-sodomy law, applicable
to male-male relations with a punishment of five years of hard labor.
There were mass arrests of homosexuals in several cities, including Moscow. Thousands were incarcerated in labor camps. Soviet
repression was episodic, however, although a frequent tactic by the
agents of the state was to use evidence of homosexuality as a tool
for blackmail. Police and secret agents often gained this evidence
through entrapment and other forms of **police harassment**. Even
with the tight control of life and ubiquitous presence of the police,
there were still cruising locations in parks and other venues in the
larger cities. In the 1970s, the situation partially eased and a few gay
authors circulated underground samizdat literature with homosexual
themes, although they did this at great personal risk. Underground
gay communities could be found in major cities. Still, until the 1980s

some gays and lesbians were forced into asylums and made to undergo **reparative therapy**. Hundreds were prosecuted every year for sodomy offenses.

In the 1990s, Russian authorities decriminalized homosexual male sex as well as de-listed homosexuality from the catalog of mental disorders. Russia does not confer legal recognition of any sort on same-sex relationships. There are also no **anti-discrimination laws**. In the post-Soviet era, the Russian Orthodox Church has gained a significant degree of influence and its leadership is strongly anti-gay. In 2006 and 2007, attempts by gay rights organizers to have marches and other public events were met with hostility, and in some cases even violence. *See also* GAY BASHING; IMMIGRATION AND NATURALIZATION LAW; LITERATURE, HOMOSEXUAL MALE; MEDICAL MODEL OF HOMOSEXUALITY.

– S –

SACRED BAND OF THEBES. Male same-sex eroticism was a component of various city-state militaries in **ancient Greece**. One of the speakers in **Plato**'s *Symposium* argues that an army comprised of pairs of lovers would be a formidable fighting unit, since each lover would be afraid of showing any cowardice in front of his beloved. In 378 B.C.E., Thebes formed such a unit, several hundred strong, called the Sacred Band of Thebes. The unit initially fought against the Spartans in order to defend their democratic constitution from the oligarchy that the Spartans had previously installed in Thebes after their victory in the Peloponnesian War. Plutarch gives the most detailed account of the Sacred Band and he presents it as a deeply impressive unit, able to defeat the fierce Spartan military even when the Spartans outnumbered them. The Sacred Band played a key role in the Theban victory at Leuctra in 371, which destroyed Sparta's military supremacy.

The Sacred Band endured for decades, continuing its composition as pairs of lovers. In 338 B.C.E., Philip II of Macedon invaded southern Greece. The key battle took place at Chaeronea. Philip's army won and the Sacred Band was killed to a man. A large marble lion memorial was erected at the site of the battle to commemorate this noble army of lovers. It still stands today. It was refurbished in 1902 by the Order of Chaeronea, a secret society of English homosexuals. *See also* MILITARY SERVICE.

SAIKAKU, IHARA (1642–1693). A **Japanese** novelist during the Genroku period, Ihara Saikaku wrote several works that explored sexual themes in largely middle-class settings. Many see his *The Great Mirror of Male Love* as one of the most powerful explorations of homosexual attraction in the pre-modern era. It is a collection of 40 stories, evenly divided between tales of love between samurai and boys, and stories of actor-prostitutes in kabuki theaters. The work evinces a deep distrust of women, even contempt. Yet an earlier work of Saikaku's, *The Life of an Amorous Man*, explored the sensual pleasures of a man who, even while happy to go to bed with either sex, did prefer women. Overall, Saikaku's work provides great insight into the relationship ideals and conventions of his age, along with flashes of humor, drama, and beauty. *See also* LITERATURE, HOMOSEXUAL MALE.

SAME-SEX MARRIAGE. There is a lively debate among historians and legal theorists as to whether any pre-modern societies accorded legal recognition to same-sex unions. The issue is complicated by the fact that what counts as "marriage" is subject to large variation itself. Also, the historical debate ends up touching on the contemporary political battle over same-sex marriage. Thus at least some persons who want to counter the charge that same-sex marriage is an innovation, a "tampering with" an age-old institution, argue that there is historical precedent. What seems clear is that historically there were limited examples of recognition of same-sex unions. Same-sex relationships were socially and semi-formally recognized in some city-states in **ancient Greece**, and legally to a limited degree in **ancient Rome**. Unions with widespread social acceptance have existed, such as in **China**. Yet it is difficult to find compelling evidence of mainstream legal acceptance of same-sex unions prior to the latter part of the 20th century.

A number of historical factors have contributed to the contemporary push for same-sex marriage recognition. The rise of companionate marriage in the modern era, premised on a deep emotional connection with another person as one of the highest goods in life, along with a concern for the social and legal recognition of that relationship, has made many perceive the denial of same-sex marriage recognition as equivalent to the denial of basic personhood. The widespread availability of contraceptives has sundered the connection between marriage and procreation and encouraged understandings of sexuality oriented toward pleasure, self-expression, and the cultivation of intimacy. The abolition of anti-miscegenation laws as well as the rise of equality between the sexes in marriage rights helped to alter traditional notions of marriage. The latter in particular weakened older ideas about the connection between sex and gender roles, such as women being passive "by nature." More recently, the greater openness of gay and lesbian communities from the 1970s to the 1990s led to a sharp increase in the number of de facto lesbian and gay families. Court rulings that struck down anti-miscegenation laws established legal precedents that have been used by same-sex marriage advocates. Finally, the **human immunodeficiency virus/ acquired immunodeficiency syndrome** epidemic also led to innumerable conflicts between bereaved partners and traditional families. Thus issues such as medical power of attorney, inheritance rights, and other legal concerns connected to marriage stopped being matters of abstract concern. So while members of the **homophile movement** sometimes mentioned same-sex marriage as a goal—for instance, the August 1954 issue of *ONE* magazine had same-sex marriage as its cover story—the movement had neither the political clout nor the same degree of personal impetus to fight for such a change.

The situation, however, was very different in the 1980s and 1990s. By that point, gay communities were more open and better organized, especially in **Europe**. At least initially, many countries and local levels of governments, such as states, have opted for lesser levels of legal recognition, including **registered partnerships** and **civil unions**, even though the former is almost legally equivalent to marriage. Many have continued to push for the strongest version of legal recognition, arguing that anything less is a form of discrimination and bigotry. This is certainly the position of the mainstream of the gay rights movement in developed countries. In contrast, some gays and lesbians argue that marriage itself is an objectionable institution. For instance, some lesbians contend that it is by nature patriarchal and therefore needs to be rejected.

Same-sex marriage accords couples rights and responsibilities equal to that of opposite-sex marriages, although some countries have been reluctant to include a few important aspects, such as **adoption** rights and joint custody of children. The Netherlands was the first country to extend legal marriage rights to same-sex couples. It did so in April 2001. Belgium did so two years later, although without allowing adoption rights. That provision of the law was subsequently changed. **Canada**, **Spain**, South Africa, and Norway also recognize same-sex marriages. The movement for same-sex marriage recognition is small or even nonexistent in most countries in **Africa**, **Asia**, and the **Middle East**. In much of **Latin America**, however, the issue of same-sex relationship recognition is openly debated, largely because the gay rights movement there is better organized than in many other regions of the developing world.

In the **United States**, Massachusetts recognizes same-sex marriages. In 2008, the California and Connecticut supreme courts ruled that legal recognition of same-sex marriage was mandatory under their state constitutions, although voters in California subsequently approved a constitutional amendment that overturned the court's decision. Under the U.S. federal system, these changes have already sparked litigation in other states. The governor of New York directed state agencies to begin recognizing same-sex marriages from other jurisdictions, in part due to the threat of legal action. Nationally gay rights are seen as controversial but same-sex marriage is especially so. Leading Republicans orchestrated a campaign to have same-sex marriage bans placed on statewide ballots in the 2004 election as a way of energizing fundamentalist **Christian** voters. The tactic helped deliver key states, such as Ohio, for President Bush. Yet the opposition in the United States and elsewhere to same-sex marriage is energizing self-described moderates to enact alternatives to marriage, such as domestic partnerships and civil unions, which arguably threaten the social and legal primacy of marriage. *See also* ASSIMILATION; AUSTRALIA; DEFENSE OF MARRIAGE ACT; DOMESTIC PARTNERSHIP; FAMILY RESEARCH COUNCIL; FOCUS ON THE FAMILY; FRANCE; HUMAN RIGHTS CAMPAIGN; IMMIGRATION AND NATU-RALIZATION LAW; ITALY; JAPAN; *LAWRENCE V. TEXAS*; METROPOLITAN COMMUNITY CHURCH; NATIONAL GAY

AND LESBIAN TASK FORCE; REGISTERED PARTNERSHIP; RELIGIOUS RIGHT.

SAPPHO (CA. 620–570 B.C.E.). One of the great lyric poets of **ancient Greece**, Sappho is believed to have been born in the city of Mytilene on the island of Lesbos. Although she composed a good amount of lyric poetry, most has been lost. What remains is a series of fragments, many less than complete lines, plus one complete poem addressed to the goddess Aphrodite. Her poetry is marked by intense emotionality, typically about other women. The language of her poetry duplicates that common to the *erastes/eromenos* pairing of men.

Given the low status of women in ancient Greece, it was unusual that Sappho was able to attain the prominence she did. There are references to her being a teacher and attracting young women to study under her, presumably in poetry and music. Little is known about female same-sex eroticism in ancient Greece; hence, inferring details about either her life or the relationships envisioned in the fragments is difficult. *See also* GREAT BRITAIN; LITERATURE, LESBIAN.

SEXUAL OFFENSES ACT (1967). In 1967, **Great Britain**'s government passed the Sexual Offenses Act. It repealed the **Act of 25 Henry VIII** that criminalized homosexual anal sex, subsequently altered by the **Labouchère Amendment** to include oral sex as well. The **Wolfenden Report** in 1957 set the stage for the reform movement by calling for the decriminalization of homosexual sex. The next year the **Homosexual Law Reform Society** was established to repeal Britain's **anti-sodomy law**. Uncharacteristically, it was a member of the House of Lords, Lord Arran, who introduced the first bill aimed at such a measure. He had a reputation as a quirky member of Parliament, with a pet badger, the nickname "Boofy," and referring to his bill as "William." With the help of the archbishops of Canterbury and York, Arran's bill passed on the third reading. It eventually ran out of parliamentary time, however.

The election of a Labor government in 1966 changed the political landscape. The new home secretary, Roy Jenkins, fought hard on behalf of the decriminalization of sodomy. The House finally passed the Sexual Offenses Act on a 101–16 vote. The vote tally for the 650-seat House was low due to the bill's supporters holding an all-night session in order to suppress opposition turnout. One hundred votes were needed for passage.

The Sexual Offenses Act retained some of the features of the Wolfenden Report. For example, it put the age of consent for homosexual sex at 21, while for heterosexual sex it was 16. The act also increased the legal penalty for those over the age of 21 who were convicted of having homosexual sex with someone aged 16 to 21. It also left standing legal penalties against "procuring" and "solicitation" of homosexual sex, even for those of age. For example, two men exchanging addresses or phone numbers in order to arrange a tryst would be breaking the law. It was an unusual situation wherein it was illegal to have a conversation that would ultimately result in a lawful act. As late as 1989, during the Tory family values campaign, more than 2,000 men were prosecuted for gross indecency. Also, the act only applied to England and Wales. Scotland did not repeal its anti-sodomy law until 1980. In Northern Ireland it took the case of *Dudgeon v. United Kingdom*, heard by the **European Court of Human Rights**, to prompt decriminalization in 1982. *See also* AGE OF CONSENT LAWS; EUROPE.

SHEPARD, MATTHEW (1976–1998). Born and raised in Casper, Wyoming, Matthew Shepard was brutally attacked outside of Laramie, where he was attending the University of Wyoming. He died a few days later. The crime and his ensuing death attracted a wave of attention, extending beyond the **United States**. Much of the coverage focused on **gay bashing** and what many saw as the need for **hate crime laws** to cover gays and lesbians.

His death and subsequent events became the basis for the play *The Laramie Project*. Shepard's murder also dramatically increased the number of gay-straight student alliances in U.S. high schools and universities. Many states passed hate crime laws after his death. A proposed federal hate crime bill that would extend protections to include sexual orientation and gender identity is named after him. *See also* RELIGIOUS RIGHT.

SOCIAL CONSTRUCTIONISM. Along with the explosion in gay and lesbian studies in the 1970s came a debate about the proper method of historical investigation. Some historians, such as John Boswell, appeared to portray homosexuality as a universal human category of sexuality, although they readily granted that its expression and inter-pretation varied significantly over time and from place to place. This view is known as **essentialism**. In contrast, a new group of historians and theorists, including **Michel Foucault**, Jeffrey Weeks, and David Halperin, more impressed by historical differences than similarities, argued that how sex is organized within a given cultural milieu is irreducibly particular. The emphasis on the social creation of sexual experience and expression led to the labeling of the viewpoint as social constructionism.

According to social constructionists, homosexuality is best un-derstood as a specifically modern, Western concept and role. Prior to the development of this construction, persons were not really "homosexual," even when they were attracted to those of the same sex. The differences between same-sex relations in, for example, **an-cient Greece**, with its emphasis upon **pederasty** and status, and the contemporary West are simply too great to collapse these divergent practices and understandings into one category. Social construction-ists argue that specific social contexts actually produce or construct sexual ways of being. There is no given sexual mode that is culturally independent; even the concept and experience of sexual orientation itself are products of history. The range of historical sexual diver-sity, and the fluidity of human possibility, is simply too varied to be adequately captured by any specific conceptual scheme thrown up by one culture or another. Thus it does not really make sense to look for like people in history, whether someone as recent as **Walt Whitman** or from centuries ago, such as **Michelangelo**. In contrast, what does make sense is the historical investigation of how specific cultural forms, including same-sex-focused ones, came to be created and what role they play or played in society.

There is a significant political dimension to this seemingly abstract historiographical debate. Social constructionists argue that essential-ism makes at least two ill-conceived concessions. First, by accepting a basic heterosexual/homosexual organizing dichotomy, essentialism wrongly concedes that heterosexuality is the norm and that homo-sexuality is therefore, strictly speaking, abnormal and the basis for a permanent minority. Second, social constructionists argue that an important goal of historical investigations should be to put into question contemporary organizing schemas about sexuality. From this perspective, acceptance of the modern framework is reactionary and forecloses the exploration of new forms of sexuality, or what Foucault called "a new economy of bodies and pleasures" (1980, 159). *See also* LITERATURE, HOMOSEXUAL MALE; QUEER; SODOMITE.

SOCIETY FOR INDIVIDUAL RIGHTS (SIR). Founded in San Francisco in 1964, the Society for Individual Rights marked an important transitional stage for the West Coast **homophile movement**. While the local chapters of the **Mattachine Society** and the **Daughters of Bilitis** (DOB) still refused to take a more confrontational approach to politics, the SIR was aggressive and unapologetic on behalf of equal rights for homosexuals. The SIR also was very effective at recruiting members since it was open to organizing social events such as dances and art classes. This was something that neither the Mattachine Society nor DOB were willing to do, lest they be accused of organizing to promote illegal activity since California still had an **anti-sodomy law**. Within three years of its founding, the SIR had close to 1,000 members. It published a glossy monthly magazine, *Vector*. Its members were also effective at fundraising, and in 1966 the SIR purchased a building and opened the first gay and lesbian community center in the **United States**.

The SIR had an ambitious and well-organized political program. It ran voter registration drives, surveyed state politicians about their stands on sex law reform and **police harassment**, and held a candidates' forum every fall, where persons running for office were invited to speak to a gay audience. It published a "Pocket Lawyer" guide for those arrested on indecency or sodomy charges. It also fought with the local police about entrapment and general harassment, and was instrumental in getting police practices to improve. After 1965, there was a marked reduction in police harassment in the city.

Although the SIR was the most activist and militant local group in its first few years of existence, after **Stonewall** it was soon outflanked by more militant organizations. Its membership declined in the late 1960s and early 1970s until the group lost its political relevance.

SODOMITE. The book of Genesis in the **Bible** has the story of Lot, who lived with his family in the city of Sodom. The men of the city were so wicked that God decided to destroy it, although the Bible is unclear about exactly how they were sinful. In the story God sends two angels to save Lot, a just man, and his family. The men of the city surround the house and demand that Lot bring out his guests so that they may "know" them, with the connotation of "know" certainly being sexual. Lot refuses, stating that they are guests. God subsequently destroys Sodom as well as another city, Gomorrah. While some take the story as concerned with hospitality, another interpretation emphasizes the homosexual aspect of the story. **Augustine** was one of the earliest and most influential proponents of this latter reading.

In the Western **Christian** tradition, this story eventually provided the basis for the terms "sodomy" and "sodomite." The medieval Christian moralists and theologians who first used terms such as *peccatum sodomitae*, which means "the sin of sodomy" or perhaps "the sin of the people of Sodom," typically laid out three distinct types of sodomy. There is sodomy due to an impermissible mode of sex; that is, the sex is heterosexual, but it is oral or anal instead of vaginal. There is sodomy due to impermissible origins, *ratione generis*, which is sex between a human and an animal. Finally, there is sodomy due to gender; that is, two persons of the same sex. Because of these different types of sodomy, not all medieval references to "sodomites" involve homosexual sex. Still, it is probable that the criminal punishments or penances ordered due to the crime of sodomy were most often due to male-male sex. What counted as sodomy under the law, or the corresponding ecclesiastical penalty, differed significantly from region to region, as well as over time.

There is some controversy over whether medieval punishments in this area were oriented toward acts or persons, which in turn is part of the larger debate between **essentialism** and **social constructionism**. According to the latter, prior to the modern era the focus was upon acts, and those attracted to members of their own sex were not seen as a distinct type of person. Without prejudging this debate, it is fair to say that many medieval texts refer to "sodomites" and portray them as a uniquely sinister threat. It is also clear that the terms "sodomite" and "sodomy" have a deeply theological background. "Sodomite" is not equivalent to "homosexual," which is a modern term that reflects the **medical model of homosexuality**.

The imprecision of the term "sodomy" continued into the modern era. For instance, in 19th-century **Great Britain** many used the term to refer to heterosexual sex that involved contraception. Any non-procreative sex thus was seen as "sodomy."

The story of Sodom's destruction has later echoes in that for centuries, and even in some quarters of contemporary societies, the alleged sin of sodomy is blamed for bringing God's wrath down on entire communities. In the 16th century, a Spanish monk inspired a mob to attack "sodomites" for having caused a plague. A 17th-century German legal theorist likewise blamed sodomites for plagues. Writers in the 18th-century Dutch republic invoked the example of Sodom and warned about God's judgment coming down on their country if the authorities showed any tolerance of sodomites, thereby contributing to the hysteria that saw hundreds prosecuted and scores put to death in 1730 and 1731. In the immediate aftermath of 11 September 2001, the American evangelist **Jerry Falwell** blamed gays and lesbians for helping cause the terrorist attacks. *See also* ENLIGHTENMENT, THE; FRANCE; INQUISITION; JUDAISM; LATIN AMERICA; OUTING; REPARATIVE THERAPY; UNITED STATES.

SOTADIC ZONE. The explorer, writer, and polyglot Sir Richard Burton coined the term "Sotadic Zone" in an essay he appended to his 17-volume translation of (as he titled it) *The Book of the Thousand Nights and a Night*. It was published in 1885. The term was inspired by the poet Sotades, who in **ancient Greece** composed overtly homoerotic verse. Burton's "Terminal Essay" argued that geographical and climatic factors altered sexuality, sometimes dramatically. While he also examined other possible influences on sexual behavior, such as restricted male access to women as a source of what has been called situational homosexuality, Burton focused upon his hypothesized zone that encompassed lands surrounding the Mediterranean, Central and Southeast Asia, China, and all of the Americas. In contrast to the restrictive patterns of sexuality common to northern Europe, Burton believed that warmer climes spurred more open attitudes to sexual behavior, including same-sex relations.

Burton's reflections were part of a general 19th-century northern European idealization of same-sex relations in places such as **Italy**, **Spain**, and northern **Africa**, at least for those who were interested in such. Due to the **Code Napoléon**, neither Italy nor Spain had an **anti-sodomy law**. **Oscar Wilde**, André Gide, and others contributed to the idealization of the region, including northern Africa.

SPAIN. As **ancient Rome**'s empire fell apart, Spain under the Visigoths rose in power. In contrast to the law codes of other Germanic tribes, the Visigoths punished sodomy. In the mid-seventh century, the Visigothic king decreed an **anti-sodomy law** with castration as the punishment. A half century later the penalties were increased to include lashes, shaving of the head, and finally banishment or death. The same rulers also persecuted Jews.

Muslim invaders conquered most of Spain in the eighth century, and portions of the country had Muslim rulers up to the end of the 15th century. During the 10th and 11th centuries, Muslim Spain had a flourishing culture that rivaled any in **Europe** at the time. A tradition of romantic poetry took hold, often with homoerotic themes. Masters described themselves as slaves to a boy's beauty, typically alongside a declaration of the purity and chastity of the romance. A female writer, Hind, compiled an anthology of love stories, including a dozen lesbian ones. The influence of the **Koran** and the hadith are clear. Same-sex attraction was seen as permissible, but sex acts themselves were seen as proscribed. The poetry of the era, often beautiful, had a deep romanticism further magnified by the idealization of chastity. There is good reason to doubt, however, how often the ideal of purity was actually realized. Male prostitution was frequent; some rulers had catamites. One work lost from this era was the *Kitab al-Sahhakat*, or *Treatise on Lesbianism*. In the 11th and 12th centuries, a Hebrew-language poetic tradition was revived. It too was strongly marked by overtly homoerotic writings, likely due to the influence of the Muslim poetry of the day.

As Muslim rulers were defeated in city after city in the 13th century, the harsh Visigothic code was re-imposed. These laws endured for centuries, sometimes with even more draconian penalties such as public castration and execution. Given Spain's role in the colonization of **Latin America**, the influence of the old Visigothic code spread well beyond its borders. The earliest records of executions, from the 13th and 14th centuries, record that the preferred mode was death by burning. In the 15th century, King Ferdinand and Queen Isabella established the Spanish **Inquisition**. While sodomy was not initially one of the offenses that inquisitors pursued, royal decree added it in the early 16th century. Eventually some districts prosecuted more persons for sodomy than for heresy. Moreover, from the legal perspective, sodomy could be pursued by either secular or religious authorities. In some Spanish-controlled areas, such as Sicily, the royal courts pursued cases with more vigor and, in that particular instance, ordered approximately a hundred executions between the mid-16th and mid-17th centuries. The Spanish Inquisition ended in the early 19th century.

Within decades of the end of the Inquisition, Spain encountered mainstream European ideas in a process that led to great intellectual and social ferment. By the early 20th century, Spanish writers were increasingly open in their exploration of homosexuality. The short-lived Second Republic promised even greater toleration, but the civil war and the rise of the Fascist regime led by General Francisco Franco cut short those social and political trends. A Fascist militia executed one of Spain's foremost poets, Federico García Lorca, allegedly by shooting him in the ass for being homosexual. Even though Franco's regime did not enact any anti-sodomy laws until 1970, it still did not tolerate any public expressions of same-sex attraction and love. A provision within the 1970 law, the Social Menace and Rehabilitation Act, called for "re-education" of those convicted. A re-education establishment was opened in 1971; it subjected those housed there to alleged treatments such as electroshock therapy. Most persons convicted under the relevant provisions, whether anti-sodomy or public decency, were simply incarcerated in jails.

The end of the Franco regime in 1976 allowed many previously silenced and excluded groups into the public sphere, including gays and lesbians. Although a few scattered, clandestine groups had formed in the early 1970s, the freedom of post-Franco Spain made it possible to issue manifestos and hold public demonstrations. One area of unity between the often fractious groups was the fight against the Social Menace and Rehabilitation Act. In 1979, the government repealed most of the law, including its provisions against homosexuals. **Police harassment**, however, continued to be a problem. Gays and lesbians largely avoided direct activism, especially in terms of a gay identity politics as was increasingly common in other Western countries, although their issues were often incorporated into the agendas of larger leftist groups. The movement had difficulty advancing its cause in the 1980s. When the police arrested two women for kissing, under a public decency statute, and then subjected them to two days of detention and abuse without even telling them of the reason for arrest, it proved to be a galvanizing event. In early 1987, public demonstrations were held throughout Spain to protest the treatment of the two women. The public decency statute was repealed the next year.

In the 1990s, gay and lesbian groups were more effective in their lobbying activities. In 1995, the government enacted a new penal code that recognized freedom of expression of one's sexual orientation as a basic right. Consequently, discrimination on the basis of sexual orientation in employment, housing, or public services became illegal. In 2005, the Socialist government of José Zapatero passed a **same-sex marriage** law, including **adoption** rights. The law also provided legal recognition to the non-biological mothers of children born through in vitro fertilization within a lesbian marriage. One notable aspect of the debate over gay rights in Spain is that the focus is not upon identity politics, in contrast to countries such as the **United States**. Instead, many persons frame the issue as one of Spain's modernization and normalization after the Franco era, and the adoption of gay rights is part of that process. In the early 21st century, Spain is unquestionably one of the foremost countries in the world as far as the equal legal treatment of gays and lesbians. *See also* GERMANY; ITALY; LITERATURE, HOMOSEXUAL MALE; SOTADIC ZONE.

STEIN, GERTRUDE (1874–1946). Even though she was born and raised in the **United States**, Gertrude Stein spent most of her life as an expatriate, primarily in Paris. There she wrote, collected art, and was an integral part of a circle of authors and artists, including Ernest Hemingway and F. Scott Fitzgerald. Through her fiction, which was at the forefront of literary modernism, and her essays on art, celebrating then-controversial figures such as Pablo Picasso, she helped to open the United States to modernism in art. Even her friendships did the same, mixing Parisian avant-garde figures with more staid Americans.

After a failed love affair with another woman while Stein was a medical student, she left medical school and went to Europe. In 1907, Alice Toklas, also an American, arrived in Paris and soon met Stein. The two quickly became a couple and remained together until Stein's death. Their relationship exemplified the roles of **butch/femme**, with Stein in the butch, or "husband," role. They freely called each other by their pet names in front of others, including the American soldiers they hosted after the liberation of France.

Stein's literary efforts were influential, although they are not widely read today. Her first novel, *Q.E.D.*, was inspired by her affair as a medical student and it is forthright in its exploration of a lesbian relationship. She did not publish it during her lifetime. Other works, such as *Tender Buttons*, are difficult and seemingly intentionally obscure. The one work that still commands attention, and is also the most accessible, is *The Autobiography of Alice B. Toklas*. While not in fact an autobiography, it is written as one from her partner's point of view, complete with references to "Miss Stein" in the third person. Direct in language and very amusing, it allows a view into the lives of expatriates in Paris. *See also* FRANCE; LITERATURE, LESBIAN.

STONEWALL. The Stonewall riots are widely seen as the central, pivotal event of the modern gay rights movement in the **United States**. Many divide the history of the movement into pre- and post-Stonewall eras. The Stonewall Inn was a popular, though seedy, gay bar in Greenwich Village. Under the New York State Liquor Authority, which licensed all bars, dissolute establishments were to be closed, and it interpreted that rule as banning same-sex dancing. The mafia ran the establishment, since they had police connections who could keep the bar open. Its patrons included transvestites, transsexuals, and drug dealers. In late June 1969, the police raided the bar, which had occurred several times previously. This time, however, the patrons resisted and a riot ensued. It continued for several nights. Rioters shouted "gay power," showing that the radicalism of the 1960s civil rights movement was being absorbed by a new generation of gays and lesbians.

The Stonewall riots received a substantial amount of media attention. While **homophile** groups responded with pleas for calm and proposed candlelight vigils, a new cadre of leaders quickly emerged. Drawn largely from New Left groups, and proud of their homosexuality, they were militant and demanded that American society change. A group of activists formed the **Gay Liberation Front** in New York City a few weeks after Stonewall.

Stonewall today often serves as shorthand for a whole series of changes that were already beginning before the actual riots. Gay and lesbian activists were slowly moving away from the strategy of showing that they fit in with establishment institutions and the mainstream culture. Instead of the **homophile movement**'s focus on **police harassment** and an attempt to carve out some private space, the new activists focused more on the public arena and the demand for equal rights. Stonewall and the media attention it received influenced the gay rights movement in **Great Britain** and **Europe** as well. In 1999, the U.S. government listed the site where the Stonewall Inn was, and its immediate vicinity, on the National Register of Historic Places, due to its role in gay and lesbian history. *See also* AIDS COALITION TO UNLEASH POWER; ANTI-DISCRIMINATION LAWS; ASIA; CANADA; CLOSET, THE; HAY, HENRY; LITERATURE, LESBIAN; MATTACHINE SOCIETY; QUEER THEORY; SOCIETY FOR INDIVIDUAL RIGHTS.

SYMONDS, JOHN ADDINGTON (1840–1893). A British historian of genuine talent, as well as a translator and poet, John Addington Symonds did not widely distribute his writings defending same-sex love. In 1872, Symonds wrote *A Problem in Greek Ethics*, although he did not even circulate it among friends until years later. In it he argued that **ancient Greece** showed that, contrary to modern stereotypes that linked male homosexuality to effeminacy, male-male love should be seen as masculine and in no way symptomatic of degeneracy or pathology. He also privately published *A Problem in Modern Ethics*, which contains what is probably the first use of the word "homosexual" in English. This work focused on criticizing the scientific views of his day regarding same-sex love. Symonds approached his friend **Havelock Ellis** about co-authoring a work on homosexuality. The resulting book, *Sexual Inversion*, only contained one essay by Symonds, but it had an international circulation.

Like his friend **Edward Carpenter**, Symonds was deeply moved by **Walt Whitman**'s *Leaves of Grass*, especially the poems in the "Calamus" section. Carpenter corresponded extensively with Whitman, although he was never able to get Whitman to clarify just what was meant by the repeated invocations of "manly love" and "the love of comrades." Symonds eventually wrote a book about Whitman, which was published on the same day that Symonds died.

– T –

TORAH. The five books that constitute the Torah are central to **Judaism**; the tradition's adherents consider them the most sacred of all religious texts. Although the Torah, or Law, is supposed to have been handed down by Moses, contemporary scholars agree that it is largely a compilation from centuries after Moses lived. The Torah most likely dates from the sixth century B.C.E. One of the books, Leviticus, contains a harsh denunciation of same-sex sexuality along with a prescribed penalty of death. Since the five books (Genesis, Exodus, Leviticus, Numbers, and Deuteronomy) were later incorporated into the **Bible**, the Torah's hostility to same-sex relations has also been central to the history of **Christianity**. Some have interpreted the proscription of same-sex relations as a primitive pro-natal policy, but the language and the context of the passage suggest concerns for ritual purity and avoidance of defilement, perhaps arising from suspicions of rival tribes that practiced same-sex cult prostitution.

Genesis relates the story of Lot, which many have taken to be yet another example of hostility to same-sex relations. Lot and his family lived in Sodom, which Yahweh (God) condemned due to its sinfulness. The nature of its evil, however, is left unclear. In the narrative, God sent two angels to save Lot and his family from the city's impending destruction. Men from the city surrounded Lot's house and demanded that he send out the two so that, the text implies, they may have sex with them. God subsequently destroyed the city. Early Jewish interpretations and commentaries, however, show that ancient scholars did not interpret the story as a denunciation of homoeroticism. Many argued that Sodom was wicked due to a lack of charity or the sin of pride.

TRANSGENDERISM. A term coined in the 1960s and reaching wider use in the 1970s and 1980s, transgenderism usually refers to persons whose presentation of self does not conform to traditional gender categories. It functions as a broader umbrella term that includes **transvestism** and **transsexualism**. The roots of the term, however, focus on persons who choose to live as the opposite gender without the hormone therapy or surgery necessary to be a transsexual. There is a rich theoretical debate, with political implications, about how transgendered persons should see themselves. Some argue that transgenderism is an affirmation of androgyny, others that it is a form of opposition to a stultifying, dichotomous mapping of gender. *See also* ASIA; UNITED NATIONS.

TRANSSEXUALISM. Coined by **Magnus Hirschfeld**, the term "transsexualism" refers to persons wanting to live as the opposite gender from what they were born, or perhaps assigned at birth. Contemporary Western understandings of transsexuality rely on a conceptual background that distinguishes between sex, as in the biological equipment one has, and gender, which is the social role or presentation of self one makes, and whether that presentation of self manifests traits that are socially understood as masculine or feminine. Transsexuals can pursue hormone therapy or sex reassignment surgery as means for bringing their self-perception of sex and gender into alignment. Many transsexuals do not self-identify as gay or lesbian, although some do. *See also* TRANSGENDERISM.

TRANSVESTISM. A term coined by **Magnus Hirschfeld**, transvestism is from the Latin for "cross" and "dress." It refers to persons who wear clothes common to the opposite sex. The range of cross-dressing practices, however, is large. In some simple societies, transvestism is part of religious rituals. Transvestism has been a significant component of the **butch/femme** subculture, as well as for drag queens and drag kings.

Historically, transvestism has often been confused with homosexuality. Some 19th-century sex researchers lumped the two together.

Hirschfeld, in a work composed primarily of case studies of cross-dressers, pointed out that most were heterosexual. Thus he felt the need to invent a neologism to help differentiate the two. *See also* ASIA; TRANSGENDERISM.

TRIBADE. Derived from the Greek verb for "to rub," the term "tribade" was used for centuries to describe women who have sex with women, especially those who are the sexual aggressors. Authors in **ancient Rome** were the first to use the term; they often borrowed words from Greek when discussing sexuality. The first extant uses date from the first century C.E., and the term was often used well into the 19th century.

Concerns with role and status played a significant role in how ancient Romans interpreted sexuality, and they assimilated female-female relations into the penetrator/penetrated dichotomy. For the fifth-century (C.E.) medical text *On Chronic Diseases*, the problematic issue was a woman taking a masculine role. The work did not discuss the passive partner, even though she was of the same sex. The *tribas* takes the penetrative role either through the use of a dildo or, allegedly, by using the overly enlarged clitoris that, according to ancient and modern authors, was the source of this unnatural sexuality.

The rediscovery of ancient Roman literature in the 16th century promoted the term and concept more than a millennium after its birth. The word entered the English language in the early 17th century. Writers in the 18th and 19th centuries used the term most frequently in pornographic literature. Shifts in hypotheses about the **etiology** of homosexuality at the turn of the 20th century, from physiological to psychological, made the notion of the tribade as a specific type of woman fall into disuse. *See also* FRANCE; LITERATURE, LESBIAN.

TURING, ALAN (1912–1954). A British mathematician and logician, many consider Turing the father of computer science. His innovative ideas about algorithms provided conceptual breakthroughs that helped in the building of early computers. He was also instrumental in the Allied effort to break the German "Enigma" Code during World War II. In late 1951, Turing met a young man, Arnold Murray, and the two briefly became lovers. In early 1952, Turing was a victim of burglary; one of Murray's friends committed the crime. During the subsequent police investigation, Turing admitted that he and Murray had had sex. The police arrested both and they were subsequently convicted. Turing avoided jail time but at the price of undergoing experimental hormone therapy. For a year he was injected with female hormones. The authorities' hope was to end his sex drive, but it did not work. After his conviction, the British government no longer allowed him to work on sensitive cryptology projects. In 1954, Turing committed suicide by eating an apple laced with cyanide.

– U –

ULRICHS, KARL HEINRICH (1825–1895). A lawyer by training, Karl Heinrich Ulrichs published a series of pamphlets in the 1860s and 1870s about same-sex love. His arguments were innovative and proved deeply influential on subsequent generations of thinkers about sexuality. He was also a political activist. He advocated legal and social reform that would accord equality regardless of what many today would call sexual orientation. Ulrichs also was open about his attraction to men at a time when that was rare and exposed one to legal risk.

Ulrichs argued that sexual attraction is innate. According to him, the embryo, in its earliest developmental stages, has a hermaphroditic stage that then transforms into a specific sex. Similarly, he contended, in utero one's adult pattern of sexual attraction also develops. Just as some persons never develop the genitalia of one sex, becoming physical hermaphrodites, others never develop a psycho-sexual orientation toward the opposite sex. Known as the "third sex" theory, Ulrichs argued that this development of attraction to one's own gender is harmless. Seeking neutral terms for same-sex love, rather than the pejorative ones of his cultural milieu, Ulrichs coined the terms *Urnings* and *Urningins* for males and females, respectively, attracted to members of their own sex. Given that this "third sex" is a natural biological variation and morally acceptable, it is nonsensical to have **anti-sodomy laws**. Furthermore, Ulrichs maintained that France's decriminalization of sodomy, under the **Code Napoléon**, did not degrade morals or threaten social order.

Ulrichs also protested Prussia's annexation of Hanover, where he was a citizen. This action, in 1866, resulted in Ulrichs' spending a year in jail. One reason for his opposition to Prussia's policy was its punitive anti-sodomy law. He attended two law congresses to get that law overturned, but to no avail.

Ulrichs' arguments about same-sex attraction as a natural, biological process proved deeply influential for sexologists such as **Havelock Ellis**. Ulrichs also helped to shape the thinking of **Magnus Hirschfeld**, the co-founder of the *Wissenschaftlich-humanitäres Komitee* (Scientific-Humanitarian Committee). In this way, Ulrichs was instrumental to the birth of the homosexual rights movement in late 19th-century **Germany**. *See also* ETIOLOGY; EUROPE; HALL, RADCLYFFE; MEDICAL MODEL OF HOMOSEXUALITY; REPARATIVE THERAPY.

UNITED NATIONS (UN). In 1994, United Nations' Human Rights Committee, which is charged with interpreting the International Covenant on Civil and Political Rights (ICCPR), ruled in *Toonen v. Australia* that Tasmania's **anti-sodomy law** violated the ICCPR's provision against arbitrary interference with an individual's privacy, home, or family. **Australia** had argued before the committee that the law concerned a moral issue best addressed domestically and that no human rights issue was at stake since no prosecutions under it had taken place in years. The complainant, Nicholas Toonen, and his lover had even gone to a police station and confessed to over 1,000 violations of the law and still had not been arrested. The committee's ruling stated that the mere existence of such a law constituted discrimination and created the possibility of breach of privacy. *Toonen* also implicitly overturned the committee's 1982 ruling in *Hertzberg v. Finland*, which had held that state discretion on moral issues permitted Finland's government to ban broadcasts that dealt with homosexuality. Tasmania complied with the decision three years later by repealing the law.

The UN General Assembly addressed the issue of homosexuality for the first time in 2008. **France** and other states put forward a nonbinding declaration calling on all member countries to stop violence, discrimination, and harassment based upon sexual orientation and gender identity, including such acts done by the state and its agents.

The declaration also emphasized the need for member states to overturn all laws that discriminate against gays, lesbians, and **transgender** persons, including anti-sodomy laws. Some countries' anti-sodomy laws allow for the death penalty. Sixty-six countries voted in favor of the declaration, mostly from **Europe** and **Latin America**, while 57 countries signed an alternative statement put forward by the Organization of the **Islamic** Conference that condemned the declaration for promoting "pedophilia." The **United States** did not support either side, stating that while it opposes discrimination, U.S. officials were worried that the non-binding declaration would have unacceptable legal implications for state and local governments. *See also* INTERNATIONAL LESBIAN AND GAY ASSOCIATION.

UNITED STATES. Given the racial and ethnic diversity within the United States, as well as a long history of geographical divisions, it is often difficult to generalize about homosexuality in the country. Some American Indian tribes had an institutionalized "third sex" role, called the **berdache**. There is virtually no evidence about lesbian relationships or attraction in traditional Native American societies. While there have been a few efforts to infer the nature of lesbianism among traditional Indians, these inquiries are reduced to speculative inferences based on social structures, religious beliefs and practices, and the like.

European colonizers brought with them a theological approach, placing much emphasis on the story of Sodom. Some early colonial **anti-sodomy laws** had language directly from the **Bible**, while others adopted the **Act of 25 Henry VIII**. The laws did not refer to sexual relations between women, with the exception of the New Haven Colony's 1656 code. New Haven amended the law a decade later, at which time the colony dropped the provision about female-female relations. While usually prescribing the death penalty, the laws appear to have been infrequently enforced. Those convicted were typically whipped, branded, or banished from the colony, or perhaps they suffered all of those punishments. On a few occasions, the convicted were executed. In 1682, Pennsylvania, under the leadership of William Penn and other Quakers, reduced the penalty for a first offense to six months of hard labor. Pastors throughout the colonies routinely denounced **sodomites** from the pulpit, although the sin was often presented as an action that anyone could fall into, given the prevalent emphasis on mankind's fallen nature and the ubiquity of temptation and evil.

By the end of the 18th century, the theological framework was partially displaced by a more juridical one. Yet the general air of condemnation did not change. Thomas Jefferson and other prominent Virginians proposed that the penalty for sodomy be reduced from death to castration. That effort failed, but states did alter punishments. State lawmakers substituted whipping, branding, and the death penalty for prison sentences, fines, and the use of the pillory. Still, convictions were rare. A man who conducted a two-year tour of American prisons wrote, in 1826, an open letter that complained about male prisoners forcing boys to submit to sex. He alleged that older prisoners often prostituted, or "kept," boys for sexual purposes. He urged legislators to separate juvenile offenders from the general prison population. Yet there is some evidence from personal correspondence of the time that among young men, especially in the South, same-sex relations were fairly common, including among the rich, and were not seen as a dire moral failing. More generally, the 19th century idealized same-sex friendships. Personal letters from the era are often marked by deep expressions of passion and longings, which showed that this cult of friendship carried so far as to often make same-sex friendships the central relationships of people's lives. Yet even though these communications were undoubtedly sincere and carried an explicit romantic aspect, it is unlikely that many of them involved overtly sexual relationships.

In the mid-19th-century United States, Victorian morality strengthened its hold. For instance, one complaint about **Walt Whitman**'s poetry was that he did not seem ashamed of his genitalia. The poet Bayard Taylor wrote more explicitly about male same-sex love. Despite the general moral climate, in most major American cities there were only a few recorded prosecutions for same-sex sodomy each year in the 19th century. The rate of prosecutions clearly increased, however, in the final years of the century. Trial records from that time also show that certain urban areas had been established for same-sex assignations. There were also gay bars in some urban areas, such as New York City. Largely catering to working-class patrons, the bars had "fairies" who dressed in women's clothes, wore makeup, and adopted feminine mannerisms.

The pronounced changes in women's lives in the latter part of the 19th century, and carrying into the next, greatly expanded their educational and economic opportunities. The newfound independence from men, combined with the older ideal of same-sex friendship, made it possible for many women to set up homes together in relationships that sometimes lasted for decades. Often called **Boston marriages**, these relationships were confined to the upper class or to well-educated women. Many saw them as the epitome of mutual regard and care. Yet the influence of European sexologists made it so that, by the end of the 19th century, these relationships were seen as problematic; even schoolgirl crushes, or "smashes," were temptations to be avoided. While working-class women usually lacked the means to set up independent houses as women, thousands of women in 19th-century America "passed" as men, taking jobs or serving in the military. While economic motives were important, many established homes with other women, marrying and presenting themselves as heterosexual couples.

In the late 19th and early 20th centuries, medical discourse about sexuality became increasingly common. The consequences were profound. Previously, theologians and ministers described sodomy as a sin into which anyone could fall. With the new terminology, "inverts" and "homosexuals" were types of persons who might lead others into degeneracy, and who manifested unfortunate natures by being overly mannish, if female, or overly effeminate, if male. Passionate same-sex relationships became suspect, rather than ideal. Previously someone like Whitman could boast of minute-long kisses with soldiers without arousing suspicions about his "nature." Social controls increasingly were oriented at "gender inversion," even through laws that forbade cross-dressing. Private groups of individuals, such as the Comstock Society in New York, organized to work for enforcement of laws involving "vices" such as male prostitution. Most states changed their anti-sodomy laws to cover male-male oral sex, and as a consequence the number of sodomy arrests and convictions increased dramatically after 1880.

Yet during the last decades of the 19th century, and more widely during the first decades of the 20th century, there were some urban enclaves where homosexuality was as least partially accepted and public. These included New York City; Washington, D.C.; Boston; Chicago; San Francisco; and Philadelphia. Greenwich Village's art scene was open to lesbianism, although more as a phase to go through prior to marriage. In the 1920s, the gay subculture was fairly open in New York. There were bathhouses frequented by gay men, along with dance parties. Even though police arrested hundreds of men each year in New York City alone for cruising in parks and elsewhere, discreetly advertised balls were generally safe and often straight persons went as sightseers. Even as the expanded dance scene helped open the gay subculture beyond fairies to conventionally masculine men, gay authors of the time, such as Robert McAlmon, presented extremely effeminate men in their fiction. McAlmon's characters used lingo recognizable in American culture today: "**queer**," "cruising," "gay," and "drag." Harlem was accepting of bisexuality, although exclusive homosexuality was more problematic. While there were speakeasies and bars that had performers in drag, and even homosexual sex shows, persons were often pushed into heterosexual marriages.

In 1925, Henry Gerber and others founded the Society for Human Rights in Chicago. It was the first homosexual rights group in the United States. It published a newsletter, but only for two issues. The group disbanded after Gerber was arrested, probably due to **police harassment** rather than any probable cause. Repression increased in the 1930s, driving the subculture even in New York further underground. In the mid-1930s, an anti-homosexual vigilante group calling itself the White Legion attacked men in Brooklyn that they suspected were homosexual. The movie trade group passed a Production Code in 1930 that prohibited displays of "sexual perversity" or anything that would lower the morals of viewers. While the overt repression continued in the 1940s, and the armed forces began trying to screen homosexuals from **military service**, World War II was a transformative experience for many. Millions went from conservative, rural environments into the military or other sex-segregated environments. Port cities grew and bustled with activity. Gay bars proliferated. There is considerable anecdotal evidence that many persons experienced same-sex relations for the first time due to the changes of this era. For many homosexual men and women, this era of self-discovery made them unwilling to return to small-town life.

After the war, however, the repression of homosexuality was as severe as ever. Psychiatry had increased legitimacy and the mainstream of the discipline at the time saw homosexuality as a mental illness. The postwar era also emphasized conformity and sexual nonconformity became linked to treason. **McCarthyism** reflected this suspicion. Yet it was also during the 1950s that a few activists began the **homophile movement** in the United States. The **Mattachine Society** and the **Daughters of Bilitis** were the most influential groups. While they were politically quiescent in their first years, in the 1960s, under the influence of new organizers such as **Frank Kameny**, the groups became more assertive. The influence of the civil rights movement also galvanized them and they began to work against police harassment and other forms of invasion of private gay space, such as crackdowns on gay bars. It was in this area that the groups achieved some genuine progress.

The **Stonewall** riots in 1969 further radicalized the movement for gay rights, so much so that the movement's history is usually divided into pre- and post-Stonewall eras. While this is in many ways shorthand for broader trends, the gays who aggressively responded to a police raid on a gay bar in Greenwich Village did launch a revolution. A few weeks later, activists had formed the influential **Gay Liberation Front** (GLF). Younger, more radicalized gays and lesbians displaced older, **homophile**-era homosexuals in leadership positions. Some of the homophile groups simply dissolved.

In the 1970s, gay rights groups proliferated. Radical, largely male groups like the GLF, and lesbian-feminist groups—like Radicalesbians on the East Coast and Gay Women's Liberation on the West Coast—uneasily coexisted with more mainstream groups. Sometimes they tried not to coexist: Radicalesbians established communes, and lesbian separatists tried to avoid men altogether, gay or straight.

Since the agendas often did not overlap, and sometimes differed from one another, it is not truly accurate to speak of "a" gay rights movement from 1970 on. Instead, a variety of movements formed. One of the central divides was between lesbians and gay men. Many lesbians strongly endorsed feminism, and while some feminist leaders did not reciprocate, during the decade, some of the most prominent feminists did defend lesbian liberation, and the National Organization for Women formally endorsed the cause. For many lesbians the emphasis was on male domination of society and the need to liberate women and female sexuality, rather than a focus upon heterosexism and gay liberation.

Gay neighborhoods in big urban centers flourished. Large numbers of men, and somewhat smaller numbers of women, left rural environs for more tolerant cities. Gays and lesbians established alternative institutions, such as gay churches, newspapers, and singing groups. As the 1970s wore on, a good portion of gay politics settled into a quasi-ethnic model, with gay leaders portraying "the movement" as another pressure group and voting bloc. The increasing prominence of gay neighborhoods and political groups contributed to a backlash. Led by individuals such as **Anita Bryant** and Phyllis Schlafly, social conservative and evangelical groups tried with some success to stop and in some cases roll back pro-gay policy changes. The right wing saw the onset of the **human immunodeficiency virus/acquired immunodeficiency syndrome** (HIV/AIDS) epidemic in the 1980s as more evidence of how gays and lesbians contributed to social decay. Some went so far as to argue for quarantining HIV-positive persons, or, as with William Buckley, mandating that they receive a tattoo identifying them as infected.

The 1990s, however, marked a turn in the political situation. More and more prominent persons came out of **the closet**, such as Martina Navratilova, one of the greatest female tennis players ever, as well as figures in the arts and even the military. In contrast to the overtly anti-gay *Bowers v. Hardwick* decision, the Supreme Court ruled, in *Romer v. Evans*, that a state anti-gay initiative had no rational or legitimate policy aim and was instead motivated by an unconstitutional bias against one class of persons. A large number of cities and several states, including New Jersey and Vermont, passed **antidiscrimination laws**.

Gay rights issues have been at the forefront of the culture wars of the 21st century. On the one hand, more companies have opted to grant **domestic partnership** benefits, yet hate crimes against gays and lesbians continue. Large urban areas have seen **assimilation**. Even **Matthew Shepard**'s hometown of Casper, Wyoming, had an openly gay mayor, yet gays and lesbians continue to be marginalized and maligned in many areas. Probably the defining debate of the first decade of the 21st century has been over **same-sex mar-**

riage. In 2004, Massachusetts became the first state to recognize gay marriage; Vermont, Connecticut, and New Jersey recognize **civil unions**. The debate has also energized the **religious right**, who take the issue as virtually definitive of society's overall moral well-being. In 2008, the California and Connecticut Supreme Courts ruled that gays and lesbians have the right to marry under their respective state constitutions, and the governor of New York mandated state agencies to begin recognizing same-sex marriages from elsewhere, including abroad. Yet anti-gay groups countered by putting a proposition on the ballot in California that would nullify the court's decision, which ultimately passed, and threatening to sue in New York. *See also* AIDS COALITION TO UNLEASH POWER; *BOUTILIER V. IMMIGRATION AND NATURALIZATION SERVICE*; CANADA; CHRISTIANITY; COMING OUT; DEFENSE OF MARRIAGE ACT; "DON'T ASK, DON'T TELL"; EMPLOYMENT NON-DIS-CRIMINATION ACT; FALWELL, JERRY, SR.; GAY BASHING; HALL, RADCLYFFE; HATE CRIME LAWS; HOMOPHILE; HO-MOPHOBIA; HUMAN RIGHTS CAMPAIGN; IMMIGRATION AND NATURALIZATION LAW; JUDAISM; KRAMER, LARRY; *LAWRENCE V. TEXAS*; LITERATURE; HOMOSEXUAL MALE; LITERATURE, LESBIAN; *MANUAL V. DAY*; MEDICAL MODEL OF HOMOSEXUALITY; MILK, HARVEY; NATIONAL GAY AND LESBIAN TASK FORCE; NEWPORT NAVAL SCANDAL; *ONE, INC. V. OLESEN*; OUTING; PARENTS AND FRIENDS OF LESBIANS AND GAYS; QUEER NATION; STEIN, GERTRUDE; UNITED NATIONS.

URNINGS. *See* ULRICHS, KARL HEINRICH.

– V –

VIAU, THÉOPHILE DE (1590–1626). A gifted French poet, and one of the most popular of his time, Théophile de Viau was also a notorious atheist and wrote poetry that proclaimed the beauty of male-male love. He urged his readers to follow the impulses of nature rather than the dictates of morality. Viau also wrote doggerel verses that delighted in scandal and the foibles of the powerful. He fell in love with another poet, Jacques Vallée des Barreaux, who was handsome and nine years younger than he was. Their relationship endured up to Viau's death.

In 1623, Parliament ordered his arrest for impiety and blasphemy, due to his writings. Viau fled, but was tried in absentia and sentenced to death. Soon he was captured but influential friends were able to secure a retrial, this time for sodomy. He was imprisoned for two years, during which he was tortured and suffered from the deplorable conditions. In 1625, the court held that Viau should be banished and his goods confiscated. His health shattered by his time in confinement, Viau died in 1626. *See also* FRANCE; LITERATURE, HOMOSEXUAL MALE.

– W –

WASHINGTON CONFIDENTIAL. In 1951, two Hearst reporters published the results of their investigation into homosexuals in the federal government. The book reflected and contributed to the "Lavender Scare," which was the idea that homosexual men and women in government constituted a security threat. As often happened during **McCarthyism**, the numbers given throughout the book were either invented or of dubious worth. The book is filled with sensationalistic language, referring to homosexual men and women as "fags" or "deviates." Regardless of its lack of adherence to traditional standards of journalism, the book sold well and reached the top spot on the *New York Times'* bestseller list soon after publication.

WELL OF LONELINESS, THE. *See* HALL, RADCLYFFE.

WHITMAN, WALTER (1819–1892). At a time when sensuality and bodily appetites were ignored or scorned, the American poet Walt Whitman brought forth a bold celebration of the physical self. He published his seminal work, *Leaves of Grass*, in 1855 and revised and added to it throughout his life. The "Calamus" section of *Leaves*, added to the third edition in 1860, praises "the love of comrades" and "manly love" repeatedly. The opening poem of the section sets the tone: in paths untrodden and away from the norms of society, the narrator of the poem will seek "athletic love," "tell the secret of my nights and days," and "celebrate the need of comrades." A pair of lines, which Whitman chose to delete in later editions, made what seems a clear reference to homosexual anal sex. Many persons read Whitman as praising male-male eros, including **John Addington Symonds** and **Edward Carpenter**.

It is difficult to sort out Whitman's own sexuality, due to both limitations of evidence and the fact that, like many persons who lived prior to the diffusion of contemporary sexual categories, it appears to have been inchoate and not sharply defined. Certainly, his central emotional ties were with young, working-class men and soldiers. He also recorded the numerous times that he met and ended up "sleeping with" various laborers. Yet Whitman lived during a time notable for the intensity of male-male friendships, when men would share a bed for months or even years and it was not seen as inappropriate or implying any sort of sexual contact. Despite the ambiguities, Whitman's life and poetry embody and praise intimate relations between persons of the same sex. *See also* LITERATURE, HOMOSEXUAL MALE; SOCIAL CONSTRUCTIONISM; UNITED STATES.

WILDE, OSCAR (1854–1900). An Irish-born author who spent most of his adult life in **Great Britain**, Oscar Wilde was famous for his plays, such as *The Importance of Being Earnest*, and other works, such as his short novel *The Picture of Dorian Gray*. Although he married and had children, Wilde was attracted to younger men. His most important long-term relationship was with Sir Alfred Douglas, who was 16 years his junior. Douglas' father, the marquess of Queensbury, was hostile to the relationship and took to harassing Wilde, including publicly accusing Wilde of posing as a **sodomite**. In response, Wilde sued the marquess for libel. Wilde lost and the evidence entered during the trial prompted the authorities to have Wilde arrested and charged under the **Labouchère Amendment**. The first prosecution resulted in a hung jury, but the authorities were able to convict Wilde in a subsequent trial. Wilde was sentenced to two years in prison with hard labor. The conditions in prison were horrendous. Wilde also had to pay for the marquess' costs from the original libel trial. As a result, his possessions were sold off. Wilde left for **France** upon his release from prison. He died in Paris as a result of an infection he had contracted in prison.

Wilde's trials were one of the great sensations of his era. While the original charge and his subsequent conviction and sentencing caused a wave of fear among British homosexuals, the ultimate effects of his tribulations are more ambiguous. The combination of the repression associated with the Labouchère Amendment, the Wilde trials, and other scandals of the era (such as the Cleveland Street scandal of 1889) helped to forge a self-consciousness among Britons who were attracted to members of their own sex. While there was not yet a modern gay identity, these events and the cultural, medical, and legal patterns behind them set the stage for the emergence of that identity. *See also* BILLING CASE; ELLIS, HAVELOCK; LITERATURE, HOMOSEXUAL MALE; SOTADIC ZONE.

WISSENSCHAFTLICH-HUMANITÄRES KOMITEE (WHK)/SCI-ENTIFIC-HUMANITARIAN COMMITTEE. Founded in 1897, the *Wissenschaftlich-humanitäres Komitee* was dedicated to educating the public about homosexuality and fighting for the repeal of **anti-sodomy laws**. **Magnus Hirschfeld** was one of the co-founders. The group quickly began circulating a petition for the repeal of **Germany**'s anti-sodomy law. Targeted primarily at prominent and influential persons, the petition eventually was signed by August Bebel (the Social Democratic Party leader), Martin Buber, Albert Einstein, **Sigmund Freud**, Karl Jaspers, Rainer Maria Rilke, and Thomas Mann. Although the petition did provoke debate in parliament, the effort ultimately proved unsuccessful.

In 1899, the WHK began publishing the *Jahrbuch für sexuelle Zwischenstufen* (Yearbook for Sexual Intermediates). The title itself reflects **Karl Heinrich Ulrichs'** influence on Hirschfeld, its editor, and other founders. The yearbook was a scholarly journal. Hirschfeld was prosecuted for publishing the results of a WHK survey that claimed that over 2 percent of Berliners were homosexual. He was acquitted. The mainstream press gave the trial substantial coverage. The group stopped publishing the yearbook in 1923.

The WHK had influence across **Europe**. Like-minded persons formed chapters in other German cities, as well as in London, Amsterdam, and Vienna. The rise of **National Socialism** proved fatal to the WHK. In 1933, Nazis stormed the WHK's headquarters in Berlin and burned the materials they had confiscated. Hirschfeld, who was the dominant force in the group, was out of the country at the time. He never returned. *See also* BRITISH SOCIETY FOR THE STUDY OF SEX PSYCHOLOGY; MEDICAL MODEL OF HOMOSEXUALITY; OUTING.

WOLFENDEN REPORT. England enacted its **anti-sodomy law** in 1533. Although subsequently modified and even broadened, it remained in place in the mid-20th century. After World War II the law was frequently used with hundreds and, in the 1950s, thousands of men being arrested each year for consensual sodomy. **Police harassment** and entrapment were often behind such arrests. The increasing arrests made the public more aware of the situation, especially since those arrested included a member of Parliament, a prominent actor, and a leading journalist. The home secretary, David Maxwell-Fyfe, asked Sir John Wolfenden to lead a committee investigation into homosexuality and prostitution, and the legal regime most appropriate to each. The Committee on Homosexual Offenses and Prostitution issued the Wolfenden Report in 1957. It recommended the decriminalization of consensual homosexual sex. The committee strongly defended the role of privacy in liberal society. It put forward an understanding of law as a morally neutral framework that is geared toward public order, rather than the imposition of private morality upon the public at large. Those who defend **natural law** theory continue to criticize this line of argument, as well as the report itself. The report also criticized stereotypes about homosexual men as especially prone to pedophilia and homosexuality as a source of moral decay.

The public did not share the Wolfenden Report's support for decriminalization of sodomy, even though the report called for putting the age of consent for homosexual sex at 21. The report received favorable coverage in the press. Over time, it helped lead to the **Sexual Offenses Act** of 1967, which decriminalized homosexual sex in England and Wales. In that later battle the former home secretary, by then named to the House of Lords, led the fight against decriminalization. Some speculate that Wolfenden's support for reform was due, in part, to his having a gay son. *See also* CANADA; GREAT BRITAIN; HOMOSEXUAL LAW REFORM SOCIETY.

WORLD LEAGUE FOR SEXUAL REFORM. *See* HIRSCHFELD, MAGNUS.

Bibliography

CONTENTS

INTRODUCTION

The amount of material pertaining to homosexuality has increased vastly over the past half century. It is also fair to say that, for the most part, the quality of the material has improved, too. The love that did not dare to speak its name is now a topic of serious moral, legal, philosophical, and historical discussion. Clearly the subject of homosexuality has long been controversial and is still so today. As a result, many of the works in this bibliography are tendentious; it is fair to say that this is especially true with works that pre-date the modern gay rights movement. That movement has not only made it possible for those who defend equality for gays and lesbians to come forward; it has also made it so that those who seek to disparage homosexuality often must defend their views rather than simply relying on stereotypes or established opinions and prejudices.

A historiographical debate between "essentialists" and "social constructionists," which peaked in the 1980s, has left its imprint on studies of homosexuality. Since then authors have had to take, at least implicitly, a stand on whether homosexuality is a largely unchanging fact about human beings, or sexuality in general—and same-sex attraction in particular—is largely constructed along lines dictated by particular social regimes. The debate has led to a greater theoretical sophistication, although often at the cost of obscurantism and prose rife with jargon. Even though this debate is now somewhat transformed and less prominent, it has forced historians and others writing about the history of homosexuality to pay more attention to the differences between cultural understandings and practices of same-sex attraction across societies.

An exhaustive bibliography would be several times longer than the one included here. The goal of this bibliography is to list the central works in various fields, as well as the sources of all the material in the dictionary entries above. Original source material has been included when it has proven to be of lasting import. Influential early studies and secondary works have also been listed, but overall the emphasis is upon more contemporary scholarship. While many of the works below are of lasting value or fine scholarship, a few are especially recommended for the reader seeking a better initial understanding of homosexuality. For those wanting a historical survey spanning ancient Greece to the modern West, Louis Crompton's *Homosexuality and Civilization* is an excellent introduction. David F. Greenberg provides a truly global survey with extensive material about archaic cultures in *The Construction of Homosexuality*. Both works also have extensive bibliographies. *Hidden from History*, a collection of historical and theoretical essays edited by Martin Duberman, Martha Vicinus, and George Chauncey, is an especially worthwhile survey that largely attends primarily to Western history.

Many still see K. J. Dover's work on ancient Greece as definitive, although some of the more recent studies look more broadly than his focus upon artwork, philosophers, and the records of one trial. David Halperin's work on ancient Greece is of lasting interest. For surveys covering more recent history, Neil Miller's *Out of the Past* provides an engrossing account of homosexuality in the late 19th century and the 20th. He emphasizes the United States, but includes discussions of developments in other countries. Jonathan Katz's *Gay American History* has a wealth of historical documents and Chris Bull's *Come Out Fighting* has a good collection of essays from the past century. Lillian Faderman's work is recognized as perhaps the best for modern lesbian history. For the modern homophile movement, John D'Emilio's *Sexual Politics, Sexual Communities* is truly essential reading.

In philosophy, a volume edited by David Estlund and Martha Nussbaum, *Sex, Preference, and Family*, provides a good introduction to main areas of argument and the basic philosophical positions involved. William Eskridge Jr. is one of the best contemporary legal theorists writing about gay and lesbian issues and law. His writings vary from rather plainspoken to the theoretically elaborate *Gaylaw*, but they are consistently smart and engaging. *The Lesbian and Gay Studies Reader*, edited by Henry Abelove, Michele Barale, and David Halperin, is comprehensive in its inclusion of influential political and philosophical essays across a range of issues. Bruce Bawer's *A Place at the Table* is eloquent in its plea for gay equality. Tanya Erzen, in *Straight to Jesus*, has put together a sensitive and balanced account of the "ex-gay" movement.

The growth of writing about homosexuality over the past three decades has led to categories of study that are noteworthy for the quality and diversity of work they include. One of these categories is studies of same-sex attraction in particular milieus, especially local or regional. George Chauncey's *Gay New York* has long stood as one of the best of these. More recently, Brian Whitaker has written an accessible work, *Unspeakable Love*, about homosexuality in the contemporary Middle East. An excellent thematic study is Henry Minton's *Departing from Deviance*, which examines the medical establishment's slow turn away from an understanding of homosexuality as pathology. Vito Russo's *The Celluloid Closet* transformed cultural studies in its area. His detailed readings of the depiction of same-sex sexuality in film not only made many people see movies in a new way, it also helped usher in a profusion of works that do the same for literature, pop culture, and the media.

Two notable archives focus on homosexuality. The Lesbian Herstory Archives in Brooklyn has a large collection and a user-friendly website. The ONE National Gay and Lesbian Archives, in Los Angeles, has an extensive and varied collection, including the private papers of various important persons from the homophile rights movement and early gay journals. The number of websites concerned with homosexuality has exploded over the past decade. The foremost international gay rights group, the International Lesbian and Gay Association, conducts research and publishes reports and first-person accounts, often of political oppression, on its website (www.ilga.org). Two good sites that focus on Europe are Pink News (www.pinknews.co.uk) and Rainbow Network (www.rainbownetwork.com). Gay Middle East also is an excellent site with a regional focus (www.gaymiddleeast.com). Useful websites based in the United States include the Advocate (www.advocate.com) and the Human Rights Campaign (www.hrc.org/), both of which provide news and resources from a pro–gay rights perspective, as does the site for Parents, Families, and Friends of Lesbians and Gays (www.pflag.org).

REFERENCE MATERIAL (ANTHOLOGIES, BIBLIOGRAPHIES, ENCYCLOPEDIAS, AND DICTIONARIES)

Aldrich, Robert, and Garry Wotherspoon, eds. *Who's Who in Gay and Lesbian History: From Antiquity to World War II*. New York: Routledge, 2001.

———. *Who's Who in Gay and Lesbian History: From World War II to the Present Day*. New York: Routledge, 2001.

Bell, Alan P., and Martin S. Weinberg, eds. *Homosexuality: An Annotated Bibliography*. New York: Oxford University Press, 1972.

Bronski, Michael, Christa Brelin, and Michael J. Tyrkus, eds. *Outstanding Lives: Profiles of Lesbians and Gay Men*. New York: Visible Ink Press, 1997.

Connor, Randy P., David Sparks, and Mariya Sparks. *Cassell's Encyclopedia of Queer Myth, Symbol and Spirit: Gay, Lesbian, Bisexual and Transgender Love*. London: Cassell Press, 1998.

Crawford, William. *Homosexuality in Canada: A Bibliography*. Toronto: Canadian Gay Archives, 1984.

Dynes, Wayne, Warren Johansson, and William A. Percy, eds. *Encyclopedia of Homosexuality*. New York: Garland Publishers, 1990.

Ellis, Alan, Liz Highleyman, Kevin Schaub, and Melissa White, eds. *The Harvey Milk Institute Guide to Lesbian, Gay, Bisexual, Transgender, and Queer Internet Research*. Binghamton, N.Y.: Harrington Park Press, 2002.

Fone, Byrne R. S., ed. *The Columbia Anthology of Gay Literature: Readings from Western Antiquity to the Present Day*. New York: Columbia University Press, 1998.

Furtado, Ken, and Nancy Hellner. *Gay and Lesbian American Plays: An Annotated Bibliography*. Metuchen, N.J.: Scarecrow Press, 1993.

Galloway, David, and Christian Sabisch, eds. *Calamus: Male Homosexuality in Twentieth-Century Literature: An International Anthology*. New York: Quill, 1982.

Gerstner, David A., ed. *Routledge International Encyclopedia of Queer Culture*. New York: Routledge, 2006.

Haggerty, George E., ed. *Gay Histories and Cultures: An Encyclopedia*. New York: Garland, 2000.

Miller, Meredith. *Historical Dictionary of Lesbian Literature*. Lanham, Md.: Scarecrow Press, 2006.

Morrow, Bruce, and Charles H. Rowell, eds. *Shade: An Anthology of Fiction by Gay Men of African Descent*. New York: Avon, 1996.

Myers, Joanne. *Historical Dictionary of the Lesbian Liberation Movement*. Lanham, Md.: Scarecrow Press, 2003.

Nelson, Emmanuel S., ed. *Contemporary Gay American Novelists: A Bio-Bibliographical Critical Sourcebook*. Westport, Conn.: Greenwood Press, 1993.

Parker, William. *Homosexuality: A Selective Bibliography of Over Three Thousand Items*. Metuchen, N.J.: Scarecrow Press, 1971.

———. *Homosexuality Bibliography: Second Supplement, 1976–1982*. Metuchen, N.J.: Scarecrow Press, 1985.

———. *Homosexuality Bibliography: Supplement, 1970–1975*. Metuchen, N.J.: Scarecrow Press, 1977.

Richardson, Diane, and Steven Seidman, eds. *Handbook of Lesbian and Gay Studies*. Thousand Oaks, Calif.: SAGE, 2002.

Ridinger, Robert B. Marks. *The Homosexual and Society: An Annotated Bibliography*. New York: Greenwood Press, 1990.

Schlager, Neil. *St. James Press Gay and Lesbian Almanac.* Detroit: St. James Press, 1998.

Smith, Raymond A., ed. *Encyclopedia of AIDS: A Social, Political, Cultural, and Scientific Record of the HIV Epidemic.* Chicago: Fitzroy Dearborn, 1998.

Stein, Marc, ed. *Encyclopedia of Lesbian, Gay, Bisexual, and Transgender History in America.* New York: Scribner, 2004.

Stewart, Charles. *Gay and Lesbian Issues: A Reference Handbook.* Santa Barbara, Calif.: ABC-CLIO, 2003.

Summers, Claude J., ed. *The Gay and Lesbian Literary Heritage: A Reader's Companion to the Writers and Their Works, from Antiquity to the Present.* New York: Routledge, 2002.

——, ed. *The Queer Encyclopedia of the Visual Arts.* San Francisco: Cleis Press, 2004.

Tin, Louis-Georges, ed. *The Dictionary of Homophobia: A Global History of Gay and Lesbian Experience.* Vancouver: Arsenal Pulp Press, 2008.

Walzer, Lee. *Gay Rights on Trial: A Reference Handbook.* Santa Barbara, Calif.: ABC-CLIO, 2002.

Weinberg, Martin S., and Alan P. Bell, eds. *Homosexuality: An Annotated Bibliography.* New York: Harper and Row, 1972.

Young, Ian. *The Male Homosexual in Literature: A Bibliography.* Metuchen, N.J.: Scarecrow Press, 1975.

Zimmerman, Bonnie, ed. *Lesbian Histories and Cultures: An Encyclopedia.* New York: Garland Press, 2000.

ARCHIVES AND LIBRARIES

Archives Gaies de Québec. 4067 St. Laurent, Bureau 202, Montreal, Québec, Canada, H2W 1Y7. Website: http://www.agq.qc.ca.

Australian Lesbian and Gay Archives. P.O. Box 124, Parkville VIC 3052, Australia. Website: http://home.vicnet.au/~alga/.

Canadian Gay Archives. P.O. Box 669, Station F, 50 Charles St. East, Toronto, Canada, M4Y 2N6. Website: http://www.clga.ca.

GLBT Historical Society. 657 Mission St., #300, San Francisco, CA, 94105. Website: http://www.glbthistory.org/.

Henry Gerber/Pearl M. Hart Library and Archives. 1127 W. Granvile Ave., Chicago, IL, 60660. Website: http://www.gerberhart.org/.

June L. Mazer Lesbian Archives. 626 N. Robertson Blvd., West Hollywood, CA, 90069. Website: http://mazerlesbianarchives.org.

Lesbian Herstory Archives. P.O. Box 1258, New York, NY 10116. Website: http://www.lesbianherstoryarchives.org.

National Archive of Lesbian, Gay, Bisexual, and Transgender History. Lesbian and Gay Community Services Center, 208 W. 13th St., New York, NY, 10011. Website: http://www.gaycenter.org/.

ONE National Gay and Lesbian Archives. 909 W. Adams Blvd., Los Angeles, CA, 90007. Website: http://www.onearchives.org/.

JOURNALS AND PERIODICALS

The Advocate. Los Angeles: LPI, 1967—.
The Body Politic. Toronto: Pink Triangle Press, 1971–1987.
Christopher Street. New York: That New Magazine, Inc., 1976–1995.
Equality. Washington, D.C.: Human Rights Campaign and Human Rights Campaign Foundation, 2003—.
The Gay and Lesbian Review/Worldwide. Boston: GLR, Inc., 1994—.
Gay Sunshine. San Francisco: Gay Sunshine Press, 1970–1982.
Journal of Homosexuality. New York: Haworth Press, 1974—.
The Ladder (16 vols.). San Francisco: Daughters of Bilitis, 1956–1972.
The Mattachine Review (12 vols.). New York: Arno Press, 1975.
One Magazine. Los Angeles: One, Inc., 1953–1968.

Local and Regional Publications

Bay Area Reporter. San Francisco: Benro Enterprises, 1971—.
Bay Windows. Boston: Bay Windows, Inc., 1983—.
Between the Lines. Livonia, Mich.: Pride Source Media Group, 1994—.
Exit. Johannesburg, South Africa: Highland Publications, 1985—.
Express Gay News. Fort Lauderdale: Window Media, 2000—.
Frontiers. Los Angeles: Frontiers Media, 1983—.
Gay and Lesbian Times. San Diego: Uptown Publications, 1988—.
Gay Community News. Dublin: National Lesbian and Gay Federation (Ireland), 1988—.
Lavender Magazine. Minneapolis: Lavender Media, 1995—.
New York Blade. New York: Window Media, 1999—.
Out Front Colorado. Denver: Q Publishing Group, 1976—.
OutSmart. Houston: Up and Out Communications, 1994—.
Philadelphia Gay News. Philadelphia: Masco Communications, Inc., 1978—.
The Pillar of the Gay Community. Salt Lake City: Pillar Publishing, 1993—.
ScotsGay Magazine. Edinburgh: Pageprint Publishing, 1994—.
Seattle Gay News. Seattle: JT&A, 1973—.

Southern Voice. Atlanta: Window Media, 1988—.
Washington Blade. Washington, D.C.: Window Media, 1969—.
Windy City Times. Chicago: Windy City Media Group, 1986—.
Xtra. Toronto: Pink Triangle Press, 1984—.

HISTORY

General Reference

Aldrich, Robert, ed. *Gay Life and Culture: A World History.* New York: Universe Publishing, 2006.

Angelides, Steven. *A History of Bisexuality.* Chicago: University of Chicago Press, 2000.

Blackwood, Evelyn, and Saskia Wieringa, eds. *Culture, Identity and Sexuality: Cross-Cultural Perspectives on Women's Same-Sex Erotic Friendships.* New York: Columbia University Press, 1998.

Crompton, Louis. *Homosexuality and Civilization.* Cambridge, Mass.: Belknap Press, 2003.

Duberman, Martin, ed. *A Queer World: The Center for Lesbian and Gay Studies Reader.* New York: New York University Press, 1997.

Duberman, Martin, Martha Vicinus, and George Chauncey Jr., eds. *Hidden from History: Reclaiming the Gay and Lesbian Past.* New York: Meridian, 1990.

Fone, Byrne R. S. *Homophobia: A History.* New York: Henry Holt, 2000.

Frantzen, Allen J. *Before the Closet: Same-Sex Love from* Beowulf *to* Angels in America. Chicago: University of Chicago Press, 1998.

Greenberg, David F. *The Construction of Homosexuality.* Chicago: University of Chicago Press, 1988.

Halperin, David M. *How to Do the History of Homosexuality.* Chicago: University of Chicago Press, 2002.

Johnson, E. Patrick, and Mae G. Henderson, eds. *Black Queer Studies: A Critical Anthology.* Durham, N.C.: Duke University Press, 2005.

Jordan, Mark D. *The Invention of Sodomy in Christian Theology.* Chicago: University of Chicago Press, 1998.

Licata, Salvatore J., and Robert P. Peterson, eds. *Historical Perspectives on Homosexuality.* New York: Haworth Press, 1981.

Livia, Anna, and Kira Hall, eds. *Queerly Phrased: Language, Gender, and Sexuality.* New York: Oxford University Press, 1997.

Mondimore, Francis Mark. *A Natural History of Homosexuality.* Baltimore: Johns Hopkins, 1996.

Murray, Stephen O. *Homosexualities.* Chicago: University of Chicago Press, 2002.

Nardi, Peter M., ed. *Social Perspectives in Lesbian and Gay Studies: A Reader.* New York: Routledge, 1998.

Stein, Edward, ed. *Forms of Desire: Sexual Orientation and the Social Constructionist Controversy.* New York: Routledge, 1992.

Swidler, Arlene, ed. *Homosexuality and World Religions.* Valley Forge, Penn.: Trinity Press International, 1993.

Ancient and Medieval

Boswell, John. *Christianity, Social Tolerance, and Homosexuality: Gay People in Western Europe from the Beginning of the Christian Era to the Fourteenth Century.* Chicago: University of Chicago Press, 1980.

———. *Same-Sex Unions in Premodern Europe.* New York: Vintage Books, 1994.

Brendel, Otto G. *Etruscan Art.* New York: Penguin Books, 1978.

Brooten, Bernadette. *Love between Women: Early Christian Responses to Female Homoeroticism.* Chicago: University of Chicago Press, 1998.

Cantarella, Eva. *Bisexuality in the Ancient World.* New Haven, Conn.: Yale University Press, 1992.

Carrasco, Rafael. *Inquisición y represión sexual en Valencia: Historia de los sodomitas (1565–1785).* Barcelona: Laertes, 1985.

Davidson, James. *Courtesans and Fishcakes: The Consuming Passions of Classical Athens.* London: HarperCollins, 1997.

———. *The Greeks and Greek Love: A Radical Reappraisal of Homosexuality in Ancient Greece.* London: Weidenfeld and Nicolson, 2007.

Dover, K. J. *Greek Homosexuality.* Cambridge, Mass.: Harvard University Press, 1978.

Goodich, Michael. *The Unmentionable Vice: Homosexuality in the Later Medieval Period.* Santa Barbara: ABC-Clio, 1979.

Halperin, David M. *One Hundred Years of Homosexuality: and Other Essays on Greek Love.* New York: Routledge, 1990.

Hubbard, Thomas K. *Homosexuality in Greece and Rome: A Sourcebook of Basic Documents.* Berkeley: University of California Press, 2003.

Murray, Jacqueline, and Konrad Eisenbichler. *Desire and Discipline: Sex and Sexuality in the Premodern West.* Toronto: University of Toronto Press, 1996.

Nissinen, Marti. *Homoeroticism in the Biblical World: A Historical Perspective.* Minneapolis: Augsburg Fortress Publishers, 2004.

Percy, William Armstrong, III. *Pederasty and Pedagogy in Archaic Greece.* Urbana: University of Illinois Press, 1996.

Richlin, Amy. *The Garden of Priapus: Sexuality and Aggression in Roman Humor.* New Haven: Yale University Press, 1983.

Sergent, Bernard. *L'Homosexualité dans la mythologie grecque.* Paris: Payot, 1984.

———. *L'Homosexualité initiatique dans l'Europe ancienne.* Paris: Payot, 1986.

Williams, Craig A. *Roman Homosexuality: Ideologies of Masculinity in Classical Antiquity.* New York: Oxford University Press, 1999.

Modern and Contemporary

Adam, Barry D. *The Rise of a Gay and Lesbian Movement.* New York: Twayne Publishers, 1995.

Adam, Barry D., Jan Willem Duyvendak, and André Krouwel, eds. *The Global Emergence of Gay and Lesbian Politics: National Imprints of a Worldwide Movement.* Philadelphia: Temple University Press, 1999.

Aldrich, Robert. *Colonialism and Homosexuality.* New York: Routledge, 2002.

Beneman, William. *Male-Male Intimacy in Early America: Beyond Romantic Friendship.* Binghamton, N.Y.: Haworth Press, 2006.

Berube, Alan. *Coming Out under Fire: The History of Gay Men and Women in World War II.* New York: Free Press, 1990.

Blasius, Mark, and Shane Phelan, eds. *We Are Everywhere: A Historical Sourcebook of Gay and Lesbian Politics.* New York: Routledge, 1997.

Bleys, Rudi C. *The Geography of Perversion: Male-to-Male Sexual Behavior outside the West and the Ethnographic Imagination, 1750–1918.* New York: New York University Press, 1995.

Bray, Alan. *Homosexuality in Renaissance England.* London: Gay Men's Press, 1982.

Bull, Chris, ed. *Come Out Fighting: A Century of Essential Writing on Gay and Lesbian Liberation.* New York: Thunder's Mouth Press/Nation Books, 2001.

Carter, David. *Stonewall: The Riots that Sparked a Gay Revolution.* New York: St. Martin's Press, 2005.

Chauncey, George. *Why Marriage? The History Shaping Today's Debate over Gay Equality.* New York: Basic Books, 2005.

D'Emilio, John. *Sexual Politics, Sexual Communities.* Chicago: University of Chicago Press, 1983.

Duberman, Martin B. *About Time: Exploring the Gay Past.* New York: Meridian, 1991.

———. *Stonewall.* New York: Dutton, 1993.

Faderman, Lillian. *Odd Girls and Twilight Lovers.* New York: Columbia University Press, 1991.

———. *Surpassing the Love of Men.* New York: William Morrow, 1981.

Gallo, Marcia M. *Different Daughters: A History of the Daughters of Bilitis and the Rise of the Lesbian Rights Movement.* New York: Carroll and Graf Publishers, 2006.

Gerard, Kent, and Gert Hekma, eds. *The Pursuit of Sodomy: Male Homosexuality in Renaissance and Enlightenment Europe.* Binghamton, N.Y.: Harrington Park Press, 1989.

Goldberg, Jonathan, ed. *Queering the Renaissance.* Durham, N.C.: Duke University Press, 1994.

———. *Sodometries: Renaissance Texts, Modern Sensibilities.* Stanford, Calif.: Stanford University Press, 1992.

Grau, Gunter, ed. *Hidden Holocaust: Gay and Lesbian Persecution in Germany, 1933–1945.* London: Cassell, 1995.

Higgs, David, ed. *Queer Sites: Gay Urban Histories since 1600.* New York: Routledge, 1999.

Jensen, Erik N. "The Pink Triangle and Political Consciousness: Gays, Lesbians, and the Memory of Nazi Persecution." *Journal of the History of Sexuality* 11, nos. 1–2 (January–April 2002): 319–349.

Johnson, David K. *The Lavender Scare.* Chicago: University of Chicago Press, 2004.

Kaiser, Charles. *The Gay Metropolis, 1940–1996.* New York: Houghton Mifflin, 1997.

Katz, Jonathan Ned, ed. *Gay American History.* New York: Thomas Y. Crowell, 1976.

———, ed. *Homosexuality: Lesbians and Gay Men in Society, History and Literature.* New York: Arno Press, 1975.

———. *Love Stories: Sex between Men before Homosexuality.* Chicago: University of Chicago Press, 2001.

Kennedy, Elizabeth Lapovsky, and Madeline Davis. *Boots of Leather, Slippers of Gold: The History of a Lesbian Community.* New York: Routledge, 1993.

Loughery, John. *The Other Side of Silence: Men's Lives and Gay Identities: A Twentieth-Century History.* New York: Henry Holt, 1998.

Martin, William. *With God on Our Side: The Rise of the Religious Right in America.* New York: Broadway Books, 1996.

McGarry, Molly, and Fred Wasserman. *Becoming Visible: An Illustrated History of Lesbian and Gay Life in Twentieth-Century America.* New York: Penguin, 1998.

Micheler, Stefan. "Homophobic Propaganda and the Denunciation of Same-Sex-Desiring Men under National Socialism." *Journal of the History of Sexuality* 11, nos. 1–2 (January–April 2002): 95–130.

Miller, Neil. *Out of the Past: Gay and Lesbian History from 1869 to the Present.* New York: Alyson Books, 2006.

Mosse, George L. *Nationalism and Sexuality: Respectability and Abnormal Sexuality in Modern Europe.* New York: Howard Fertig, 1997.

Nealon, Christopher S. *Foundlings: Lesbian and Gay Historical Emotion Before Stonewall.* Durham, N.C.: Duke University Press, 2001.

Plant, Richard. *The Pink Triangle: The Nazi War against Homosexuals.* New York: Henry Holt, 1986.

Ridinger, Robert B., ed. *Speaking for Our Lives: Historic Speeches and Rhetoric for Gay and Lesbian Rights, 1892–2000.* Binghamton, N.Y.: Harrington Park Press, 2004.

Rupp, Leila J. *A Desired Past: A Short History of Same-Sex Love in America.* Chicago: University of Chicago Press, 1999.

Saslow, James M. *Ganymede in the Renaissance: Homosexuality in Art and Society.* New Haven, Conn.: Yale University Press, 1986.

Sears, James T. *Behind the Mask of the Mattachine: The Hal Call Chronicles and the Early Movement for Homosexual Emancipation.* New York: Harrington Park Press, 2006.

———. *Lonely Hunters: An Oral History of Lesbian and Gay Southern Life, 1948–1968.* Boulder, Colo.: Westview Press, 1997.

———. *Rebels, Rubyfruit, and Rhinestones: Queering Space in the Stonewall South.* New Brunswick, N.J.: Rutgers University Press, 2001.

Steakley, James D. *The Homosexual Emancipation Movement in Germany.* New York: Arno Press, 1975.

Weeks, Jeffrey. *Coming Out.* London: Quartet Books, 1977.

———. *Sexuality and Its Discontents: Meanings, Myths and Modern Sexualities.* New York: Routledge, 1985.

Williams, Walter L., and Yolanda Retter. *Gay and Lesbian Rights in the United States: A Documentary History.* Westport, Conn.: Greenwood Press, 2003.

PHILOSOPHY

Bentham, Jeremy. "Jeremy Bentham's Essay on Paederasty, Part Two." *Journal of Homosexuality* 4 (1978): 91–107.

———. "Offenses against One's Self: Paederasty, Part One." *Journal of Homosexuality* 3 (1978): 389–405.

Blasius, Mark. *Gay and Lesbian Politics: Sexuality and the Emergence of a New Ethic.* Philadelphia: Temple University Press, 1995.

Butler, Judith P. *Bodies That Matter: On the Discursive Limits of Sex.* New York: Routledge, 1993.

———. *Gender Trouble: Feminism and the Subversion of Identity.* New York: Routledge, 1990.

———. *Undoing Gender.* New York: Routledge, 2004.

Crompton, Louis. "Jeremy Bentham's Essay on 'Paederasty': An Introduction." *Journal of Homosexuality* 3 (Summer 1978): 383–387.

Estlund, David M., and Martha C. Nussbaum, eds. *Sex, Preference, and Family: Essays on Law and Nature.* New York: Oxford University Press, 1997.

Finnis, John. *Aquinas: Moral, Political, and Legal Theory.* New York: Oxford University Press, 1999.

Foucault, Michel. *The History of Sexuality.* Vol. 1, *An Introduction.* New York: Vintage Books, 1980.

George, Robert P. *In Defense of Natural Law.* New York: Oxford University Press, 1999.

Halperin, David M. *Saint Foucault: Towards a Gay Hagiography.* New York: Oxford University Press, 1995.

Jagose, Annamarie. *Queer Theory: An Introduction.* New York: New York University Press, 1996.

Malinowitz, Harriet. "Queer Theory: Whose Theory?" *Frontiers* 13 (1993): 168–184.

Nussbaum, Martha C. *Sex and Social Justice.* New York: Oxford University Press, 1999.

Phelan, Shane. *Sexual Strangers: Gays, Lesbians and Dilemmas of Citizenship.* Philadelphia: Temple University Press, 2001.

Plato. *The Laws.* Translated by T. J. Saunders. New York: Penguin Classics, 1970.

———. *Phaedrus and Letters VII and VIII.* Translated by Walter Hamilton. New York: Penguin Classics: 1973.

———. *The Republic.* Translated by Desmond Lee. New York: Penguin Classics, 1955.

———. *The Symposium.* Translated by Walter Hamilton. New York: Penguin Classics, 1951.

Rich, Adrienne. "Compulsory Heterosexuality and Lesbian Existence." In *The Lesbian and Gay Studies Reader*, ed. Henry Abelove, Michèle Aina Barale, and David M. Halperin, 227–255. New York: Routledge, 1993.

Sandel, Michael. "Moral Argument and Liberal Toleration: Abortion and Homosexuality." In *New Communitarian Thinking: Persons, Virtues, Institutions and Communities,* ed. Amitai Etzioni, 71–87. Charlottesville: University Press of Virginia, 1995.

Sedgwick, Eve Kosofsky. *Epistemology of the Closet.* Berkeley: University of California Press, 1990.

———. *Tendencies.* Durham, N.C.: Duke University Press, 1993.

Snyder, R. Claire. *Gay Marriage and Democracy: Equality for All.* Lanham, Md.: Rowman & Littlefield, 2006.

Spargo, Tasmin. *Foucault and Queer Theory.* New York: Totem Books, 1999.

Stychin, Carl F. "Being Gay." *Government and Opposition* 40 (2005): 90–109.

Turner, William B. *Genealogy of Queer Theory.* Philadelphia: Temple University Press, 2000.

Whitehead, Kenneth D., ed. *Marriage and the Common Good.* South Bend, Ind.: St. Augustine's Press, 2001.

LAW

Baird, Robert M., and Stuart E. Rosenbaum, eds. *Same-Sex Marriage: The Moral and Legal Debate.* Amherst, N.Y.: Prometheus Books, 1997.

Cretney, Stephen. *Same-Sex Relationships, from "Odious Crime" to "Gay Marriage."* New York: Oxford University Press, 2006.

Editors of the Harvard Law Review. *Sexual Orientation and the Law.* Cambridge, Mass.: Harvard University Press, 1989.

Eskridge, William N., Jr. *The Case for Same-Sex Marriage: From Sexual Liberty to Civilized Commitment.* New York: The Free Press, 1996.

———. *Equality Practice: Civil Unions and the Future of Gay Rights.* New York: Routledge, 2001.

———. *Gaylaw: Challenging the Apartheid of the Closet.* Cambridge, Mass.: Harvard University Press, 1999.

Eskridge, William N., Jr., and Nan D. Hunter. *Sexuality, Gender, and the Law.* Westbury, N.Y.: Foundation Press, 1997.

Eskridge, William N., Jr., and Darren R. Spedale. *Gay Marriage: For Better or Worse? What We've Learned from the Evidence.* New York: Oxford University Press, 2006.

Finnis, John. "Law, Morality, and 'Sexual Orientation.'" *Notre Dame Law Review* 69 (1994): 1049–1076.

George, Robert P. "Public Reason and Political Conflict: Abortion and Homosexuality." *Yale Law Journal* 106 (1997): 2475–2504.

George, Robert P., and Gerard V. Bradley. "Marriage and the Liberal Imagination." *Georgetown Law Journal* 84 (1995): 301–320.

Gerstmann, Evan. *The Constitutional Underclass: Gays, Lesbians, and the Failure of Class-based Equal Protection.* Chicago: University of Chicago Press, 1999.

Macedo, Stephen. "Homosexuality and the Conservative Mind." *The Georgetown Law Journal* 84 (1995): 261–300.

———. "Reply to Critics." *The Georgetown Law Journal* 84 (1995): 329–337.

Merin, Yuval. *Equality for Same-Sex Couples: The Legal Recognition of Gay Partnerships in Europe and the United States.* Chicago: University of Chicago Press, 2002.

Mezey, Susan. *Queers in Court: Gay Rights Law and Public Policy.* Lanham, Md.: Rowman & Littlefield, 2007.

Mohr, Richard D. *Gays/Justice: A Study of Ethics, Society, and Law.* New York: Columbia University Press, 1988.

Murdoch, Joyce, and Deb Price. *Courting Justice: Gay Men and Lesbians v. the Supreme Court.* New York: Basic Books, 2001.

Ottosson, Daniel. "State-Sponsored Homophobia: A World Survey of Laws Prohibiting Same-Sex Activity between Consenting Adults" (an ILGA Report, May 2008).

Pickett, Brent. "Natural Law and the Regulation of Sexuality: A Critique." *Richmond Journal of Law and the Public Interest* 8 (2004): 39–54.

Pierceson, Jason. *Courts, Liberalism, and Rights: Gay Law and Politics in the United States and Canada.* Philadelphia: Temple University Press, 2005.

Polikoff, Nancy D. *Beyond (Straight and Gay) Marriage: Valuing All Families under the Law.* Boston: Beacon Press, 2008.

Posner, Richard. *Sex and Reason.* Cambridge, Mass.: Harvard University Press, 1992.

Rollins, Joe. *AIDS and the Sexuality of the Law: Ironic Jurisprudence.* New York: Palgrave Macmillan, 2004.

Rubenstein, William B., ed. *Lesbians, Gay Men, and the Law.* New York: New Press, 1993.

Simonson, Gary J. "Beyond Interstate Recognition in the Same-Sex Marriage Debate." *UC Davis Law Review* 40 (2006): 313–383.

West, Donald J., and Richard Green, eds. *Sociolegal Control of Homosexuality: A Multi-Nation Comparison.* New York: Kluwer Academic Publishers, 2002.

Wintemute, Robert, and Mads Andenaes, eds. *Legal Recognition of Same-Sex Partnerships: A Study of National, European, and International Law.* Portland, Ore.: Hart Publishing, 2001.

Wolfson, Evan. *Why Marriage Matters: America, Equality, and Gay People's Right to Marry.* New York: Simon & Schuster, 2005.

POLITICS

Abelove, Henry, Michèle Aina Barale, and David M. Halperin, eds. *The Lesbian and Gay Studies Reader*. New York: Routledge, 1993.

Baird, Robert M., and Katherine Baird, eds. *Homosexuality: Debating the Issues*. Amherst, N.Y.: Prometheus Books, 1995.

Bawer, Bruce, ed. *Beyond Queer: Challenging Gay Left Orthodoxy*. New York: Free Press, 1996.

———. *A Place at the Table: The Gay Individual in American Society*. New York: Poseidon Press, 1993.

Berlet, Chip. *Eyes Right! Challenging the Right Wing Backlash*. Boston: South End Press, 1995.

Bernstein, Elizabeth, and Laurie Schaffner, eds. *Regulating Sex: The Politics of Intimacy and Identity*. New York: Routledge, 2005.

Bull, Chris, and John Gallagher. *Perfect Enemies: The Religious Right, the Gay Movement, and the Politics of the 1990s*. Toronto: Madison Books, 2001.

Calhoun, Cheshire. *Feminism, the Family, and the Politics of the Closet: Lesbian and Gay Displacement*. New York: Oxford University Press, 2002.

Caramagno, Thomas C. *Irreconcilable Differences? Intellectual Stalemate in the Gay Rights Debate*. Westport, Conn.: Praeger, 2002.

D'Emilio, John. *Making Trouble: Essays on Gay History, Politics, and the University*. New York: Routledge, 1992.

Duberman, Martin. *Left Out: The Politics of Exclusion, Essays 1964–2002*. Cambridge, Mass.: South End Press, 2002.

Gross, Larry P. *Contested Closets: The Politics and Ethics of Outing*. Minneapolis: University of Minnesota Press, 1993.

Hekma, Gert, Harry Oosterhuis, and James Steakley, eds. *Gay Men and the Sexual History of the Political Left*. Binghamton, N.Y.: Harrington Park Press, 1995.

Hendriks, Aart, Rob Tielman, and Evert van der Veen, eds. *The Third Pink Book: A Global View of Lesbian and Gay Liberation and Oppression*. Buffalo, N.Y.: Prometheus, 1993.

Herman, Didi. *The Antigay Agenda*. Chicago: University of Chicago Press, 1997.

Hull, Kathleen. *Same-Sex Marriage: The Cultural Politics of Love and Law*. New York: Cambridge University Press, 2006.

Johnson, William Stacy. *A Time to Embrace: Same-Gender Relationships in Religion, Law, and Politics*. Grand Rapids Mich.: William B. Eerdmans Publishing, 2006.

Kenney, Moira Rachel. *Mapping Gay L.A.: The Intersection of Place and Politics*. Philadelphia: Temple University Press, 2001.

Mello, Michael. *Legalizing Gay Marriage*. Philadelphia: Temple University Press, 2005.

Mohr, Richard D. *Gay Ideas: Outing and Other Controversies*. Boston: Beacon Press, 1992.

Olyan, Saul M., and Martha C. Nussbaum, eds. *Sexual Orientation and Human Rights in American Religious Discourse*. New York: Oxford University Press, 1998.

Parker, Richard G., Regina Maria Barbosa, and Peter Aggleton, eds. *Framing the Sexual Subject: The Politics of Gender, Sexuality, and Power*. Berkeley: University of California Press, 2000.

Pinello, Daniel R. *America's Struggle for Same-Sex Marriage*. New York: Cambridge University Press, 2006.

Rauch, Jonathan. *Gay Marriage: Why It Is Good for Gays, Good for Straights, and Good for America*. New York: Times Books, 2004.

Rimmerman, Craig A., Kenneth D. Wald, and Clyde Wilcox, eds. *The Politics of Gay Rights*. Chicago: University of Chicago Press, 2000.

Rimmerman, Craig A., and Clyde Wilcox, eds. *The Politics of Same-Sex Marriage*. Chicago: University of Chicago Press, 2007.

Shanley, Mary Lyndon, Joshua Cohen, and Deborah Chasman, eds. *Just Marriage*. New York: Oxford University Press, 2004.

Sullivan, Andrew. *Virtually Normal: An Argument about Homosexuality*. New York: Alfred A. Knopf, 1995.

Teal, Donn. *The Gay Militants*. New York: Stein and Day, 1971.

Vaid, Urvashi. *Virtual Equality: The Mainstreaming of Gay and Lesbian Liberation*. New York: Anchor Books, 1995.

SOCIAL ISSUES

Andriote, John-Manuel. *Victory Deferred: How AIDS Changed Gay Life in America*. Chicago: University of Chicago Press, 1999.

Badgett, M. V. Lee. *Money, Myths, and Change: The Economic Lives of Lesbians and Gay Men*. Chicago: University of Chicago Press, 2001.

Benkov, Laura. *Reinventing the Family: The Emerging Story of Lesbian and Gay Parents*. New York: Crown, 1994.

Besen, Wayne R. *Anything but Straight: Unmasking the Scandals and Lies behind the Ex-Gay Myth*. Binghamton, N.Y.: Haworth Press, 2003.

Cantor, Donald J., Elizabeth Cantor, James C. Black, and Campbell D. Barrett. *Same-Sex Marriage: The Legal and Psychological Evolution in America*. Middletown, Conn.: Wesleyan University Press, 2006.

Comstock, Gary David. *Violence against Lesbians and Gay Men*. New York: Columbia University Press, 1991.

Epps, Brad, Keija Valens, and Bill Johnson González, eds. *Passing Lines: Sexuality and Immigration*. Cambridge, Mass.: Harvard University Press, 2005.

Erzen, Tanya. *Straight to Jesus: Sexual and Christian Conversions in the Ex-Gay Movement*. Berkeley: University of California Press, 2006.

Estes, Steve. *Ask and Tell: Gay and Lesbian Veterans Speak Out*. Chapel Hill: University of North Carolina Press, 2007.

Ford, Michael. *Disclosures: Conversations Gay and Spiritual*. Lanham, Md.: Rowman & Littlefield, 2005.

Fuss, Diana, ed. *Inside/Out: Lesbian Theories/Gay Theories*. New York: Routledge, 1991.

Greenberg, Steven. *Wrestling with God and Men: Homosexuality in the Jewish Tradition*. Madison: University of Wisconsin Press, 2005.

Herek, Gregory M., and Kevin T. Berrill, eds. *Hate Crimes: Confronting Violence against Lesbians and Gay Men*. London: Sage, 1992.

Jordan, Mark D., ed. *Authorizing Marriage? Canon, Tradition, and Critique in the Blessing of Same-Sex Unions*. Princeton, N.J.: Princeton University Press, 2006.

———. *Blessing Same-Sex Unions: The Perils of Queer Romance and the Confusions of Christian Marriage*. Chicago: University of Chicago Press, 2005.

———. *The Silence of Sodom: Homosexuality in Modern Catholicism*. Chicago: University of Chicago Press, 2000.

Kahn, Rabbi Yoel H. "Judaism and Homosexuality: The Traditionalist/Progressive Debate." *Journal of Homosexuality* 18, nos. 3–4 (1989/1990): 47–82.

Kramer, Larry. *Reports from the Holocaust: The Making of an AIDS Activist*. New York: St. Martin's Press, 1995.

Lehring, Gary L. *Officially Gay: The Political Construction of Sexuality by the U.S. Military*. Philadelphia: Temple University Press, 2003.

Lewin, Ellen. *Out in Theory: The Emergence of Lesbian and Gay Anthropology*. Champaign: University of Illinois Press, 2002.

Lewin, Ellen, and William L. Leap, eds. *Out in the Field: Reflections of Lesbian and Gay Anthropologists*. Champaign: University of Illinois Press, 1996.

Luibhéid, Eithne. *Entry Denied: Controlling Sexuality at the Border*. Minneapolis: University of Minnesota Press, 2002.

Luibhéid, Eithne, and Lionel Cantu, eds. *Sexuality, U.S. Citizenship, and Border Crossings*. Minneapolis: University of Minnesota Press, 2005.

Murray, Stephen O. *American Gay*. Chicago: University of Chicago Press, 1996.

Rofes, Eric. *A Radical Rethinking of Sexuality and Schooling: Status Quo or Status Queer?* Lanham, Md.: Rowman & Littlefield, 2005.

Schulman, Sarah. *My American History: Lesbian and Gay Life during the Reagan/Bush Years*. New York: Routledge, 1994.

Sears, James T., ed. *Gay, Lesbian, and Transgender Issues in Education: Programs, Policies, and Practices*. New York: Harrington Park Press, 2003.

Shilts, Randy. *And the Band Played On: Politics, People, and the AIDS Epidemic*. New York: St. Martin's Press, 1987.

———. *Conduct Unbecoming: Gays and Lesbians in the U.S. Military*. New York: St. Martin's Press, 1993.

Warner, Michael, ed. *Fear of a Queer Planet: Queer Politics and Social Theory*. Minneapolis: University of Minnesota Press, 1993.

———. *The Trouble with Normal: Sex, Politics, and the Ethics of Queer Life*. Cambridge, Mass.: Harvard University Press, 1999.

Weston, Kath. *Families We Choose: Lesbians, Gays, Kinship*. New York: Columbia University Press, 1991.

Wright, Kai. *Drifting toward Love: Black, Brown, Gay, and Coming of Age on the Streets of New York*. Boston: Beacon Press, 2008.

REGIONAL STUDIES

Andreadis, Harriette. *Sappho in Early Modern England: Female Same-Sex Literary Erotics, 1550–1714*. Chicago: University of Chicago Press, 2001.

Bedell, Geraldine. "Coming Out of the Dark Ages." *Observer*, June 24, 2007.

Benstock, Shari. *Women of the Left Bank*. Austin: University of Texas Press, 1986.

Blackmore, Josiah, and Gregory S. Hutcheson, eds. *Queer Iberia: Sexualities, Cultures, and Crossings from the Middle Ages to the Renaissance*. Durham, N.C.: Duke University Press, 1999.

Blackwood, Evelyn, ed. *Anthropology and Homosexual Behavior*. New York: Haworth Press, 1986.

———. "Sexuality and Gender in Certain Native American Tribes: The Case of Cross-Gender Females." *Signs* 10, no. 4 (1984): 27–42.

Bleys, Rudi. *The Geography of Perversion: Male-to-Male Sexual Behavior outside the West and the Ethnographic Imagination, 1750–1918*. New York: New York University Press, 1999.

Boag, Peter. *Same-Sex Affairs: Constructing and Controlling Homosexuality in the Pacific Northwest*. Berkeley: University of California Press, 2003.

Boellstorff, Tom. *A Coincidence of Desires: Anthropology, Queer Studies, Indonesia*. Durham, N.C.: Duke University Press, 2007.

———. *The Gay Archipelago: Sexuality and Nation in Indonesia*. Princeton, N.J.: Princeton University Press, 2005.

Brown, Judith C. *Immodest Acts: The Life of a Lesbian Nun in Renaissance Italy.* New York: Oxford University Press, 1986.

Buruma, Ian. *On Sexual Demons, Sacred Mothers, Transvestites, Gangsters, and Other Japanese Heroes.* New York: Pantheon Books, 1984.

Carrier, Joseph M. *De Los Ostros: Intimacy and Homosexuality among Mexican Men.* New York: Columbia University Press, 1995.

Carvajal, Federico Garza. *Butterflies Will Burn: Prosecuting Sodomites in Early Modern Spain and Mexico.* Austin: University of Texas Press, 2003.

Chauncey, George. *Gay New York: Gender, Urban Culture, and the Making of the Gay Male World, 1890–1940.* New York: Basic Books, 1995.

Crompton, Louis. *Byron and Greek Love: Homophobia in Nineteenth-Century England.* Berkeley: University of California Press, 1985.

Cuncun, Wu. *Homoerotic Sensibilities in Late Imperial China.* New York: Routledge, 2004.

Dean, Carolyn. *The Frail Social Body: Pornography, Homosexuality, and Other Fantasies of Interwar France.* Berkeley: University of California Press, 2000

Donoghue, Emma. *Passions between Women: British Lesbian Culture, 1668–1801.* London: Scarlet Press, 1993.

El-Rouayheb, Khaled. *Before Homosexuality in the Arab-Islamic World, 1500–1800.* Chicago: University of Chicago Press, 2005.

Engelstein, Laura. *The Keys to Happiness: Sex and the Search for Modernity in Fin-de-siécle Russia.* Ithaca, N.Y.: Cornell University Press, 1992.

Graupner, Helmut, and Phillip Tahmindjis, eds. *Sexuality and Human Rights: A Global Overview.* New York: Haworth Press, 2005.

Green, James N. *Beyond Carnival: Male Homosexuality in Twentieth-Century Brazil.* Chicago: University of Chicago Press, 1999.

Gunther, Scott. *The Elastic Closet: A History of Homosexuality in France, 1942–Present.* New York: Palgrave Macmillan, 2009.

Gupinath, Gayatri. *Impossible Desires: Queer Diasporas and South Asian Public Cultures.* Durham, N.C.: Duke University Press, 2005.

Haliczer, Stephen. *Inquisition and Society in the Kingdom of Valencia, 1478–1834.* Berkeley: University of California Press, 1990.

Hanan, Patrick. *The Invention of Li Yu.* Cambridge, Mass.: Harvard University Press, 1988.

Herdt, Gilbert, ed. *Ritualized Homosexuality in Melanesia.* Berkeley: University of California Press, 1984.

Hoare, Philip. *Oscar Wilde's Last Stand: Decadence, Conspiracy, and the Most Outrageous Trial of the Century.* New York: Arcade Publishing, 1997.

Houlbrook, Matt. *Queer London: Perils and Pleasures in the Sexual Metropolis, 1918–1957.* Chicago: University of Chicago Press, 2005.

Hynes, Samuel. *A War Imagined: The First World War and English Culture.* New York: Atheneum, 1991.

Kulick, Don. *Travesti: Sex, Gender, and Culture among Brazilian Transgendered Prostitutes.* Chicago: University of Chicago Press, 1998.

Labi, Nadya. "The Kingdom in the Closet." *Atlantic* 299, no. 4 (May 2007): 70–82.

Lancaster, Roger. *Life Is Hard: Machismo, Danger, and the Intimacy of Power in Nicaragua.* Berkeley: University of California Press, 1992.

Laurent, Erick. "Sexuality and Human Rights: An Asian Perspective." In *Sexuality and Human Rights: A Global Overview*, ed. Helmut Graupner and Phillip Tahmindjis. New York: Harrington Park Press, 2005.

Leiner, Marvin. *Sexual Politics in Cuba: Machismo, Homosexuality and AIDS.* Boulder, Colo.: Westview Press, 1994.

Lévi-Provençal, Evariste. *Histoire de l'Espagne musulmane jusqu'à la conquête d'Andalousie par les Almovarids.* Nouv. éd. 3 vols. Paris: G.-P. Maisonneuve, 1950.

Lumsden, Ian. *Machos, Maricones and Gays: Cuba and Homosexuality.* Philadelphia: Temple University Press, 1996.

Lunsing, Wim. *Beyond Common Sense: Sexuality and Gender in Contemporary Japan.* London: Kegan Paul, 1997.

Luongo, Michael, ed. *Gay Travels in the Muslim World.* New York: Haworth Press, 2007.

McLelland, Mark. *Queer Japan from the Pacific War to the Internet Age.* Lanham, Md.: Rowman & Littlefield, 2005.

McLelland, Mark, Katsuhiko Suganuma, and James Welker, eds. *Queer Voices from Japan: First Person Narratives from Japan's Sexual Minorities.* Lanham, Md.: Rowman & Littlefield, 2007.

Merrick, Jeffrey, and Bryant T. Ragan, eds. *Homosexuality in Early Modern France: A Documentary Collection.* New York: Oxford University Press, 2000.

———. *Homosexuality in Modern France.* New York: Oxford University Press, 1996.

Molloy, Sylvia, and Robert Mckee Irwin, eds. *Hispanisms and Homosexualities.* Durham, N.C.: Duke University Press, 1998.

Monter, William. *Frontiers of Heresy: The Spanish Inquisition from the Basque Lands to Sicily.* Cambridge, Mass.: Cambridge University Press, 1990.

Murray, Stephen O., and Will Roscoe, eds. *Boy-Wives and Female Husbands: Studies of African Homosexualities.* New York: St. Martin's Press, 1998.

———. *Islamic Homosexualities: Culture, History, and Literature.* New York: New York University Press, 1997.

Najmabadi, Afsaneh. *Women with Mustaches and Men without Beards: Gender and Sexual Anxieties of Iranian Modernity*. Berkeley: University of California Press, 2005.

Parker, Richard G. *Beneath the Equator: Cultures of Desire, Male Homosexuality, and Emerging Gay Communities in Brazil*. New York: Routledge, 1999.

——. *Bodies, Pleasures and Passions: Sexual Culture in Contemporary Brazil*. Boston: Beacon Press, 1991.

Prieur, Annick. *Mema's House, Mexico City: On Transvestites, Queens, and Machos*. Chicago: University of Chicago Press, 1998.

Puff, Helmut. *Sodomy in Reformation Germany and Switzerland, 1400–1600*. Chicago: University of Chicago Press, 2003.

Reddy, Gayatri. *With Respect to Sex: Negotiating Hijra Identity in South India*. Chicago: University of Chicago Press, 2004.

Reinfelder, Monika, ed. *Amazon to Zami: Towards a Global Lesbian Feminism*. London: Cassell, 1996.

Rocke, Michael. *Forbidden Friendships: Homosexuality and Male Culture in Renaissance Florence*. New York: Oxford University Press, 1998.

Roscoe, Will. *Changing Ones: Third and Fourth Genders in Native North America*. New York: Palgrave Macmillan, 2000.

——. *The Zuni Man-Woman*. Albuquerque: University of New Mexico Press, 1992.

Rose, Kieran. *Diverse Communities: The Evolution of Gay and Lesbian Politics in Ireland*. Cork: Cork University Press, 1994.

Sang, Tze-Lan D. *The Emerging Lesbian: Female Same-Sex Desire in Modern China*. Chicago: University of Chicago Press, 2002.

Schmitt, Arno, and Jehoeda Sofer, eds. *Sexuality and Eroticism among Males in Moslem Societies*. Binghamton, N.Y.: Haworth Press, 1991.

Sigal, Pete, ed. *Infamous Desire: Male Homosexuality in Colonial Latin America*. Chicago: University of Chicago Press, 2003.

Sinnott, Megan. *Toms and Dees: Transgender Identity and Female Same-Sex Relationships in Thailand*. Honolulu: University of Hawai'i Press: 2004.

Vainfas, Ronaldo. *Trópico dos Pecados*. Rio de Janeiro: Editora Campus, 1989.

Vanita, Ruth. *Queering India: Same-Sex Love and Eroticism in Indian Culture and Society*. New York: Routledge, 2001.

Vanita, Ruth, and Saleem Kidwai, eds. *Same-Sex Love in India: Readings from Literature and History*. New York: Palgrave Macmillan, 2001.

Whitaker, Brian. *Unspeakable Love: Gay and Lesbian Life in the Middle East*. Berkeley: University of California Press, 2006.

Williams, Walter L. *The Spirit and the Flesh: Sexual Diversity in American Indian Culture*. Boston: Beacon Press, 1986.

Young, Allen. *Gays under the Cuban Revolution*. San Francisco: Grey Fox Press, 1981.

MEDICAL AND SCIENTIFIC ISSUES

Aggleton, Peter. *Bisexualities and AIDS: International Perspectives.* London: Taylor and Francis, 1996.

Bagemihl, Bruce. *Biological Exuberance: Animal Homosexuality and Natural Diversity.* New York: St. Martin's Press, 1999.

Bayer, Ronald. *Homosexuality and American Psychiatry: The Politics of Diagnosis.* Princeton, N.J.: Princeton University Press, 1987.

Bland, Lucy, and Laura Doan, eds. *Sexology in Culture: Labelling Bodies and Desires.* Chicago: University of Chicago Press, 1999.

———. *Sexology Uncensored: The Documents of Sexual Science.* Chicago: University of Chicago Press, 1999.

Chauncey, George. "From Sexual Inversion to Homosexuality: Medicine and the Changing Conceptualization of Female Deviance." *Salmagundi* 58–59 (Fall 1982—Winter 1983): 114–146.

Cohler, Bertram J., and Robert M. Galatzer-Levy. *The Course of Gay and Lesbian Lives: Social and Psychoanalytic Perspectives.* Chicago: University of Chicago Press, 2000.

Dean, Tim, and Christopher Lane, eds. *Homosexuality and Psychoanalysis.* Chicago: University of Chicago Press, 2001.

Diamond, Lisa M. *Sexual Fluidity: Understanding Women's Love and Desire.* Cambridge, Mass.: Harvard University Press, 2008.

Ellis, Havelock. *Studies in the Psychology of Sex.* New York: Random House, 1936.

Fausto-Sterling, Anne. *Sexing the Body: Gender Politics and the Construction of Sexuality.* New York: Basic Books, 2000.

Freud, Sigmund. *Three Essays on Sexuality.* New York: Basic Books, 1963.

Gagnon, John H., Peter M. Nardi, and Martin P. Levine, eds. *In Changing Times: Gay Men and Lesbians Encounter HIV/AIDS.* Chicago: University of Chicago Press, 1997.

Green, Richard. *Sexual Science and the Law.* Cambridge, Mass.: Harvard University Press, 1992.

Hirschfeld, Magnus. *Die homosexualität des mannes und des weibes.* Berlin: W. de Gruyter, 1984.

Homer, Dean. *Science of Desire: The Gay Gene and the Biology of Behavior.* New York: Touchstone, 1995.

Kirby, Michael. "The 1973 Deletion of Homosexuality as a Psychiatric Disorder: 30 Years On." *Australian and New Zealand Journal of Psychiatry* 37 (2003): 674–677.

Krafft-Ebing, Richard von. *Psychopathia Sexualis.* New York: Stein and Day, 1978.

LeVay, Simon. *Queer Science: The Use and Abuse of Research into Homosexuality.* Cambridge, Mass.: MIT Press, 1996.

Lewes, Kenneth. *The Psychoanalytic Theory of Homosexuality.* New York: Simon & Schuster, 1988.

Minton, Henry L. *Departing from Deviance: A History of Homosexual Rights and Emancipatory Science in America.* Chicago: University of Chicago Press, 2002.

Money, John. *Gay, Straight, and In-Between: The Sexology of Erotic Orientation.* New York: Oxford University Press, 1988.

Shernoff, Michael. *Without Condoms: Unprotected Sex, Gay Men and Barebacking.* New York: Routledge, 2005.

Stein, Edward. *The Mismeasure of Desire: The Science, Theory, and Ethics of Sexual Orientation.* New York: Oxford University Press, 2001.

Ulrichs, Karl Heinrich. *The Riddle of "Man-Manly" Love: The Pioneering Work on Male Homosexuality.* 2 vols. Buffalo, N.Y.: Prometheus Books, 1994.

Wilson, Glenn D., and Rahman Qazi. *Born Gay: The Psychobiology of Sex Orientation.* Chester Springs, Pa.: Peter Owen, 2005.

CULTURAL STUDIES

Aldrich, Robert. *The Seduction of the Mediterranean: Writing, Art, and Homosexual Fantasy.* New York: Routledge, 1993.

Benshoff, Harry M., and Sean Griffin. *Queer Images: A History of Gay and Lesbian Film in America.* Lanham, Md.: Rowman & Littlefield, 2005.

Bergman, David. *Gaiety Transfigured: Gay Self-Representation in American Literature.* Madison: University of Wisconsin Press, 1991.

Bergmann, Emile L., and Paul Julian Smith, eds. *¿Entiendes? Queer Readings, Hispanic Writings.* Durham, N.C.: Duke University Press, 1995.

Bersani, Leo. *Homos.* Cambridge, Mass.: Harvard University Press, 1995.

Borhan, Pierre. *Man to Man: A History of Gay Photography.* New York: Vendome Press, 2007.

Bronski, Michael. *The Pleasure Principle: Sex, Backlash, and the Struggle for Gay Freedom.* New York: St. Martin's Press, 1998.

Butters, Ronald R., John M. Clum, and Michael Moon, eds. *Displacing Homophobia: Gay Male Perspectives in Literature and Culture.* Durham, N.C.: Duke University Press, 1989.

Clum, John M. *Still Acting Gay: Male Homosexuality in Modern Drama.* New York: St. Martin's Press, 2000.

Cooper, Emmanuel. *The Sexual Perspective: Homosexuality and Art in the Last 100 Years in the West.* New York: Routledge, 1986.

Craft, Christopher. *Another Kind of Love: Male Homosexual Desire in English Discourse, 1850–1920.* Berkeley: University of California Press, 1994.

Cuseo, Allan A. *Homosexual Characters in YA Novels: A Literary Analysis, 1969–1982.* Metuchen, N.J.: Scarecrow Press, 1992.

Cvetkovich, Ann. *An Archive of Feelings: Trauma, Sexuality, and Lesbian Public Cultures.* Durham, N.C.: Duke University Press, 2003.

De Jongh, Nicholas. *Not in Front of the Audience: Homosexuality on Stage.* New York: Routledge, 1992.

Dollimore, Jonathan. *Sexual Dissidence: Augustine to Wilde, Freud to Foucault.* New York: Oxford University Press, 1991.

Dyer, Richard. *Now You See It: Studies on Lesbian and Gay Film.* New York: Routledge, 1990.

Feidman, Steven. *Beyond the Closet: The Transfomation of Gay and Lesbian Life.* New York: Routledge, 2003.

Forster, Thomas, Carol Siegel, and Ellen E. Berry, eds. *Sex Positives? The Cultural Politics of Dissident Sexualities.* New York: New York University Press, 1997.

Foster, David William. *Gay and Lesbian Themes in Latin American Writing.* Austin: University of Texas Press, 1991.

Gever, Martha, John Greyson, and Pratibha Parmar, eds. *Queer Looks: Perspectives on Lesbian and Gay Film and Video.* New York: Routledge, 1993.

Halberstam, Judith. *In a Queer Time and Place: Transgender Bodies, Subcultural Lives.* New York: New York University Press, 2005.

Harris, Daniel. *The Rise and Fall of Gay Culture.* New York: Hyperion, 1997.

Harris, Laura, and Elizabeth Crocker, eds. *Femme: Feminists, Lesbians, and Bad Girls.* New York: Routledge, 1997.

Hazm, Ibn. *The Ring of the Dove: A Treatise on the Art and Practice of Arab Love.* London: Luzac Oriental Press, 1997.

Hubbs, Nadine. *The Queer Composition of America's Sound: Gay Modernists, American Music, and National Identity.* Berkeley: University of California Press, 2004.

Hughes, Howard L. *Pink Tourism: Holidays of Gay Men and Lesbians.* New York: Oxford University Press, 2006.

Jay, Karla, and Joanne Glasgow, eds. *Lesbian Texts and Contexts: Radical Revisions.* New York: New York University Press, 1990.

Jay, Karla, and Allen Young, eds. *Lavender Culture: The Unrecognized Influence of Gay Culture.* New York: New York University Press, 1994.

Kopelson, Kevin. *Love's Litany: The Writing of Modern Homoerotics.* Stanford, Calif.: Stanford University Press, 1994.

Love, Heather. *Feeling Backward: Loss and the Politics of Queer History.* Cambridge, Mass.: Harvard University Press, 2007.

McIntosh, Mary. "The Homosexual Role." *Social Problems* 16, no. 2 (Autumn 1968): 182–192.

Moon, Dawne. *God, Sex, and Politics: Homosexuality and Everyday Theologies.* Chicago: University of Chicago Press, 2004.

Muñoz, Josè Esteban. *Disidentifications: Queers of Color and the Performance of Politics.* Minneapolis: University of Minnesota Press, 1999.

Murphy, Timothy F., and Suzanne Poirier, eds. *Writing AIDS: Gay Literature, Language, and Analysis.* New York: Columbia University Press, 1993.

Nestle, Joan. *A Restricted Country.* Ithaca, N.Y.: Firebrand Books, 1987.

Rupp, Leila J., and Verta A. Taylor. *Drag Queens at the 801 Cabaret.* Chicago: University of Chicago Press, 2003.

Russo, Vito. *The Celluloid Closet.* New York: Harper and Row, 1981.

Schulman, Sarah. *Stagestruck: Theater, AIDS, and the Marketing of Gay America.* New Haven, Conn.: Yale University Press, 1999.

Sedgwick, Eve Kosofsky. *Between Men: English Literature and Male Homosocial Desire.* New York: Columbia University Press, 1986.

——, ed. *Novel Gazing: Queer Readings in Fiction.* Durham, N.C.: Duke University Press, 1997.

Sherry, Michael S. *Gay Artists in Modern American Culture: An Imagined Conspiracy.* Chapel Hill: University of North Carolina Press, 2007.

Shneer, David, and Caryn Aviv, eds. *American Queer, Now and Then.* Boulder, Colo.: Paradigm Publishers, 2006.

Sinfield, Alan. *Out on Stage: Lesbian and Gay Theatre in the Twentieth Century.* New Haven, Conn.: Yale University Press, 1999.

Stockton, Kathryn. *Beautiful Bottom, Beautiful Shame: Where "Black" Meets "Queer."* Durham, N.C.: Duke University Press, 2006.

Straayer, Chris. *Deviant Eyes, Deviant Bodies: Sexual Re-Orientations in Film and Video.* New York: Columbia University Press, 1996.

Thompson, Mark, ed. *Leatherfolk.* Los Angeles: Daedalus Publishers, 2004.

Waugh, Thomas. *Hard to Imagine: Gay Male Eroticism in Photography and Film from Their Beginnings to Stonewall.* New York: Columbia University Press, 1996.

Wright, J. W., Jr., and Everett K. Rowson, eds. *Homoeroticism in Classical Arabic Literature.* New York: Columbia University Press, 1997.

Yingling, Thomas E. *Hart Crane and the Homosexual Text: New Thresholds, New Anatomies.* Chicago: University of Chicago Press, 1990.

LITERATURE, MEMOIRS, AUTOBIOGRAPHIES, AND BIOGRAPHIES

Arenas, Reinaldo. *Before Night Falls*. New York: Viking, 1993.

Baker, Michael. *Our Three Selves: The Life of Radclyffe Hall*. New York: William Morrow, 1985.

Barnes, Djuna. *Ladies Almanack*. New York: New York University Press, 1992.

———. *Nightwood*. New York: New Directions, 2006.

Bronski, Michael, ed. *Pulp Friction: Uncovering the Golden Age of Gay Male Pulps*. New York: St. Martin's Griffin, 2003.

Brundage, James A. *Richard Lion Heart*. New York: Scribner, 1974.

Colette. *The Pure and the Impure*. New York: Farrar, Straus and Giroux, 1966.

Doty, Mark. *Fire to Fire: New and Selected Poems*. New York: HarperCollins, 2008.

———. *Heaven's Coast: A Memoir*. New York: HarperPerennial, 1997.

Duberman, Martin B. *Cures: A Gay Man's Odyssey*. New York: Dutton, 1991.

———. *Midlife Queer: Autobiography of a Decade: 1971–1981*. New York: Scribner, 1996.

Fallenberg, Evan. *Light Fell*. New York: Soho Press, 2007.

Forster, E. M. *Maurice: A Novel*. New York: Morton, 1971.

Gay, Peter. *Freud: A Life for Our Time*. New York: W.W. Norton, 1988.

Grosskurth, Phyllis. *John Addington Symonds, a Biography*. London: Longmans, 1964.

———, ed. *The Memoirs of John Addington Symonds*. London: Hutchison, 1984.

Hare, Thomas Blenman. *Zeami's Style: The Noh Plays of Zeami Motokiyo*. Stanford, Calif.: Stanford University Press, 1986.

Hodges, Andrew. *Alan Turing*. New York: Simon & Schuster, 1984.

Isherwood, Christopher. *Christopher and His Kind, 1929–1939*. New York: Farrar, Straus and Giroux, 1976.

Kaplan, Justin. *Walt Whitman: A Life*. New York: Simon & Schuster, 1980.

Kennedy, Hubert. *Ulrichs: The Life and Works of Karl Heinrich Ulrichs: Pioneer of the Modern Gay Movement*. Boston: Alyson Publications, 1988.

Kramer, Larry. *Faggots*. New York: Grove Press, 2000.

———. *The Normal Heart and the Destiny of Me*. New York: Grove Press, 2000.

———. *Reports from the Holocaust: The Story of an AIDS Activist*. New York: St. Martin's Press, 1994.

Leleux, Robert. *The Memoirs of a Beautiful Boy*. New York: St. Martin's Press, 2007.

Lind, Earl. *Autobiography of an Androgyne*. New York: Arno Press, 1975.

Lorde, Audre. *Zami: A New Spelling of My Name*. Trumansburg, N.Y.: Crossing Press, 1983.

Lucey, Michael. *Gide's Bent: Sexuality, Politics, Writing*. New York: Oxford University Press, 1995.

Malinowski, Sharon, and Christa Berlin, eds. *The Gay and Lesbian Literary Companion*. Detroit: Visible Ink Press, 1995.

Mallon, Thomas. *Fellow Travelers*. New York: Pantheon, 2007.

Mass, Lawrence D. *"We Must Love One Another or Die": The Life and Legacies of Larry Kramer*. New York: St. Martin's Press, 1997.

Maupin, Armistead. *Tales of the City*. New York: Ballantine Books, 1979.

McAlmon, Robert. *Miss Knight and Others*. Albuquerque: University of New Mexico Press, 1992.

Mishima, Yukio. *Confessions of a Mask*. New York: New Directions, 1968.

Mixner, David. *Stranger among Friends*. New York: Bantam Books, 1996.

Monette, Paul. *Becoming a Man: Half a Life Story*. New York: Harcourt Brace, 1992.

———. *Borrowed Time: An AIDS Memoir*. New York: Harcourt Brace, 1988.

Nicolson, Nigel. *Portrait of a Marriage*. New York: Atheneum, 1973.

O'Brien, Sharon. *Willa Cather: The Emerging Voice*. New York: Oxford University Press, 1986.

Peters, Robert L., and Herbert M. Schueller, eds. *The Letters of John Addington Symonds*. 3 vols. Detroit: Wayne State University Press, 1967–1969.

Picano, Felice. *Like People in History*. New York: Viking, 1995.

Pollard, Patrick. *Andre Gide: Homosexual Moralist*. New Haven, Conn.: Yale University Press, 1991.

Porter, Kevin, and Jeffrey Weeks, eds. *Between the Acts: Lives of Homosexual Men, 1885–1967*. New York: Routledge, 1991.

Rechy, John. *About My Life and the Kept Woman: A Memoir*. New York: Grove Press, 2008.

———. *City of Night*. New York: Grove Press, 1994.

Rowbotham, Sheila, and Jeffrey Weeks. *Socialism and the New Life: The Personal and Sexual Politics of Edward Carpenter and Havelock Ellis*. London: Pluto Press, 1977.

Rule, Jane. *Desert of the Heart*. Tallahassee, Fla.: Bella Books, 2005.

Saikaku, Ihara. *The Great Mirror of Male Love*. Stanford, Calif.: Stanford University Press, 1990.

Shilts, Randy. *The Mayor of Castro Street: The Life and Times of Harvey Milk*. New York: St. Martin's Press, 1982.

Stein, Gertrude. *The Autobiography of Alice B. Toklas*. New York: Vintage Books, 1990.

———. *Fernhurst, Q.E.D., and Other Early Writings*. New York: Liveright, 1971.

Sturgis, Howard. *Belchamber*. New York: NYRB Classics, 2008.

Symonds, John Addington. *Walt Whitman: A Study*. New York: B. Blom, 1967.

Timmons, Stuart. *The Trouble with Harry Hay: Founder of the Modern Gay Movement*. Boston: Alyson Publications, 1990.

Tsuzuki, Chushichi. *Edward Carpenter, 1844–1929*. New York: Cambridge University Press, 1980.

Whitman, Walt. *Leaves of Grass*. New York: Bantam Books, 1983.

Willy. *The Third Sex*. Champagne: University of Illinois Press, 2007.

Woods, Gregory. *A History of Gay Literature: The Male Tradition*. New Haven, Conn.: Yale University Press, 1998.

Woolf, Virgina. *Orlando*. New York: Vintage, 2005.

About the Author

Brent L. Pickett (Ph.D., University of Colorado at Boulder) is associate dean in the Outreach School, director of the University of Wyoming/Casper College Center, and associate professor of political science. He teaches courses in political philosophy and comparative politics and has published in the areas of postmodern and communitarian political thought. Dr. Pickett has also produced work on sexuality and how societies regulate the body, such as through anti-sodomy laws and health policy. He is the author of *On the Use and Abuse of Foucault for Politics* (2005) and has published in journals such as the *Cambridge Review of International Affairs*, *Journal of Politics*, *Richmond Review of Law and the Public Interest*, and the *Political Research Quarterly*. Dr. Pickett is a member of the Casper chapter of Parents and Friends of Lesbians and Gays and frequently gives talks in defense of full legal and social equality for gays and lesbians.